Tolkien Criticism:
An Annotated Checklist

# Tolkien Criticism:

## An Annotated Checklist
## Revised Edition

Richard C. West

University of Wisconsin-Madison

The Kent State University Press

*The Serif Series: Number 39*
*Bibliographies and Checklists*

Dean H. Keller, General Editor
Kent State University

**Library of Congress Cataloging in Publication Data**

West, Richard C.
  Tolkien criticism.

  (The Serif series : bibliographies and checklists; no. 39)
  Includes index.
  1. Tolkien, J. R. R. (John Ronald Reuel), 1892–1973—Bibliography.  I.
Title.  II.  Series: Serif series : bibliographies and checklists; no. 39.
Z8883.45.W45  1981          [PR6039.032]          81-8135
ISBN 0-87338-256-0          016.828'91209          AACR2

Library of Congress Catalog Card Number 81–8135
ISBN: 0-87338-256-0
Manufactured in the United States of America

For Perri, my wife,
who advised against waiting
until this was perfect before
publishing it

# Contents

# Introduction

During the eleven years that have elapsed since the appearance of the first edition of this bibliography, critical and scholarly study of the oeuvre of J. R. R. Tolkien has proliferated to the extent that this volume is some five times the size of its predecessor. I would like to think that this represents something more than the verbosity of the authors. For mere numbers of essays can prove only that there is considerable interest in a subject, while artistic stature can be properly assessed only after enough time has passed (one or more centuries, say) to make it possible to see the enduring qualities of artists and works of art. It is, therefore, early yet to be sure that Tolkien will join the immortals. Most (though not all) of the writers listed here seem to be fairly confident that he will.

The enormous popularity of Tolkien's fiction stems in large part, I think, from its being so multifaceted that a reader of almost any age or degree of literary sophistication can enjoy it on one or more levels. *The Lord of the Rings*, in particular, offers relatively simple, but very satisfying, pleasures as an exciting narrative and an imaginary world that is remarkably complete and self-consistent in its details. Yet it also repays critical exegesis from a great many points of view: in its linguistic textures, in its structure, in its psychological and mythic and symbolic resonances. Moreover, Tolkien can be seen as a major figure in the development of various traditions. There has in this century been a movement in Western letters away from "realism" to more "fantastic" modes, which can be discerned in such different writers as Joyce, Faulkner, Grass, Borges—and Tolkien, who is thus in some ways very much in the literary mainstream. He is also part of popular culture and of the genres of science fiction and fantasy, areas in which his work has been highly influential, and to which (in part due to his attraction) considerable academic interest is now being paid. Tolkien had roots in the Victorian and Edwardian periods of his childhood and upbringing, and also in the classical and medieval ages that were his primary field of study; and thus he partakes of the present vogue for works that draw inspiration from those of earlier times. Whether one is a classicist, medievalist, or modernist, a psychologist or a student of language or mythology, or a lover of a good story, Tolkien's work has something to offer, and moreover continues to do so after repeated readings. It is not so very surprising that he should have found a wide readership.

The studies listed here all explore Tolkien's works and try to illuminate their appeal and their value—in the terminology of C. S. Lewis, their Deliciousness and their Truth. Let me describe the format of the checklist.

Section I is a list of Tolkien's published work: juvenilia, poetry, scholarship, fiction, letters. It is arranged chronologically, but the individual titles are listed alphabetically in Section IV-A. Section I owes much to Humphrey Carpenter's work (see II-86), and to the research by members of England's own Tolkien Society. It is not a descriptive bibliography in the full sense, for it records only the standard bibliographical information and not a detailed description of all features. It does list the major (though not all) editions of all of Tolkien's work published through 1980. It is certainly not yet a complete list, however, for more juvenile and anonymous works are still being discovered, and much that is in manuscript remains to be published. Christopher Tolkien, literary executor for his father, continues to put us ever deeper in his debt by editing these papers for publication; he is at this writing reportedly at work (with Humphrey Carpenter) on a volume of his father's letters, and on a volume of his father's scholarly essays. Also, Tolkien's edition of and commentary on *The Old English Exodus* is scheduled to be published by Oxford University Press in 1981.

It should be noted that, while most of Tolkien's papers remain in the possession of his heirs, there are two important collections in the United States. The Archives of the Marquette University Library in Milwaukee, Wisconsin, purchased from Tolkien a number of papers dealing with *The Hobbit*, *Farmer Giles of Ham*, "Mr. Bliss" (the unique manuscript of an unpublished short story), and, most notably, the holograph, two typescripts, and two sets of galley proofs for *The Lord of the Rings*. The Wade Collection at Wheaton College in Wheaton, Illinois, has gathered material relating to Tolkien and to six other authors of Christian and mythopoeic relevance. The Wade Collection also now sponsors *Seven*, an annual journal devoted to critical essays on these authors.

Section II constitutes the main body of this volume. It consists of critical and scholarly writings on Tolkien's work: reviews, essays, dissertations, monographs, pamphlets, books, and commentaries. These are arranged alphabetically by author, except for a few articles which were published anonymously and are therefore listed by title. There is also an index by title in Section IV-C. Bibliographical information is provided for each entry, to enable the reader to locate a copy of the item. In almost all cases I have verified the citations myself; exceptions are marked "Not seen." In my annotations I have not tried to provide full summaries, but succinct descriptions of the major points and salient features, so that a researcher might judge the relevance of a piece to his or her particular line of investigation. I have also tried to cross-reference items dealing with similar matters. Nor are my annotations meant to provide critiques. Probably my judgment of the worth (or lack of it) of the studies will, in some cases at least, be discernable between the lines in spite of my efforts to remain impartial. I have quoted or paraphrased the original as often as I thought warranted, in an attempt to keep my annotations objective. I have also dispensed with placing an asterisk next to items I judged to be the most valuable, a practice which I had followed in the first edition.

Section III is a checklist of book reviews, with Part A devoted to reviews of Tolkien's own work, and Part B to reviews of books about Tolkien. Most reviews appear also in Section II, and so rather than give the full citation again I have merely made reference back to that section. Reviews that for one reason or another did not fit into Section II are also listed here, and for these I have provided full bibliographical information.

Section IV consists of indexes, designed to assist in the use of the other sections. Part A is a list of Tolkien's writings arranged alphabetically by title and refers back to Section I where the same works are listed chronologically. Part B is a checklist of full-length books, shorter monographs and pamphlets, and essay collections on Tolkien, arranged by author, and refers to Section II for fuller treatment of these items. Part C lists the works in Section II alphabetically by title. Part D is a checklist of Ph.D. dissertations and M.A. theses relating to Tolkien, and also refers to Section II where these are listed and annotated. Part E gives information on some of the major fan organizations and publications devoted wholly or in large part to Tolkien.

So much for the overall format. Something needs to be said about what is included in, and excluded from, this bibliography. In brief, what is included is everything relating to Tolkien's scholarly and fictive work that is definitely of real importance, from the time that he began publishing in the 1920s down through the greater part of 1980, while what is excluded is much of what I consider peripheral. In the first edition, though there had already been a great deal published on Tolkien, still I could afford to take note of a few tangential items (e.g., Charles Grean's "Ballad of Bilbo Baggins" as sung by Leonard Nimoy). Now the body of work has grown to such proportions that I cannot afford that luxury, and some parameters must be set to keep this bibliography within workable limits.

You will find nothing here on anything relating to merchandising Tolkieniana: no games, puzzles, toys or the like. I have listed one poster, since it was the first publication of a poem by Tolkien (see I-71). Otherwise, I have omitted all such prints or illustrations, even those for the annual Tolkien calendars that have been issued since 1973 by Allen and Unwin in the U.K. and by Ballantine in the U.S. (but see I-80). I have included a number of illustrated volumes which provide some commentary on Tolkien's work (see Wenzel, II-705, and Wyatt, II-746). All such material, while it may be enjoyable in itself, is rarely of much value for criticism. For those interested, let me say that the American Tolkien Society (see IV-D) reviewed such items in its publications for many years, until this task became too burdensome.

I have not listed translations of Tolkien's work into other languages, nor the reviews of those translations. I have, however, included foreign-language essays on Tolkien.

I have also left out adaptations of Tolkien's works into other media, and articles relating to those. Hence there is nothing here on the film of *The Lord of the Rings, Part One* directed by Ralph Bakshi (Fantasy Films, 1978), nor the Rankin-Bass animated versions of *The Hobbit* (1977) or *The Return of the King* (1980), nor phonorecords such as Nicol Williamson's reading in 1974 of *The Hobbit* (Argo Records ZPL 1196/9), nor any of the various stage or radio dramatizations, nor such items as Bo Hansson's *Music Inspired by Lord of the Rings* in 1972 (Buddah Records CAS 1059), and so forth. To be consistent, I have not listed even Christopher Tolkien's records of *The Silmarillion* in 1978 (Caedmon TC 1564 and TC 1579). I have listed Tolkien's own recordings, however (see I-66, I-74 and I-75). I have listed an article on the subject of adaptation into another medium if it was included in a collection of essays, in order to provide a complete account of the contents of the book (e.g., see Weir, II-702).

I have ruled out most mock-scholarly articles which pretend that Middle-earth is the "real" or (in Tolkien's terminology) Primary World and expound on it from within that frame of reference. While this sort of whimsy may be amusing, it is more fiction than criticism. Nor have I included fiction or poetry inspired by Tolkien's work.

I have not listed books or essays which make only a brief, passing reference to Tolkien.

I have largely omitted newspaper articles, with obvious exceptions such as reviews in major organs such as the *New York Times Book Review*. I have tried to note the particularly substantial pieces, but I realize that this is a subjective judgment. As an example of the sort of thing which I have deliberately left out, let me mention that, while it is of some interest to read on p. 18 of the *London Times* for 2 November 1973 that an old desk of Tolkien's fetched £340 at auction, I find such an item peripheral and easily expendable.

I have not endeavored to list every biographical sketch of Tolkien published, though I have included the more prominent ones. Indeed, Humphrey Carpenter's excellent volume (II-86) makes most of the other biographical forays look almost superfluous.

Finally, and most importantly, I have felt it necessary to exclude most of the material in the numerous "fanzines" or fan magazines published by Tolkien aficionados. I had also omitted such articles from the first edition (to the dissatisfaction of some of the reviewers) for reasons which still seem cogent to me. I demurred in my foreword to that edition that these fanzines were many and unindexed, so that the task was difficult and daunting. There are still many of them (though some titles have ceased publication, others have taken their places), and they are still unindexed. Moreover, even were my own collection of fanzines complete (and it is not), I would hesitate to refer people to publications which go out of print quickly, are rarely collected by libraries, and whose editors move frequently. Of what use is it to cite such items if a researcher cannot find them? Yet it is certainly true that a great deal of very valuable material is published in the fanzines. Some of this has been reprinted in book form, and that I can cite with a clear conscience. I have also noted the reprinting in a fanzine of articles from the more standard journals. Moreover, I have included essays and reviews from three of the leading "fanzines" (i.e., *Mythlore*, *Orcrist*, and *Tolkien Journal*), because they have already been indexed for some years now in the annual *PMLA* bibliography, because several libraries do collect them, and because most back issues are available from the Mythopoeic Society (see IV-E) or from University Microfilms International. These parameters do not permit the inclusion of most material from such very worthwhile fanzines as those of the American Tolkien Society or of England's Tolkien Society, and I do regret that. As some compensation, in Section IV, Part E, I have listed and briefly described some (but by no means all) of the major fan groups and fanzines.

That is what is not included, and no doubt what is peripheral in my view may be just the thing that someone else wants. Yet I am reasonably confident that most of the major critical and scholarly writing on Tolkien is here. The besetting sin of a bibliographer is the sin of omission, and additions and corrections to this checklist are herewith invited, encouraged, and indeed urged.

There will, of course, be more work published. Another anthology of essays edited by Neil D. Isaacs and Rose A. Zimbardo (*Tolkien: New Critical Perspectives* from the University Press of Kentucky) and a new study by Randel Helms (*Tolkien and the Silmarils: Imagination and Myth in The Silmarillion* from Houghton Mifflin) have been announced and should see print before this bibliography does. Jared Lobdell's *England and Always: Tolkien's Lord of the Rings* and T. A. Shippey's *The Road to Middle-earth* should be published in the near future. We may look forward to many more studies to enrich our experience of Tolkien's work.

Numerous scholarly tools have made it possible to research this bibliography: *Assess: The Supplementary Index to Periodicals, Book Review*

*Digest, Book Review Index, British Humanities Index, Catholic Periodical and Literature Index, Current Index to Journals in Education, Dissertation Abstracts International, Education Index, Essay and General Literature Index,* "The Year's Scholarship in Science Fiction and Fantasy" in *Extrapolation, Index to Book Reviews in the Humanities, Library Literature, Masters Abstracts, Monthly Periodical Index,* "Inklings Bibliography" in *Mythlore, New Periodicals Index, New York Times Index,* the annual *PMLA* bibliography, *Popular Periodical Index, Reader's Guide to Periodical Literature, Science Fiction Book Review Index,* and *Social Science and Humanities Index* (formerly *International Index*). I have also been fortunate in having access to many fine libraries while I was at work on both editions of this checklist, particularly those in the Boston area (notably Bapst Library at Boston College, and the Boston Public Library) and those at the University of Wisconsin-Madison (particularly its Memorial Library and Library School Library), and also the Library of the Wisconsin Historical Society. I must particularly thank Leonard Black, Frances Wood and the rest of the staff of the Interlibrary Loan Department of the Wendt Library at the University of Wisconsin-Madison, who tracked down copies of many obscure items for me. Frances Wood and John Luedtke of the Wendt Library were also of invaluable assistance in running a computer search of relevant data bases. It is a pleasure to thank them and all of the other people who, over the years, have contributed items to this bibliography, particularly James Allan, Richard Binkowski, Patrick Callahan, Carleton W. Carroll, Paulette Carroll, Fr. Brendan Connolly, W. Gordon Cunliffe, Richard Ellmann, Anne Etkin, Jan Howard Finder, Glen GoodKnight, Robert A. Hall, Marci Helms, Philip Helms, William C. James, Joseph Kelley, C. S. Kilby, Laurence Krieg, Martha Krieg, Ken Nahigian, John Nieminski, Henry Noel, Deborah Webster Rogers, Ivor A. Rogers, James Woods, and Elsy Zanen. I owe special thanks to Nat Lester for providing photocopies of many items, and to Charles Noad and Jessica Yates of the Tolkien Society for a great deal of material of British provenance. The members of the Tolkien Society of the University of Wisconsin-Madison and of the Madison Science Fiction Group have provided help and encouragement. I must give special mention to the invaluable assistance afforded by my colleague bibliographers: Bonniejean Christensen, J. R. Christopher, Wayne G. Hammond, Roger C. Schlobin, George H. Thomson, and Marshall B. Tymn. My deepest debt is expressed in the dedication.

R. C. W.
February, 1981

# List of Abbreviations

| | |
|---|---|
| *A&I* | "The Lay of Aotrou and Itroun" |
| *ATB* | *The Adventures of Tom Bombadil* |
| CT | Christopher Tolkien |
| *FCL* | *The Father Christmas Letters* |
| *FGH* | *Farmer Giles of Ham* |
| *FR* | *The Fellowship of the Ring* |
| *GGK* | *Sir Gawain and the Green Knight* |
| *GGKPO* | *Sir Gawain and the Green Knight, Pearl and Sir Orfeo* |
| *H* | *The Hobbit* |
| *HB* | "The Homecoming of Beorhtnoth Beorhthelm's Son" |
| JRRT | John Ronald Reuel Tolkien |
| *LBN* | "Leaf by Niggle" |
| *LOTR* | *The Lord of the Rings* |
| *OFS* | "On Fairy-Stories" |
| *PSME* | *Poems and Songs of Middle Earth* |
| *RGEO* | *The Road Goes Ever On* |
| *RK* | *The Return of the King* |
| *Silm* | *The Silmarillion* |
| *SWM* | *Smith of Wootton Major* |
| *T&L* | *Tree and Leaf* |
| *TR* | *The Tolkien Reader* |
| *TT* | *The Two Towers* |
| *UT* | *Unfinished Tales* |

# I. Tolkien's Writings, Arranged Chronologically

1911  I-1  "The Battle of the Eastern Fields." *The King Edward's School Chronicle*, 26, No. 186 (March, 1911), 22–27. Reprinted in *Mallorn*, No. 12 (1978), pp. 24–28.

Poem dating from Tolkien's school days at King Edward's in Birmingham. Jessica Yates notes that the poem is a parody of Macauley's "The Battle of Lake Regillus" (see her "Commentary" in *Mallorn*, No. 13, 1979, pp. 3–5). Carpenter (II-86) observes that Tolkien also reported the meetings of the school's debating society for the *Chronicle* between November, 1910 and June, 1911, and that he wrote editorials for the June and July, 1911 issues.

1913  I-2  "From the many-willow'd margin of the immemorial Thames." *The Stapeldon Magazine*, 4, No. 20 (December, 1913), 11.

Published for Exeter College by B. H. Blackwell, Oxford. Unsigned poem.

1915  I-3  "Goblin Feet." *Oxford Poetry, 1915*. Ed. G. D. H. C[ole] and T. W. E[arp]. Oxford: B. H. Blackwell, 1915, 64–65.

This early poem has been reprinted several times: in *Oxford Poetry, 1914–1916* (Oxford: B. H. Blackwell, 1917), 120–21; in *The Book of Fairy Poetry*, ed. Dora Owen (London: Longmans, Green & Co., 1920), pp. 177–78; in *Fifty New Poems for Children* (Oxford: Basil Blackwell, 1922), pp. 26–27; in *An Inheritance of Poetry*, ed. Gladys L. Adshead and Annis Duff (Boston: Houghton Mifflin, 1948), 66–67; and in J. S. Ryan, *Tolkien: Cult or Culture?* (Armidale, New South Wales, Australia: Univ. of New England, 1969), Appendix A, p. 209 (see II-580). Carpenter (II-86), pp. 74–75 prints a slightly variant version of the first two stanzas. The speaker of the poem is enchanted (in both senses) by the fairy folk in the midnight woods, but cannot follow them.

1918  I-4  Introductory note in *A Spring Harvest*, poems by Geoffrey Bache Smith. London: Erskine Macdonald, 1918.

Tolkien and C. L. Wiseman edited this collection of poetry by G. B. Smith, a close friend who was killed during World War I.

1920  I-5  "The Happy Mariners." *The Stapeldon Magazine*, 5, No. 26 (June, 1920), 69–70.

Published for Exeter College by B. H. Blackwell, Oxford. Poem. See also I-11.

1922  I-6   *A Middle English Vocabulary*. Oxford: Clarendon, 1922.

> This was meant to be used with *Fourteenth-Century Verse and Prose*,
> ed. Kenneth Sisam (Oxford: Clarendon, 1921), and appears as the
> Glossary in later printings of this anthology of medieval texts. It also
> continued to be issued separately.

1923  I-7   "Iumonna Gold Galdre Bewunden" ["The Hoard"]. *The Gryphon*, NS 4, No. 4 (January, 1923), 130.

> Published by Leeds University. Poem. See also I-34, I-54.

    I-8   "Holy Maidenhood." *Times Literary Supplement*, 26 April 1923, p. 281.

> Unsigned review of *Hali Meidenhad*, ed. F. J. Furnivall for the Early
> English Text Society.

    I-9   "The City of the Gods." *The Microcosm*, 8, No. 1 (Spring, 1923), 8.

> Poem. This magazine was edited by Dorothy Una Ratcliffe and
> published privately in Leeds.

    I-10  "Henry Bradley, 3 December 1845–23 May 1923." *Bulletin of the Modern Humanities Research Association*, No. 20 (October, 1923), pp. 4–5.

> Obituary.

    I-11  "Tha Eadigan Saelidan (The Happy Mariners)," "Why the Man in the Moon Came Down Too Soon," and "Enigmata Saxonica Nuper Inventa Duo." *A Northern Venture: verses by members of the Leeds University English School Association*. Leeds: Swan, 1923, pp. 15–20.

> Poems. See also I-5, I-54.

    I-12  "The Cat and the Fiddle: A Nursery Rhyme Undone and its Scandalous Secret Unlocked." *Yorkshire Poetry*, 2, No. 19 (October-November, 1923), 1–3.

> Published by the Swan Press in Leeds. An early version of "The Man
> in the Moon Stayed Up Too Late" in *ATB* (I-54) and in *LOTR*,
> Book I, Ch. 9.

1924  I-13  "Philology: General Works." *The Year's Work in English Studies*, 4 (1923), 20–37.

> See also I-18, I-20.

1925  I-14  "Some Contributions to Middle-English Lexicography." *Review of English Studies*, 1 (April, 1925), 210–15.

I-15  "Light as Leaf on Lindentree." *The Gryphon*, NS 6, No. 6 (June, 1925), 217.

Published by Leeds University. An early version of a poem in *LOTR*, Book I, Ch. 11.

I-16  "The Devil's Coach-Horses." *Review of English Studies*, 1, No. 3 (July, 1925), 331–36.

Notes on Middle English "aeveres."

I-17  *Sir Gawain and the Green Knight*. Oxford: Clarendon, 1925.

Coedited with E. V. Gordon. Reprinted many times. Second edition revised by Norman Davis, 1967.

1926  I-18  "Philology: General Works." *The Year's Work in English Studies*, 5 (1924), 26–65.

See also I-13, I-20.

1927  I-19  "The Nameless Land." In *Realities: An Anthology of Verse*. Ed. G. S. Tancred. Leeds: Swan; London: Gay and Hancock, 1927, pp. 24–25.

Poem.

I-20  "Philology: General Works." *The Year's Work in English Studies*, 6 (1925), 32–66.

See also I-13, I-18. These review articles deal with etymology, lexicography, phonology, place-names, grammar and other aspects of the study of language. Tolkien often mentions his own ideas and interests (his specialty in Germanic languages, enthusiasm for the shadowy history of Celtic Britain, delight in different languages offering different visions of life, etc.).

1928  I-21  Foreword to Walter E. Haigh, *A New Glossary of the Dialect of the Huddersfield District*. London: Oxford Univ. Press, 1928, pp. xiii–xviii.

Praises the work for its fullness of entries and for the excellence, humor, and idiomatic richness of its illustrative quotations. Notes the interest of the dialect for students of Old and Middle English.

1929  I-22  "Ancrene Wisse and Hali Meiðhed." *Essays and Studies*, 14 (1929), 104–26.

Philological essay on two medieval religious works.

1930  I-23  "The Oxford English School." *The Oxford Magazine*, 48, No. 21 (29 May 1930), 778–82.

Proposal for reforming the syllabus.

1932 I-24 "The Name 'Nodens.' " In *Report on the Excavation of the Prehistoric, Roman, and Post-Roman Sites in Lydney Park, Gloucestershire.* By Sir R. E. M. Wheeler and T. V. Wheeler. London: Oxford Univ. Press, 1932, Appendix I, pp. 132–37.

I-25 "Sigelwara Land: Part I." *Medium Aevum*, 1 (December, 1932), 183–96.
> See also I-29, and review by Daunt (II-133).

1933 I-26 "Errantry." *The Oxford Magazine*, 52, No. 5 (9 November, 1933), 180.
> Poem. See I-54.

1934 I-27 "Looney." *The Oxford Magazine*, 52, No. 9 (18 January, 1934), 340.
> Poem. An early version of "The Sea-bell" in *ATB* (see I-54).

I-28 "The Adventures of Tom Bombadil." *The Oxford Magazine*, 52, No. 13 (15 February 1934), 464–65.
> Poem. See I-54.

I-29 "Sigelwara Land: Part II." *Medium Aevum*, 3 (June, 1934), 95–111.
> See also I-25. Old English philological study.

I-30 "Chaucer as a Philologist: The Reeve's Tale." *Transactions of the Philological Society* (1934), pp. 1–70.
> This paper was read at a meeting of the Society in Oxford on Saturday, 16 May 1931. Discusses Chaucer's conscious use of a northern dialect of Middle English in one of the *Canterbury Tales*.

1936 I-31 *Songs for the Philologists.* Privately printed in the Department of English at University College, London, 1936.
> These humorous verses were written by Tolkien, E. V. Gordon, and others, but none are signed. Carpenter (II-86) ascribes to Tolkien's authorship: "From One to Five," "Syx Mynet," "Ruddoc Hana," "Ides Ælfscyne," "Bagme Bloma," "Eadig Beo þu," "Ofer Widne Garsecg," "La, Huru," "I Sat Upon a Bench," "Natura Apis," "The Root of the Boot" (see Johnston, II-310, for a comparison of this with its revised version, "The Stone Troll," in *ATB*, I-54), "Frenchman Froth," and "Lit and Lang."

1937 I-32 "The Dragon's Visit." *The Oxford Magazine*, 55, No. 11 (4 February 1937), 342.
> Poem. See also I-59.

I-33    "Knocking at the Door: Lines induced by sensations when waiting for an answer at the door of an Exalted Academic Person." *The Oxford Magazine*, 55, No. 13 (18 February 1937), 403.

> Poem, signed "Oxymore." Early version of "The Mewlips" In *ATB* (see I-54).

I-34    "Iumonna Gold Galdre Bewunden" ["The Hoard"]. *The Oxford Magazine*, 55, No. 15 (4 March 1937), 473.

> Poem. See also I-7, I-54.

I-35    "Beowulf: The Monsters and the Critics." *Proceedings of the British Academy*, 22 (1936), 245–95.

> The Sir Israel Gollancz Memorial Lecture, 25 November 1936. Reprinted separately by the Oxford University Press, 1958. Reprinted in *An Anthology of Beowulf Criticism*, ed. Lewis E. Nicholson (Notre Dame: Univ. of Notre Dame Press, 1963), pp. 51–103. Again reprinted for the Twentieth Century Views Series in *The Beowulf Poet*, ed. Donald K. Fry (New Jersey: Prentice-Hall, 1968), pp. 8–56. This seminal study of the Anglo-Saxon poem's literary qualities is too rich for brief annotation; basically Tolkien reads the poem as divided into two parts which contrast the hero's youth and glory with his old age and death. Although Gardner (II-220) and Rubey (II-574) hold a distinctly minority view that this essay did not mark any particular watershed in Old English studies, most scholars would agree that it was a largely pioneering effort that gave a tremendous impetus to literary criticism (as distinct from philological, anthropological, or historical study) of *Beowulf*. See the assessment by Kaske (II-319).

I-36    *The Hobbit: or There and Back Again*. London: George Allen and Unwin, 1937.

> Four color plates were added to the second impression in 1937, and this 1st ed. was reprinted in 1942 and 1946; 2nd ed., 1951; 3rd ed., 1966; all eds. reprinted many times. First U.S. ed., Boston: Houghton Mifflin, 1938; 2nd ed., 1958. 3rd U.S. ed., New York: Ballantine, 1965; reprinted many times, sometimes with minor revisions. No definitive study has yet been made of Tolkien's revisions of the text of *H*, but see Christensen (II-97).

1938    I-37    Letter regarding *The Hobbit. Observer* (London), 20 February 1938, p. 9.

> Reply to a letter published in this newspaper on 16 January 1938, in regard to sources for *H*.

1940   I-38   Preface to *Beowulf and the Finnesburg Fragment: A Translation into Modern English Prose*, by John R. Clark Hall, revised by C. L. Wrenn. London: George Allen and Unwin, 1940, pp. ix–xliii.

> On the alliterative meter of Anglo-Saxon poetry in particular, and other aspects of the poems.

1945   I-39   "Leaf by Niggle." *The Dublin Review*, 216 (January, 1945), 46–61.

> Short story. Reprinted in *T&L* (I-58) and *TR* (I-62).

     I-40   "The Lay of Aotrou and Itroun." *The Welsh Review*, 4 (December, 1945), 254–66.

> A modern English poem in the manner of a Breton lay.

1947   I-41   " 'iþþlen' in *Sawles Warde*." *English Studies*, 28 (December, 1947), 168–70.

> Philological essay written in collaboration with S. R. T. O. d'Ardenne.

     I-42   "On Fairy-Stories." In *Essays Presented to Charles Williams*. Ed. C. S. Lewis. London: Oxford Univ. Press, 1947, 38–89.

> A photolithographic reprint of this *Festschrift* was published in 1966 by the William B. Eerdmans Publishing Company of Grand Rapids, Michigan. An abbreviated form of this essay was delivered as the Andrew Lang Memorial Lecture at St. Andrews in Scotland in 1938. Revised and reprinted in *T&L* (I-58), this revised essay was also reprinted in *TR* (I-62). Selections from the revised essay have been reprinted in several anthologies of criticism: e.g., "Children and Fairy Stories" in *Only Connect: Readings on Children's Literature*, ed. Sheila Egoff, G. T. Stubbs, and L. F. Ashley (Oxford Univ. Press, 1969), pp. 111–20; and "Fantasy" in *Pastoral and Romance: Modern Essays in Criticism*, ed. Eleanor Terry Lincoln (New York: Prentice-Hall, 1969), pp. 202–07.

1948   I-43   "MS. Bodley 34: A re-collation of a collation." *Studia Neophilologica*, 20 (1947–48), 65–72.

> A philological essay written in collaboration with S. R. T. O. d'Ardenne.

1949   I-44   *Farmer Giles of Ham*. London: George Allen and Unwin, 1949. Boston: Houghton Mifflin, 1950.

> Illustrated by Pauline Baynes. Reprinted in *TR* (I-62). Also issued jointly with *SWM* (I-63) by Ballantine Books in 1969 (I-68). All of these editions have been reprinted many times.

1953 I-45 "A Fourteenth-Century Romance." *Radio Times*, London, 4 December 1953.

> Foreword to the broadcasts by the British Broadcasting Corporation Third Programme of Tolkien's translation of *Sir Gawain and the Green Knight* (see I-73).

I-46 "The Homecoming of Beorhtnoth Beorhthelm's Son." *Essays and Studies*, NS 6 (1953), 1–18.

> A modern English sequel to *The Battle of Maldon*, together with an essay on the Old English poem. Reprinted in *TR* (I-62). See also II-158, II-732.

I-47 "Middle English 'Losenger': Sketch of an Etymological and Semantic Enquiry." *Essais de Philologie Moderne* (Paris: Société d'édition "Les Belles Lettres," 1953), pp. 63–76.

> A paper presented to the Congrès International de Philologie Moderne at Liège in September, 1951. Tolkien shows how the different and changing senses in the development of this word, "losenger," indicate the contacts of Germanic and Latin in Northern Gaul.

1954 I-48 *The Fellowship of the Ring: being the first part of The Lord of the Rings.* London: George Allen and Unwin, 1954; 2nd ed., 1966. Boston: Houghton Mifflin, 1954; 2nd ed., 1967. New York: Ace, 1965. Revised ed., New York: Ballantine, 1965.

> See also I-49, I-50.

I-49 *The Two Towers: being the second part of The Lord of the Rings.* London: George Allen and Unwin, 1954; 2nd ed., 1966. Boston: Houghton Mifflin, 1955; 2nd ed., 1967. New York: Ace, 1965. Revised ed., New York: Ballantine, 1965.

> See also I-48, I-50.

1955 I-50 *The Return of the King: being the third part of The Lord of the Rings.* London: George Allen and Unwin, 1955. Boston: Houghton Mifflin, 1956; 2nd ed., 1967. New York: Ace, 1965. Revised ed., New York: Ballantine, 1965.

> See also I-48, I-49. All of these editions (except that by Ace Books, the first paperback edition, but an unauthorized one that was allowed to go out of print) were reprinted many times. There were also English-language editions in Canada and Australia, and *LOTR* has also been translated into more than a dozen languages. Although it is often mistakenly referred to as a "trilogy," *LOTR* is in fact a single work that was serialized in three volumes because of its great length.

(Indeed, in 1968 Allen and Unwin did issue a one-volume edition in paperback, minus most of the appendixes.) Tolkien stated that the three volumes were an accident of publication and that the significant structural units were the six Books (see Everett, II-187). The original titles of the six Books were: I, "The First Journey"; II, "The Journey of the Nine Companions"; III, "The Treason of Isengard"; IV, "The Journey of the Ring-bearers"; V, "The War of the Ring": and VI, "The End of the Third Age" (see West, II-713). For a textual study of the different editions of *LOTR*, see Nored (II-472).

I-51    "Imram." *Time and Tide*, 36 (3 December 1955), 1561.

Verse dialogue between St. Brendan and an inquirer into the Saint's fabulous sea voyage. The title is Gaelic for "voyage" and refers to an Old Irish genre of such stories. Illustrations by Robert Gibbings.

I-52    Preface to *The Ancrene Riwle*, translated into Modern English by M. B. Salu (London: Burns and Oates, 1955; Notre Dame: Univ. of Notre Dame Press, 1956), p. v.

Tolkien calls the Middle English dialect of the original "a natural, easy, and cultivated speech, familiar with the courtesy of letters, able to combine colloquial liveliness with a reverence for the already long tradition of English writing," and he thinks that the translator has succeeded in representing this in modern terms.

1958    I-53    Prefatory Note in *The Old English Apollonius of Tyre*. Ed. Peter Goolden. London: Oxford Univ. Press, 1958.

Tolkien notes that publication of the edition was delayed due to the loss of the editor's finished manuscript in a fire. In the interim another edition, by Dr. Joseph Raith, was published, but the Goolden edition still has valuable features which justify publishing it as well.

1962    I-54    *The Adventures of Tom Bombadil and other verses from The Red Book*. London: George Allen and Unwin, 1962. Boston: Houghton Mifflin, 1962.

Preface by Tolkien. Illustrated by Pauline Baynes. The sixteen poems included are: "The Adventures of Tom Bombadil" (see I-28); "Bombadil goes Boating"; "Errantry" (see I-26); "Princess Mee"; "The Man in the Moon stayed up Too Late" (see I-12); "The Man in the Moon came down Too Soon" (see I-11); "The Stone Troll" (see I-31); "Perry-the-Winkle"; "The Mewlips" (see I-33); "Oliphaunt"; "Fastitocalon"; "Cat"; "Shadow-bride"; "The Hoard" (see I-7, I-34); "The Sea-bell" (see I-27) and "The Last Ship." *ATB* reprinted in *TR* (see I-62). "The Hoard" reprinted in *The Hamish Hamilton Book of Dragons*, ed. Roger Lancelyn Green (London: Hamish Hamilton, 1970), pp. 246–48.

I-55  *Ancrene Wisse: The English Text of the Ancrene Riwle.*
Introduction by N. R. Ker. Early English Text Society,
Original Series No. 249. London: Oxford Univ. Press,
1962.

> Edition of the medieval Rule for Anchoresses based on MS. Corpus
> Christi College Cambridge 402.

1963  I-56  "English and Welsh." *Angles and Britons* (Cardiff: Univ. of
Wales Press, 1963; Mystic, Conn.: Verry, Lawrence, 1963),
pp. 1–41.

> The O'Donnell Lectures, Vol. I. The essay is primarily linguistic in
> focus, but contains some autobiographical reminiscence and a brief
> footnote on the relation of Tolkien's linguistic interests to his
> invented languages. See also II-730.

1964  I-57  Letter to *I Palantir*, No. 3 (April, 1964), p. 19.

> Tolkien comments on an article by Arthur K. Weir in a previous
> issue of this fanzine.

I-58  *Tree and Leaf.* London: George Allen and Unwin, 1964.
Boston: Houghton Mifflin, 1965.

> Reprints *LBN* (I-39) and a revised version of *OFS* (I-42). The whole
> work is reprinted in *TR* (I-62).

1965  I-59  "Once Upon a Time" and "The Dragon's Visit," in *Winter's
Tales for Children: 1*, ed. Caroline Hillier (London:
Macmillan, 1965; New York: St. Martin's, 1965), pp. 44–45
and 84–87.

> Both poems reprinted in *The Young Magicians*, ed. Lin Carter (New
> York: Ballantine, 1969), pp. 254–62. See also I-32.

1966  I-60  "Tolkien on Tolkien." *Diplomat*, 18 (October, 1966), 39.

> Comment on his life and work prepared by Tolkien for his
> publishers.

I-61  *The Jerusalem Bible.* London: Darton, Longman and
Todd, 1966. Garden City, N.Y.: Doubleday, 1966.

> Tolkien is listed as one of the editors. Ready (II-543) states that he
> worked on the Book of Job; but Carpenter (II-86) notes that
> Tolkien's sole contribution was to prepare the first draft of the
> translation of the Book of Jonah.

I-62  *The Tolkien Reader.* New York: Ballantine, 1966.

> Reprints in one volume *HB* (I-46), *T&L* (I-58), *FGH* (I-44), and *ATB*
> (I-54), with an introduction by Beagle (II-30). Reprinted many times.

1967   I-63   *Smith of Wootton Major.* London: George Allen and Unwin, 1967. Boston: Houghton Mifflin, 1967.

> Illustrated by Pauline Baynes. Reprinted together with *FGH* (I-44) in a single volume (see I-68). It was also published, illustrated by Milton Glaser, in the magazine *Redbook*, 130 (December, 1967), 58–61, 101, 103–07; see also the editorial on p. 6 discussing the contents of this issue.

I-64   "For W. H. A." *Shenandoah*, 18, No. 2 (Winter, 1967), 96–97.

> An alliterative poem written in honor of W. H. Auden's sixtieth birthday, appearing both in Old English and in a modern English translation.

I-65   *The Road Goes Ever On: A Song Cycle.* Boston: Houghton Mifflin, 1967; 2nd revised ed., 1978. London: George Allen and Unwin, 1968; 2nd revised ed., 1978.

> Donald Swann's musical settings for poems by Tolkien. Comments by Tolkien include discussion of Elvish, literal English translations of some Elvish passages, and notes on the religion of Middle-earth. See also I-66, I-71.

I-66   *Poems and Songs of Middle Earth.* Caedmon Record TC1231. New York: Caedmon Records, 1967.

> Issued at the same time as *RGEO* (I-65). On one side William Elvin sings the material from *RGEO* accompanied by Swann on the piano; on the other side Tolkien reads some of his poetry. Some reflections on the verse by W. H. Auden are printed on the back of the record jacket; an illustration by Pauline Baynes graces the front of the jacket.

1968   I-67   Letter to *Tolkien Journal*, 3, No. 3, Whole No. 9 (Summer, 1968), 3.

> Tolkien avows that Ready's *Tolkien Relation* (II-543) was not published with his assistance or approval.

1969   I-68   *Smith of Wootton Major and Farmer Giles of Ham.* New York: Ballantine, 1969.

> Reprints *SWM* (I-63) and *FGH* (I-44) in one paperback volume, with the original illustrations by Pauline Baynes. Later reprints substitute a cover by the Brothers Hildebrandt.

I-69   "A Letter from J. R. R. Tolkien." In *The Image of Man in C. S. Lewis.* By William Luther White. Nashville, Tenn.: Abingdon, 1969, pp. 221–22.

> Tolkien talks about the Inklings and the origin of the name.

1972   I-70   "Beautiful place because trees are loved." *Daily Telegraph* (London), Tuesday, 4 July 1972, p. 16.

Letter on the theme that "In all my works I take the part of trees as against all their enemies."

1974   I-71   "Bilbo's Last Song (at the Grey Havens)." London: George Allen and Unwin, 1974. Boston: Houghton Mifflin, 1974.

Poem issued as a poster; the British edition has an illustration by Pauline Baynes as the background for the text, while the U.S. poster has a photograph by Robert Strindberg of a coastal scene. Poem reprinted in 2nd ed. of *RGEO* (I-65).

1975   I-72   "Guide to the Names in The Lord of the Rings" (ed. Christopher Tolkien). In *A Tolkien Compass*. Ed. Jared Lobdell. La Salle, Ill.: Open Court Publishing Co., 1975, pp. 153–201.

See also II-388. Tolkien prepared these notes on nomenclature in Middle-earth as a guide for translators.

I-73   *Sir Gawain and the Green Knight, Pearl and Sir Orfeo*, translated into modern English; edited and with a preface by Christopher Tolkien. London: George Allen and Unwin, 1975. Boston: Houghton Mifflin, 1975. New York: Ballantine, 1980.

I-74   *J. R. R. Tolkien reads and sings his The Hobbit and The Fellowship of the Ring.* Caedmon Record TC1477. New York: Caedmon Records, 1975.

Includes *H*, Ch. 5, "Riddles in the Dark," and selected prose passages and verse from *FR*. Recordings made by George Sayer in August, 1952 (see II-595). The note on the jacket that Side B, band 16 features an unpublished poem is in error: this was published in *LOTR*, Book III, Ch. 6.

I-75   *J. R. R. Tolkien reads and sings his The Lord of the Rings: The Two Towers, The Return of the King.* Caedmon Record TC1478. New York: Caedmon Records, 1975.

Selections from *TT* and *RK*, with one Elvish passage from *FR*. See also I-74.

I-76   Letter. *Mythlore*, 3, No. 2, Whole No. 10 (1975), 19.

Letter to Herbert Schiro dated 17 November 1957. Tolkien notes that *LOTR* is not about power but "Death and the desire for deathlessness." See GoodKnight (II-232).

1976   I-77   *Drawings by Tolkien.* Oxford: The Ashmolean Museum, 1976.

> Foreword by K. J. Garlick. Introduction by Baillie Tolkien. Biographical note by Humphrey Carpenter. Catalogue of an exhibition of Tolkien's illustrations for *H, FCL,* and *LOTR,* held at the Ashmolean Museum in Oxford from 14 December 1976 to 27 February 1977, and at the National Book League in London from 2 March to 7 April 1977.

    I-78   *The Father Christmas Letters.* Ed. Baillie Tolkien. London: George Allen and Unwin, 1976. Boston: Houghton Mifflin, 1976.

> Letters written by Tolkien, using the persona of Father Christmas, to his children between 1925 and World War II, with illustration by the author.

1977   I-79   *The Silmarillion.* Ed. Christopher Tolkien. London: George Allen and Unwin, 1977. Boston: Houghton Mifflin, 1977. New York: Ballantine, 1979.

1979   I-80   *Pictures by J. R. R. Tolkien.* London: George Allen and Unwin, 1979. Boston: Houghton Mifflin, 1979.

> Foreword and notes by Christopher Tolkien. Drawings by Tolkien of scenes from *H, LOTR,* and *Silm,* and one from *FCL.* Most were published previously in the Tolkien calendars issued by Allen and Unwin between 1973 and 1979.

    I-81   "Valedictory Address to the University of Oxford, 5 June 1959." In *J. R. R. Tolkien, Scholar and Storyteller: Essays In Memoriam.* Ed. Mary Salu and Robert T. Farrell. Ithaca and London: Cornell Univ. Press, 1979, pp. 16–32.

> Tolkien makes a strong plea that there be no artificial separation between the study of *Lang.* and *Lit.* (that is, between linguistics and the study of literature).

1980   I-82   *Unfinished Tales of Númenor and Middle-earth.* Ed. Christopher Tolkien. London: George Allen and Unwin, 1980. Boston: Houghton Mifflin, 1980.

    I-83   Letter. Deborah Webster Rogers and Ivor A. Rogers, *J. R. R. Tolkien* (Boston: Twayne, 1980), pp. 125–26.

> Letter dated 25 October 1958 on Tolkien's "tastes, habits, [and] characteristics."

# II. Critical Works on Tolkien

II-1 Aadnanes, Per M. "Diktekunsten og eventyrlandet: J. R. R. Tolkiens *The Lord of the Rings*—eit ekko av det Kristne evangeliet?" *Edda: Nordisk Tidsskrift for Litteraturforskning*, 77, No. 4 (1977), 227–35.

Not seen.

II-2 Ace Books. *Tolkien Journal*, 2, No. 2 (1966), 4.

Publicity release. Ace has paid the full sum (rather than the customary one quarter for an English author) in back royalties to Tolkien. Ace has always been willing to pay royalties to Tolkien, but not to his publisher who forfeited his copyright. See also Ace (II-3), Dempsey (II-151), Lee (II-361), Nored (II-472), Plotz (II-524), and Scott (II-603).

II-3 "Ace books reaches agreement with Tolkien." *Publishers Weekly*, 189 (14 March 1966), pp. 37–38.

See above (II-2). A reply by Rayner Unwin was printed in the 9 May 1966 issue of this journal on p. 31: "It is noteworthy that the net result of this affair has been to distract an author of genius for six months from all creative work."

II-4 Adams, Clara. Review of *FGH*. *Library Journal*, 75 (1 December 1950), 2084. Reprinted in *Starred Books from the Library Journal*. Ed. Peggy Melcher. New York: Library Journal, 1952, p. 50.

II-5 Adams, Robert M. "The Hobbit Habit." *New York Review of Books*, 24 (24 November 1977), 22–24.

Review-essay on *Silm*. Although *H* and *LOTR* are uneven, they do have real literary qualities (e.g., exotic visual effects, rich linguistic textures, fascinating creatures). Those who enjoyed them and wish to prolong the pleasure would be better advised to go to Tolkien's own sources rather than to *Silm*, in which the epic elements are smothered by an overgrowth of genealogy.

II-6 Allan, James D. "The Decline and Fall of the Osgiliathan Empire." *Mythcon III Proceedings* (July, 1972). Ed. Glen H. GoodKnight. Whittier, Calif.: The Mythopoeic Society, 1974, pp. 3–6, 32, 36.

Notes possible influence on *LOTR* of situations in Europe from the seventh to the eleventh centuries. Cf. Epstein (II-179).

II-7 ———. *A Glossary of the Eldarin Tongues*. Privately published in Ontario, Canada, 1972.

Subsumed into, and superseded by, *An Introduction to Elvish* (II-302).

II-8      _____. "More Tolkien Exploitation." *Mythlore*, 3, No. 2, Whole No. 10 (1975), 26–27.

> Review of Ready, *The Lord of the Rings, The Hobbit Notes* (see II-542).

II-9      _____. *A Speculation on The Silmarillion*. Baltimore: T-K Graphics, n.d. [1977].

> This monograph has twenty-four unnumbered pages providing a corrected text of Allan's *An Extrapolation on The Silmarillion* (Liverpool, England: Tolkien Society, 1975), a thirty-six-page monograph which was itself a revision of his "The Story of The Silmarillion" which appeared in two parts in the British fanzine, *Mallorn*, Nos. 7 and 8. Gathers references to the First and Second Ages from Tolkien's writings and from his communications to some of his readers. Guesses (sometimes correctly, sometimes not) how the story line of *Silm* will be. For other information and speculation available prior to the publication of *Silm*, see Gilson (II-227, II-228), Jones (II-312), Kilby (II-338), Kocher (II-348), Noad (II-467).

_____. See also II-301, II-302.

II-10     Allen, Bruce. "At the Creation." *Saturday Review/World*, 1 (15 June 1974), 25–27.

> Review of Helms, *Tolkien's World* (II-270). Helms contributes a sense of the autobiographical reasons for the coherence in Tolkien's work. He has good discussions of the themes of heroic adventure as maturation ritual, the realistic presentation of evil, and consolation as equivalent to tragic catharsis. His recantation of his Freudian reading of *H* sounds almost completely phony, and he is erratic in his analyses of the lesser works, but he has a good, detailed critique of *LOTR*. He makes awkward errors of emphasis and proportion, he is sometimes arbitrary and simplistic, and he repeats points needlessly; but he examines Tolkien's rhetoric very well.

Anderson, Poul. See II-301

II-11     Andrews, Bart, with Bernie Zuber. *The Tolkien Quiz Book*. New York: Signet, 1979.

> A thousand and one questions, arranged in one hundred quizzes, ninety-nine with ten questions each and one with eleven, on all of Tolkien's fiction. This is mostly useful for trivia games, but the detail can be informative. Cf. Buchholz (II-74). For reviews, see III-B-1.

II-12     Aquino, John. *Fantasy in Literature*. Washington, D.C.: National Education Association, 1977. Document numbers: ED 144 097; also CS 203 625. Available either in paper copy from the NEA or on microfiche from ERIC (Educational Research Information Center).

> Argues that fantasy, as an activity of the mind and as literature, is useful for promoting language development and appreciation of literature. *OFS* is

cited passim, and there is a discussion of *LOTR* on pp. 42-44. *LOTR* is a storehouse of fantasy motifs, including transformations, animate nature, quest with a band of experts, epic hero, unlikely hero, stricken king, intermarriage of mortal and immortal, and magic ring. Various themes treated are responsibility, good versus evil, life versus death, fate, and love. Its flaws are stiff women characters, lack of humor, and skimpy destruction of evil at the end.

II-13    Ardenne, S. R. T. O. d'. "The Man and the Scholar." In *J. R. R. Tolkien, Scholar and Storyteller* (II-590), pp. 33–37.

An important aspect of Tolkien's wonderful humanity was his deeply felt role as *paterfamilias*. His great fiction grew out of stories for his children, informed by his love of languages.

II-14    Atchity, Kenneth. "Two Views of J. R. R. Tolkien." *San Francisco Review of Books*, January, 1978. Reprinted in Becker (II-37), pp. 96–100.

Review article on *Silm* and Carpenter, *Tolkien: a biography* (II-86).

II-15    Auden, W. H. "At the End of the Quest, Victory." *New York Times Book Review*, 22 January 1956, p. 5. Reprinted in Becker (II-37), pp. 44–48.

Review of *RK*. "If, as I believe, Mr. Tolkien has succeeded more completely than any previous writer in this genre in using the traditional properties of the Quest, the heroic journey, the Numinous Object, the conflict between Good and Evil while at the same time satisfying our sense of historical and social reality, it should be possible to know how he has succeeded" (p. 5). Argues that JRRT has created a vastly detailed world which is different from ours but which never violates our sense of the credible. Sees the victory of Good over Evil as deepened artistically by an awareness of the moral neutrality of physical and mental power: Evil has every advantage except that it is inferior in imagination, and Sauron cannot conceive that his enemies could try to destroy the Ring rather than use it themselves.

II-16    _____. "Good and Evil in *The Lord of the Rings*." *Tolkien Journal*, 3, No. i (1967), 5–8. Reprinted in *Critical Quarterly*, 10 (1968), 138–42.

Moral choice seems to be related to the power of speech. There are eight talking species in Middle-earth: Elves (who are unfallen), Dwarves, Hobbits, Wizards, Ents, Men (all of whom are capable of both good *and* evil), Trolls and Orcs (who appear to be irredeemably evil). JRRT has made his Good powerful and his Evil even more so, but Evil fails because of the mistakes it cannot, by its very nature, help making: it cannot imagine good motives, is irrationally cruel, and all alliances of Evil are necessarily unstable. Cf. Ellwood (II-174), Hayes and Renshaw (II-262), Hodgart (II-282), Webster (II-700). For the Elves as "fallen" beings, see *Silm*.

II-17    _____. "The Hero Is a Hobbit." *New York Times Book Review*, 31 October 1954, p. 37.

> Review of *FR*, praising it as a various, exciting, and realistic (not literalistic) Quest adventure, "reminiscent of the Icelandic sagas."

II-18    _____. "The Quest Hero." *Texas Quarterly*, 4, No. 4 (Winter, 1961), 81–93. Reprinted in Isaacs and Zombardo (II-307), pp. 40–61. Reprinted in *Perspectives in Contemporary Criticism*. Ed. Sheldon Norman Grebstein. New York: Harper and Row, 1968, pp. 370–81.

> Essay on the characteristics of the traditional Quest story, with discussion of *LOTR* as illustration. Expands some ideas touched on in his earlier articles.

II-19    _____. "A World Imaginary, but Real." *Encounter*, 3 (November, 1954), 59–62.

> Review of *FR*. Discusses JRRT's characterization (he "manages very cleverly to give his types an uncommon depth and solidity by providing each of them with a past which is more that of the group to which he belongs than a personal one; what Aragorn, for instance, talks about is the history of the Rangers, not of himself"), the linguistic invention, and the danger of drawing contemporary historical parallels.

_____. See also I-64, I-66, II-143.

II-20    Bailey, Anthony. "Power in the Third Age of the Middle Earth." *Commonweal*, 64 (11 May 1956), 154.

> Review of *LOTR*. It is "not a great epic, though it does have some epic qualities: a certain imaginative stature, considerable creative eloquence," because of its lack of moral and psychological complexity.

II-21    Ballif, Sandra. "Elvish Dictionary: A Sindarin-Quenya Dictionary, More or Less, Listing All Elvish Words Found in *The Lord of the Rings, The Hobbit*, and *The Road Goes Ever On* by J. R. R. Tolkien." Part 1 (*a* to *Curunir*) in *Mythlore*, 1, No. 1 (January, 1969), 41–44; Part 2 (*-dacil* to *Huorn*) in *Mythlore*, 1, No. 2 (April, 1969), 33–36; Part 3 (*Hurin* to *menel*) in *Mythlore*, 1, No. 4 (October, 1969), 23–26.

> Gives, where known, lexical information and English translation, but usually does not cite occurrences in the texts. Alpajpuri (pseudonym of Paul Novitski) offers some corrections in a letter in *Mythlore*, 1, No. 2 (April, 1969), 53–54. See also Allan (II-7), Noel (II-469), and especially II-302.

II-22    Bannon, B[arbara] A. Review of *TR*. *Publishers Weekly*, 8 August 1966, p. 61.

> Short review, listing contents. ". . . Peter S. Beagle's introduction [see II-

30] is charming and appropriate as a prelude to these delightful selections and may also be read as an introduction to hobbit-land and beyond. We hope this new volume will widen the Tolkien circle further."

II-23    Barber, Dorothy K. "The Meaning of *The Lord of the Rings*," in "The Tolkien Papers" (II-663), pp. 38–50.

JRRT "has incorporated metaphysical Christian qualities into the physical nature of Middle-earth and into the physical and mental qualities of its peoples" (p. 38). All objects in the Tolkien world possess intelligence and free will, so that, for example, the Ring chooses to bear Gollum into the Fire rather than remain with a creature it hates. Speculates about what the world of a green sun would be like.

II-24    Barber, Dorothy Elizabeth Klein. "The Structure of *The Lord of the Rings*." Ph.D. diss., University of Michigan, 1965.

Discusses building with words a secondary world with the inner consistency of reality. See *DA*, 27 (1966), 470A.

II-25    Barbour, Douglas. " 'The Shadow of the Past': History in Middle Earth." *University of Windsor Review*, 8, No. i (Fall, 1972), 35–42.

Tolkien the critic admired in *Beowulf* "the illusion of surveying a past . . . that itself reached backward into a dark antiquity," and as an artist he made such an effect one of his main concerns in *LOTR*. The past impinges on the present in a variety of ways, and the characters know (or come to realize) this and have free choice in how they respond to that impingement. There is real loss in the fading of the mythic past, but also real eucatastrophe in Middle-earth being saved for humankind. Cf. Zgorzelski (II-751).

II-26    Barnes, Myra Jean Edwards. "Linguistics and Languages in Science Fiction-Fantasy." Ph.D. diss., East Texas State University, 1971. New York: Arno, 1974.

Science fiction is a literature of communication, of late increasingly interested in the problem of communicating with beings from other worlds, and the science of communication—linguistics—may benefit criticism of this genre. Analyzes selections of invented languages by JRRT among other authors. See *DAI*, 32 (1972), 5210–11A.

Barnett, Allen. See II-134.

II-27    Barr, Donald. "Shadowy World of Men and Hobbits." *New York Times Book Review*, 1 May 1955, p. 4.

Review of *TT*. "It is . . . pure excitement, unencumbered narrative, moral warmth, barefaced rejoicing in beauty, but excitement most of all; yet a serious and scrupulous fiction, nothing cozy, no little visits to one's childhood . . . the author has had intimate access to an epic tradition stretching back and back and disappearing in the mists of Germanic history, so that his story has a kind of echoing depth behind it, wherein we hear Snorri Sturluson and Beowulf, the sagas and the Nibelungenlied, but civilized by the gentler genius of modern England."

Barrett, Ann N. See II-613.

II-28    Barron, Neil. Review of Urang, *Shadows* (II-675). *Luna Monthly*, Nos. 41/42 (October-November, 1972), p. 48.

The book derives from a thesis in literature and theology on C. S. Lewis, Charles Williams, and JRRT. The chapter on Tolkien (Ch. 3) is a revision of his essay in Hillegas (see II-277, II-676). This is a valuable scholarly study of the religious (largely Christian) concerns of the three authors and of their sources in past literature and folklore.

II-29    Basney, Lionel. "The Place of Myth in a Mythical Land: Two Notes (Converging)." *Mythlore*, 3, No. 2, Whole No. 10 (1975), 15–17.

Two related techniques used by Tolkien to give the world of *LOTR* such sensuous solidity are that of the realizing imagination (providing sharp detail) and that of deliberate, suggestive vagueness.

Bayha, Maureen. See Becker (II-37).

II-30    Beagle, Peter S. "Tolkien's Magic Ring." *Holiday*, 39, No. 6 (June, 1966), 128, 130, 133–34. Reprinted in *TR*, pp. ix–xvi.

A warmly appreciative tribute by another master of fantasy.

II-31    Beard, Henry N. and Douglas C. Kenney. *Bored of the Rings, or Tolkien Revisited*. New York: Signet, 1969.

Harvard Lampoon parody of *LOTR*. Cf. parodies by Carroll, "The Picnic," in Becker (II-37) and by Kathleen Huber, "Hello, Frodo!" in Berman and Nahigian (II-45).

II-32    Beatie, Bruce A. "Folk Tale, Fiction, and Saga in J. R. R. Tolkien's *The Lord of the Rings*." In "The Tolkien Papers" (II-663), pp. 1–17.

Introductory speech at the 1966 JRRT Symposium at Mankato. Interprets *LOTR* in relation to the characteristic components of traditional epic as described by classicist Rhys Carpenter. Surveys the differing critical opinions about JRRT's work.

II-33    _____. "*The Lord of the Rings*: Myth, Reality, and Relevance." *Western Review*, 4, No. 2 (Winter, 1967), 58–59.

One reason for the popularity of *LOTR* is that Tolkien satisfies a modern need by providing an imagined universe that is an ordered, moral world in which commitment and individual choice are important.

II-34    _____. "The Tolkien Phenomenon." *Nisus* (October, 1967), 4–5, 8.

Examines the reactions to *LOTR* in three chronological phases: 1954–56 (reviews), 1957–64 (scholars and general readers), and 1965 to date of article (widespread popularity and cult status). See also Beatie (II-35).

II-35    _____. "The Tolkien Phenomenon: 1954–1968." *Journal of Popular Culture*, 3, No. 4 (Spring, 1970), 689–703.

Expansion of earlier article in *Nisus* (II-34). Notes the progress of JRRT's popularity from the early reviews to the early scholarly critiques to literary respectability and the cult. Critics, scholars, and general readers (sometimes incarnate in the same individual) are involved in the phenomenon, and Tolkien is popular with older business and professional people as well as with students and academics. *LOTR* can be read as pure narrative adventure, but people are too concerned with its moral structure for this to be the whole answer, as Menen in "Professor Tolkien and the Hobbits" (II-534) suggested. Our generation finds overtones of the atomic threat in *LOTR*, but no other work with such a center has had such an effect. The many-leveled artistry of *LOTR* may explain the breadth of its appeal, but the depth and intensity of that appeal are more likely due to the work's mythic roots. JRRT (like Grass, Updike, and Peake) is part of a tendency to move away from "realism" toward imaginative creation of internally coherent "myths." JRRT offers a world with an ordered commitment and choice, and is thus meaningful to our culture which (as Apollo 11 showed) has identified myth and present reality. See also Lerner (II-368), Thomson (II-651), Ward (II-695), and West (II-714).

II-36    Bechtel, Louise S. Review of *FGH*. *New York Herald Tribune Book Review*, 12 November 1950, p. 14.

*FGH* is a minor masterpiece of nonsense, spoofing all the legends of knights and dragons broadly, briefly, and merrily; but it may have in mind our modern need of native wit and courage against crafty dragons and stupid kings.

II-37    Becker, Alida, ed. *The Tolkien Scrapbook*. Philadelphia: Running Press, 1978 (paper). New York: Grosset and Dunlap, 1978 (hardbound).

A potpourri of songs, poems, puzzles, pictures, parody, bibliography, recipes, fiction and essays. Songs: "The Passing of the Elven-kind" by Ted Johnstone (reprinted from *Entmoot*, No. 4, Spring, 1967); "High Fly the Nazgul, Oh!" by Ted Johnstone, et al. (reprinted from *I Palantir*, No. 1, August, 1961); the anonymous "Middle-earth" and "Smaug the Magic Dragon" (reprinted from Berman and Nahigian, II-45) and "The Orcs' Marching Song" by George Heap (reprinted from *Niekas*, No. 8, March 1964). Poems: "Christmas at the South Pole" (reprinted from *Minas Tirith Evening-Star*, 6, No. 4, October, 1976) and "A Baroque Memorial: J. R. R. Tolkien" (reprinted from *Mythlore*, 3, No. 2, Whole No. 10, 1975, pp. 11–12), both by J. R. Christopher; and "Haiku Portraits" by Don Studebaker, Ted Johnstone, et al. (reprinted from *I Palantir*, No. 2, August, 1961, and No. 3, April, 1964). Puzzles by Mel Rosen. Pictures: photographs of scenes and people associated with JRRT; black and white drawings by Michael Green; color drawings by Tim Kirk (reprinted from Ballantine's

1975 Tolkien Calendar). Parody, "The Picnic," by Paulette Carroll (reprinted from *Orcrist*, 1, 1966, pp. 50–51). There are lists of Tolkien clubs and fanzines, and Bonniejean Christensen's "Tolkien Bibliography" (see Christensen, II-100). "The Middle-earth Gourmet" by Maureen Bayha and Alida Becker provides recipes (see also Nancy Smith, "Pleasures of the Hobbit Table" in "Professor Tolkien and the Hobbits," II-534). Fiction: "In the Service of the King" by Marci Helms (reprinted from *Minas Tirith Evening-Star*, 5, No. 1, October, 1975); and "Tales Told by the Lonely Mountain" by Margaret Howes. "The Coinage of Gondor and the Western Lands" by Dainis Bisenieks is a mock-scholarly article (reprinted from *Niekas*, 16, June, 1966). For other essays, see Atchity (II-14), Auden (II-15), Cater (II-91), Helms (II-266), McClusky (II-412), Searles (II-606), Weir (II-702), Wilson (II-728), and Wilson (II-729). For reviews, see III-B-2.

II-38    Becker, May Lamberton. "Books for Young People." *New York Herald Tribune Books*, 20 February 1938, p. 7.

Review of *H*. Wonders if American children will like such "an odyssey compressed . . . a story so close-packed, one of whose chapters would make a book elsewhere," but if they don't, so much the worse for them. The world of the book "is peopled thickly with tribes, not one of them human and each with its own sharply defined characteristics." It is the reassuring quality of all true fairy tales like this that you know where you stand, and even timid children read through it unscared and unscathed, knowing they are on the side of good and safe. Like *Alice*, "the story has unmistakeable signs of having been told to intelligent children," but its style is more like Dunsany's than Carroll's. Prints JRRT's drawing of the hall at Bag End.

II-39    "Before King Arthur." *Chicago Sunday Tribune, Magazine of Books*, 12 November 1950, p. 17.

Two brief paragraphs by "M. B. K." describing the plot of *FGH*.

II-40    Begg, Ean C. M. *The Lord of the Rings and the Signs of the Times*. London: H. H. Greaves, 1975. The Guild of Pastoral Psychology Lecture No. 178.

A twenty-four-page monograph. Some imaginative literature, and especially *LOTR*, shows signs of our fundamental principles turning away from the lamentable drive for power and dominance to a better consciousness of the "feminine principle" of "relatedness, beauty, feeling, the heart" (p. 12). Discusses, in particular, the Hobbits, Aragorn, Gandalf, and various women characters in *LOTR*. See review by Moran (II-448).

II-41    Bell, Judy Winn. "The Language of J. R. R. Tolkien in *The Lord of the Rings*." *Mythcon I Proceedings* (4–7 September 1970). Ed. Glen GoodKnight. Los Angeles: Mythopoeic Society, 1971, pp. 35–40.

"This paper will discuss: 1) his [Tolkien's] attitudes toward his characters; 2) his own use of language—or his style—in telling his story and building his world of Middle-Earth; and 3) the styles of prose and poetry—and the separate languages—of the characters and groups of characters who inhabit the complex world he has created" (p. 35).

II-42    Bergier, Jacques. "J. R. R. Tolkien ou *Le Seigneur des anneaux*." Ch. 6 in his *Admirations*. Paris: Christian Bourgois Editeur, 1970, pp. 171–99.

> In French. Only *H* was available in French translation when this was written, and the essay provides an overview of Tolkien's work, theory of fantasy, and appeal to the young.

II-43    Bergmann, Frank. "The Roots of Tolkien's Tree: The Influence of George MacDonald and German Romanticism upon Tolkien's Essay 'On Fairy-Stories.' " *Mosaic: A Journal for the Comparative Study of Literature and Ideas*, 10, No. 2 (Winter, 1977), 5–14.

> George MacDonald's 1893 essay on "The Fantastic Imagination" and German Romantics (notably Fouqué, Hoffmann, and Novalis) anticipated and perhaps influenced some of Tolkien's ideas in *OFS*, such as the Gospels as story, and the transcendental happy ending. See also Helms (II-270), Reilly (II-549), and Wojcik (II-737) for other discussions of possible sources for *OFS*.

II-44    Berman, Ruth. "Here an Orc, There an Ork." *Mythlore*, 1, No. 1 (January, 1969), 8–10.

> With reference to *Beowulf, Paradise Lost, The Scarecrow of Oz, LOTR*, and the *Oxford English Dictionary*, she notes English meanings of "orc" as "sea-monster" and as "ogre." In a letter in *Mythlore*, 1, No. 2 (April, 1969), 51–52, Nan Braude comments on this article with reference to Ariosto and to Grendel in *Beowulf*.

II-45    Berman, Ruth, ed., and Ken Nahigian, coeditor. *The Middle-earth Songbook*. Rancho Cordova, Calif.: AJD Graphics, n.d. [1975].

> A publication of the American River College Science Fiction Club. Gathers, from numerous fanzines, musical settings by fans for poems by JRRT, and original songs on Tolkienian themes by fans (usually to traditional melodies). Includes, on pp. 106–21, Kathleen Huber's "Hello, Frodo! or What Ever Happened to Sauron's Ring?" reprinted from the fanzine, *I Palantir*, No. 4 (August, 1966), pp. 27–41 (see also parodies by Beard and Kenney, II-31, and by Carroll in Becker, II-37). Includes about sixty-three songs.

Berman, Ruth. See also Becker (II-37).

II-46    Binsse, Harry Lorin. Review of *H. Commonweal*, 29 (2 December 1938), 155.

> *H* is a "brilliantly told modern fairy story of Bilbo Baggins, the Hobbit, and his journey in search of the dragon's hoard of gold."

II-47   Bisenieks, Dainis. "The Hobbit Habit in the Critic's Eye."
        *Tolkien Journal*, 3, No. 4, Whole No. 10 (November, 1969),
        3–4. Corrected version reprinted in *Tolkien Journal*, No. 15
        (Summer, 1972), pp. 14–15.

> The critiques by Hodgart (II-282), Mathewson (II-410), and West (II-706)
> reveal more about the authors than about JRRT: all believe that a story
> should be as complex and ambiguous as life, but what would such a
> doctrine *not* condemn? Tolkien has given his hobbits real enemies (without
> good faith) and real allies (without any credibility gap); the cards are
> stacked in favor of the hobbit heroes. The hobbits are tested and the evil of
> Sauron does not need to be investigated (cf. West, II-706). Tolkien's
> opinion of machinery is not one-sided (cf. Brown, II-73). The medievalist
> element is not the most important in his work.

II-48   _____. "Power and Poetry in Middle-earth." *Mythlore*, 3, No.
        2, Whole No. 10 (1975), 20–24.

> Those who dislike *LOTR* would prefer it to be a regular modern novel,
> which it is not, but nevertheless it is not psychologically naïve. The quest of
> the Ringbearer calls for sheer plodding determination more than for
> courage; but the hobbits, besides a body and a will, have intellect and
> imagination, and it is the relation to learning, and especially to poetry and
> story, that gives *LOTR* such power.

II-49   _____. "Reading and Misreading Tolkien." In "The Tolkien
        Papers" (see II-663), pp. 98–100.

> *LOTR* should be taken more seriously than as a mere adventure story. The
> Tolkien cult may keep many judicious people from ever reading the work,
> but such light activites as wearing Tolkien buttons are only for fun and
> should not affect literary judgment.

        _____. See also Becker (II-37).

II-50   Blackmun, Kathryn. "The Development of Runic and Feanorian
        Alphabets for the Transliteration of English." In "The Tolkien
        Papers" (II-663), pp. 76–83.

> To make these alphabets a workable mode of expression for English, it is
> necessary to add a few new characters and reassign the values of others.

II-51   _____. "Translations from the Elvish." In "The Tolkien
        Papers" (II-663), pp. 95–97.

> A translation of "A Elbereth Gilthoniel" based on evidence scattered
> through *LOTR*. Cf. I-65, Cox (II-124), and Noel (II-469).

II-52   Blair, H. A. "Myth or Legend." *Church Quarterly Review*, 156
        (January–March, 1955), 121–22.

> Review of *FR*. "This is a religious book, pre-Christian, its theology that of
> the Zendavesta at its best: it is the original dualism of Zarathustra, in which
> the only true reality is in goodness and light. But there are Christian echoes
> and emphases: baptism . . . self-commitment . . . exodus . . . paradise

. . . absolution" (p. 122; cites references in *LOTR*). Cf. Barber (II-23) and Wilson (II-727).

II-53    Blissett, William. "Despots of the Rings." *South Atlantic Quarterly*, 58 (Summer, 1959), 448–56.

> *LOTR* is a heroic romance, "perhaps the last literary masterpiece of the Middle Ages" (p. 449). "By 'heroic' I mean that the action is narrated as an 'exploit' of crucial importance to the actor and his world, and that . . . the accomplishment of the central exploit is finally dependent on the hero's own inner power and virtue—a virtue partly his from the outset and partly confirmed in him through self-abnegation and endurance in the face of adversity and cruel opposition" (p. 449). See also Foster (II-209), Levitin (II-370), Moorman (II-445), and Reckford (II-545). "The work is a romance . . . in the sense that it discovers a world of wonder—discovers it so that we, returning, may find in this world a like world of wonder" (p. 451). On romance, see also Brewer (II-70), Thomson (II-650). Also draws a parallel with Wagner's Ring Cycle, on which see also Hall (II-251) and Stein (II-637).

II-54    Blount, Margaret. *Animal Land: The Creatures of Children's Fiction*. London: Hutchinson and Co. (Publishers), 1974. New York: William Morrow & Co., 1975.

> References to Tolkien, particularly to *H* and *FGH*, will be found on pp. 104, 126–29, 233, 275, 279–81, and 300. Discusses animal characters, chiefly Smaug, Chrysophylax, and Shelob. Finds influences on JRRT in the work of George MacDonald, H. Rider Haggard, and H. G. Wells, and in traditional stories such as "Jack the Giant Killer."

II-55    Boardman, John. "The Hereditary Pattern of Immortality in Elf-Human Crosses." *Tolkien Journal*, 2, No. 1 (1966), 10–11.

> Suggests that "immortality is a recessive characteristic, and is transmitted to the descendants of an elf-human cross by the Mendelian law" (p. 11). Letters of comment were published from Bob Foster, Peter Sloman, and Ned Brooks in *Tolkien Journal*, 2, No. 2 (1966), 10–12, and from David Friedman in *Tolkien Journal*, 3, No. 3, Whole No. 9 (1968), 14. See also Wallace (II-692).

II-56    Bonjour, Adrien. "Monsters Crouching and Critics Rampant: or The *Beowulf* Dragon Debated." *PMLA*, 68 (1953), 304–12.

> In spite of the objections raised by Gang (II-219), there is good reason to accept Tolkien's interpretation of the dragon in *Beowulf* as symbolic of an evil hostile to humanity.

II-57    Boswell, George W. "Proverbs and Phraseology in Tolkien's *Lord of the Ring* Complex." *University of Mississippi Studies in English*, 10 (1969), 59–65.

> Notes various linguistic devices used by JRRT in *H* and *LOTR*, including inversion, set phrases, riddles, significant names, curses, blessings, exhortations, magical songs, and especially proverbs.

II-58    _____. "Tolkien as Littérateur." *South Central Bulletin*, 32, No. 4 (Winter, 1972), 188–97.

> Though some connect *LOTR* with "history," and it is a geographically and linguistically substantial account of the affairs of Middle-earth, it is more poetic and imaginative than historical. It is a species of myth, including such elements as premonition, prophecy, and symbolism. Of the folktale plots analyzed in Stith Thompson's *Motif-Index of Folk-Literature*, twenty-two can be found in Tolkien's work (pp. 193–94). Numerous rhetorical devices occur: often metaphor, personification, and onomatopoeia, with some irony. Counts the number of rhetorical devices used in the twenty-nine proverbs and seventy-one songs and other verses in *LOTR* (p. 195). Notes a number of themes in *LOTR*, such as considerateness, courage, cooperation, comradeship, dependability, perseverance in one's duty, and —the central communication of the entire work—the Christian theme of vicarious sacrifice.

II-59    _____. "Tolkien's Riddles in *The Lord of the Rings*." *Tennessee Folklore Society Bulletin*, 35, No. 2 (June, 1969), 44–49.

> The word "riddle" (which properly means a legitimately soluble description of an object in terms intended to suggest something entirely different) is sometimes loosely used in the *LOTR* complex, but there are nine true riddles in the complex, all in *H*. Variants of some of these are known, but some are original with Tolkien, and all are original in wording, all "sterling examples of artistically ornamented folk riddles" (p. 48). The riddle game also serves to give Gandalf evidence of Gollum's kinship with hobbits, since he and Bilbo knew similar riddles.

II-60    Boucher, Anthony. Review of *FR*. *The Magazine of Fantasy and Science Fiction*, 8, No. 4 (April, 1955), 82.

> For wholly created and self-consistent absolute fantasy, written in superb prose and replete with both adventure and humor, the only book even remotely comparable is E. R. Eddison's *Worm Ouroboros*. This introductory section of the trilogy, at least, lacks Eddison's depth of characterization and his sense of narrative form, but it is hard to judge from a weighty and unrounded fragment, and there are rich treasures of beauty and imagination here.

II-61    _____. Review of *TT*. *The Magazine of Fantasy and Science Fiction*, 9, No. 2 (August, 1955), 93.

> The volumes of the trilogy are not self-sufficient, and one should read all parts of this epic of enchantment together. The length is sometimes needlessly demanding: whole paragraphs or even chapters could be lopped away without affecting form or content. Still, it is a compelling mythology, and vividly alive.

II-62    _____. Review of *LOTR*. *The Magazine of Fantasy and Science Fiction*, 11, No. 1 (July, 1956), 91–92.

*LOTR* is one of the unquestioned classics of the century; it is not likely to appear on best seller lists, but it will never be forgotten. Its length makes it possible for Tolkien to create the entire history and culture of Middle-earth down to every least minutia. It is, however, sometimes unnecessarily verbose; *RK* suffers least from this weakness, and is a masterly narration of tremendous and terrible climactic events. The hobbits provide gentle, down-to-earth humor, and all the races of Middle-earth, each a wholly credible individual creation, combine meaningfully to represent the infinite facets of the human soul.

II-63    Bradley, Marion Zimmer. *Men, Halflings and Hero Worship.* FAPA (Fantasy Amateur Press Association) booklet, 1961. Reprinted with corrections in *Niekas*, 16 (June, 1966), 25–44. Reprinted as a booklet, Baltimore: T-K Graphics, n.d. [c. 1973]. Abridged and reprinted in Isaacs and Zimbardo (see II-307), pp. 109–27.

"I hope to prove, first, that *The Lord of the Rings* is adult in structure, thesis, and emphasis; that the human relationships are adequately motivated; and second that the trilogy has a valid, basically self-consistent theme and progressive development in character and style, documenting a universal experience illuminated by fantasy: the end of the Heroic Age in the individual, as well as in Middle-earth." The abridgment in the anthology by Isaacs and Zimbardo retains the body of the article but omits the discussion of style and of the broader tradition of adventure literature. The booklet from T-K Graphics (which is illustrated by Judith Weiss) omits about a page of material on men's adventure books but is otherwise complete; it adds a brief sketch "About the Author" at the end, and Bradley has a four-page "Introduction" on the printing history of this monograph and on fantasy as an unconscious (in both senses) expression of the writer's personality.

II-64    Brady, Charles A. Review of *FGH*. *Renascence*, 3 (Spring, 1951), 191–95.

*FGH* is a very fetching "dragonnade" about a reluctant dragon and an even more reluctant dragoon. Quotes from a letter from C. S. Lewis to Brady, saying that *H* is the adaptation to children of part of a huge private mythology (invented by a Christian, not a mere aesthete) in which the whole cosmic struggle is mediated through an imaginary world. Also reviews *Dymer* and *The Lion, the Witch and the Wardrobe* by Lewis and *The Thirteen Clocks* by James Thurber.

II-65    Bratman, David S. "Books about J. R. R. Tolkien and His Works." *Science-Fiction Collector,* No. 5 (1977), pp. 26–28.

Checklist of the available books and pamphlets, excluding privately published and fan publications.

II-66    Braude, Nan. "Sion and Parnassus: Three Approaches to Myth." *Mythlore*, 1, No. 1 (January, 1969), 6–8.

> It may be argued that JRRT, C. S. Lewis, and Charles Williams formed a group only by accident (there are plenty of people who enjoy one or two of them but not all), but all three of them may be subsumed under the term "mythopoeic." Tolkien is engaged not in a retelling but a recombining of old elements (primarily from Teutonic and Celtic myth) into a new whole. Lewis is concerned with building a small and secular myth that will imitate a great and theological *mythos*, Christianity. Williams uses religious and mystical symbols, always giving them a Christian interpretation. In her letter in *Mythlore*, 1, No. 2 (April, 1969), 51–52, Braude comments that *LOTR* does not allude to our twentieth-century primary-world realities, but is relevant to them.

II-67    _____. "Tolkien and Spenser." *Mythlore*, 1, No. 3 (July, 1969), 8–10, 13.

> While both *LOTR* and *Faerie Queen* are interlaced quest stories, *LOTR* is far more successful as a story pattern while *FQ* is more satisfying as an image of human experience. Tolkien's basic purpose is aesthetic where Spenser's is moral.

_____. See also Berman (II-44).

II-68    Brett, Cyril. Review of *GGK*, 1st ed. *Modern Language Review*, 22 (October, 1927), 451–58.

> "Clearness, conciseness, scholarship, and common-sense are the marks of this edition." Suggests improvements for any later edition.

II-69    Brewer, Derek. "Fathers' fantasies." *Times Literary Supplement*, 1 October 1976, p. 1239.

> Review of *FCL*. The letters are delightfully fresh and original, written very unaffectedly and directly to young children, surely with no thought for publication. The humor is light, unforced, knockabout comedy. Though there are darker things here, there is nothing to disturb a child, and much to amuse him. Tolkien had the capacity to reach down to the huge fears and excitements, as well as to the simple pleasures, of childhood.

II-70    _____. "*The Lord of the Rings* as Romance." In Salu and Farrell, *J. R. R. Tolkien, Scholar and Storyteller* (see II-590), pp. 249–64.

> *LOTR* is not properly understood if regarded as a novel, for it belongs to the essentially opposite tradition (here briefly outlined) of the romance. For all its archaism, *LOTR* can achieve a contemporary feeling, as in its keen environmental awareness and its apocalyptic anxiety. Tolkien also makes brilliant use of such romance themes as the quest, confrontation with death (though it is a flaw that so many of the major characters survive), and the rite of passage to maturity. See also Blissett (II-53) and Thomson (II-650).

II-71    Briggs, K. M. *The Fairies in English Tradition and Literature.*
         London: Routledge and Kegan Paul, 1967. Chicago: Univ. of
         Chicago Press, 1967.

> Fairy lore in literature reaches its high-water mark in *H* and *LOTR*, but
> "Even in these books, where the Elves are in full power and activity the end
> is one of diminishment and vanishing" (p. 210).

II-72    Brookhiser, Richard. "Kicking the Hobbit." *National Review*, 9
         December 1977, pp. 1439–40.

> Review of *Silm*. There is some basis for the carping of people who feel
> cheated that *Silm* is not more like *LOTR*. It is not one story but a
> collection of tales, and, since Tolkien never chose one of the various
> framing devices he experimented with, it reads like a chronicle. Tolkien's
> gift for naming is still unsurpassed, but in his language "crafted sonorities
> float in a linguistic void" (p. 1439). His workaday prose is unexceptionable,
> but, while his excursions into loftier modes can be brilliant or at least
> harmless, *Silm* is written entirely in his wan substitute for the melancholy
> delicacy of Dunsany and the rugged vigor of Eddison. The conventional
> wisdom is that the unheroic hobbits were the reason for *LOTR*'s success,
> but Tolkien's interest is not in them but in the moral situations they
> confront, and this remains true in *Silm*, however godlike the characters. An
> overarching sense of decline holds *Silm* together; evil never triumphs, but
> the losses it causes are real. It is a worthy precursor to *LOTR*.

Brooks, Ned. See Boardman (II-55).

Broomhead, Susantony. See Burrow (II-77).

II-73    Brown, G. R. "Pastoralism and Industrialism in 'The Lord of
         the Rings.' " *English Studies in Africa: A Journal of the
         Humanities*, 19, No. 2 (September, 1976), 83–91.

> Isengard, and the Shire under Saruman, "are greatly simplified, caricatured
> versions of the impact of science and technology on human life and the
> natural world" (p. 84), though they contain some truth. Tolkien
> consistently associates industrialism with evil and pastoralism with good
> (and also with a major theme in *LOTR*, that free choice is needed for either
> an individual or a society to develop), but these relationships are not causal
> though his narrative skill is enough that we may be lulled into thinking so.
> Cf. Bisenieks, II-47 and "Saga," II-581.

II-74    Buchholz, Suzanne. *The Middle-earth Quiz Book*. Boston:
         Houghton Mifflin, 1979.

> Contains 101 quizzes, with ten questions each, on *H, LOTR*, and *Silm*. Cf.
> Andrews (II-11).

II-75    Buechner, Frederick. "For Devotees of Middle-earth." *New
         York Times Book Review*, 16 November 1980, pp. 15, 20.

> Review of *UT*. There is a wealth of lore here for the addict of Middle-earth

and Númenor, but the ordinary reader may be disappointed. There are indeed moments of high adventure, but they are seen from a great distance of time and space and recounted with epic stateliness. These fragments lack the extraordinary intimacy and concern for human and sensuous detail found in *LOTR* and the uncanny sense that Tolkien at his fabulist's best can convey of participating in the events of a world as real as our own.

II-76    Bunda, Robert A. "Color Symbolism in *The Lord of the Rings*." *Orcrist*, No. 8 (1977), pp. 14–16.

The colors associated with the characters in *LOTR* reflect their moral nature. Tolkien's use of color is extensive and it is vital to the development of his moral scheme.

II-77    Burrow, J. W. "Tolkien lives?" *The Listener*, 8 November 1973, pp. 634–36.

Tolkien's work is easily enjoyed, but not so easily defended. It is irrelevant to object to its form, which looks back to myth, epic, and romance. Its content may seem whimsical at worst, but is redeemed by the richness of its philological and topographical imagination. The article elicited several letters of comment: two by Tom Davis in the issues for 22 November 1973, p. 704 and in that for 6 December 1973, p. 780; by Burrow again and by Diana Reed and Susantony Broomhead in the issue for 29 November 1973, p. 748; and by Broomhead again in the issue for 20 December 1973, p. 856.

II-78    Butsch, Richard James. "Person Perception in Scientific and Medieval World Views: A Comparative Study of Fantasy Literature." Ph.D. diss., Rutgers University, 1975.

*LOTR* and Isaac Asimov's Foundation trilogy are compared using a multidimensional scaling of their character descriptions. See *DAI*, 36 (1975), 2519B.

II-79    Callahan, Patrick J. "Animism and Magic in Tolkien's *The Lord of the Rings*." *Riverside Quarterly*, 4, No. 4 (March, 1971), 240–49.

Middle-earth is a panvitalistic world: "The ladder of living things—from rock to tree to beast to the intelligent—is at its every level capable of expressing a beneficent or malific *will*" (p. 240). Magic is the means by which the intelligences of Middle-earth interact with their living world. The good are in rapport with this vitalism and are careful of the freedom of each creature; the evil are essentially opposed to the animate universe and death-oriented, for they seek to turn all creatures into mere objects under their domination. Since magic is an extension of the directing will, and so a moral force whether benevolent or malific, it can be counteracted by other moral forces such as love, loyalty, honor, or courage.

II-80    _____. "Tolkien, Beowulf, and the Barrow-wights." *The Notre Dame English Journal*, 7, No. 2 (Spring, 1972), 4–13.

The Barrow-wight episode introduces little that figures later in the story, yet it is not a breach of unity, for, as in the parallel situation of Beowulf's fight with a barrow-dragon, action is a medium by which to delineate major themes. Though the wight is actually defeated by Bombadil's magic, Frodo, in calling on this spirit of life, invokes a vitality in the fabric of the universe itself; the moral victory is Frodo's, and he proves worthy to be on the quest. Evil can be destroyed only by an antithetical good: as Frodo's act of selfless courage abrogates the selfishness and greed represented by the cursed treasure in the mound.

II-81  _____. "Tolkien's Dwarves and the Eddas." *Tolkien Journal*, No. 15 (Summer, 1972), p. 20.

Tolkien borrows eight dwarf names from the *Edda* and models his others on the Eddaic names (see also Carter, II-89 and Hoffman, II-283). Translates some names from Old Norse and suggests appropriateness of the English meaning for the character (e.g., Gríma's name comes from the Old Norse for "night," which Wormtongue symbolically serves).

II-82  _____. "Two Studies on Tolkien." *Wascana Review*, 4, No. 1 (Summer, 1969), 91–93.

Reviews of *The Tolkien Relation* by William Ready (see II-543) and of *Tolkien and the Critics* by Isaacs and Zimbardo (see II-307). Not seen.

II-83  Caluwé-Dor, Juliette de. Review of *GGK*, 2nd ed. (1967). *Revue Belge de Philologie et d'Histoire*, 47 (1969), 279–81.

In French. Norman Davis, Tolkien's student and later his successor at Oxford, is well qualified to update the excellent edition by Tolkien and E. V. Gordon. He has rethought the material and has taken advantage of later scholarship to provide a careful, detailed edition.

II-84  Carpenter, Humphrey. "Handlist of The Published Writings of J. R. R. Tolkien." In Salu and Farrell, *J. R. R. Tolkien, Scholar and Storyteller* (see II-590), pp. 317–22.

Lists books, essays, and prefaces published between 1922 and 1975. Omits juvenilia and poems published in magazines or anthologies, but these, and other items from 1975 and 1976, are listed in Appendix C, pp. 268–75, in his biography of Tolkien (II-86).

II-85  _____. *The Inklings: C. S. Lewis, J. R. R. Tolkien, Charles Williams, and their friends.* London: George Allen and Unwin, 1978. Boston: Houghton Mifflin, 1979.

Biography of this group, with the focus on Lewis as the acknowledged center of this literary association. Delves into Tolkien's friendships with Lewis and the others, and their reactions to his work. See also Carter (II-88), Christopher (II-106), GoodKnight (II-233), Green (II-243), II-305, Moorman (II-447), Robson (II-561), Ryan (II-580), Wain (II-684), and West (II-716). For reviews, see III-B-3.

II-86     ———. *Tolkien: a biography*. London: George Allen and
Unwin, 1977. Boston: Houghton Mifflin, 1977.

> Authorized biography, making extensive use of Tolkien's letters, diaries,
> manuscripts and other writings both published and unpublished, and
> reminiscences by his associates. For another biography, see Grotta (II-249)
> and Grotta-Kurska (II-250). For shorter biographical sketches, see Burrow
> (II-77), Carter (II-89), Colby (II-112), De Camp (II-145 and II-146), Hardy
> (II-256), II-316, McClusky (II-412), Morrison (II-451), Ready (II-543),
> Rogers (II-566), Ryan (II-580), II-657, II-658, II-659, II-660, II-661, II-662,
> Wakeman (II-685), and Woods (II-742). See also Castell (II-90), Milward
> (II-433), and Norman (II-473 and II-474). For reviews, see III-B-4.

———. See also I-77 and Sievert (II-613).

Carroll, Paulette. See Becker (II-37).

Carson, Nina. See II-302.

II-87     Carter, Lin. "Horvendile: A Link Between Cabell and Tolkien."
*Kalki*, 3, No. iii (1969), 85–87.

> James Branch Cabell's Horvendile and JRRT's Eärendil the Mariner both
> derive (independently) from the Norse myth of Orvandel, whose big toe,
> broken off by Thor after it was frozen, was tossed into the sky to become
> the Morning Star. Discusses the evolution of this myth in the Eddas, Old
> English literature, and Saxo Grammaticus.

II-88     ———. "The Inklings Produce a Classic: The Achievement of
Tolkien and His Influence." In his *Imaginary Worlds: The Art
of Fantasy* (New York: Ballantine, 1973), pp. 109–30.

> No author of fantasy has created as convincingly detailed or
> overwhelmingly realistic an imaginary world as Tolkien did in *LOTR*, and
> the story is very colorful. Yet in the last analysis it is memorable only for
> certain favorite scenes and beloved characters, rather than as a whole. Its
> prose style sometimes achieves passion and power but is usually
> undistinguished; its characterizations are stereotyped; and it is essentially
> shallow in its philosophy, especially in its depiction of evil. T. H. White's
> *The Once and Future King* must be accorded the premier position among
> fantasy novels, while E. R. Eddison's *The Worm Ouroboros* is the best in
> the tradition of the imaginary world; *LOTR* is, however, one of the five or
> six supreme works in the genre. For reviews, see III-B-5.

II-89     ———. *Tolkien: A Look Behind The Lord of the Rings*. New
York: Ballantine, 1968.

> Contains a brief biography of JRRT (see Carpenter, II-86), plot summaries
> of *H* and *LOTR*, a treatment of Tolkien's ideas on fantasy, and a
> discussion of a tradition of fantasy from *Gilgamesh* to the present day
> (sweeping over classical epic, French *chansons de geste*, Spanish and Italian
> epic, Spenser, William Morris, Lord Dunsany, Eddison, Pratt, Peake,

Kendall, Garner, and Alexander), with the Scandinavian Eddas and sagas seen as the major wellspring of Tolkien's inspiration. For reviews, see III-B-6.

II-90    Castell, Daphne. "The Realms of Tolkien." *New Worlds*, 50 (November, 1966), 143–54. Reprinted in *Carandaith*, 1, No. 2 (1969), 10–15, 27.

Interview by a former student of Tolkien's. Quotes JRRT on the story of Queen Berúthiel, his interest in language, his favorite passages in *LOTR*.

II-91    Cater, William. "The Filial Duty of Christopher Tolkien." *Sunday Times Magazine* (London), 25 September 1972. Reprinted in Becker (II-37), pp. 90–95.

Interview with CT on preparing *Silm*; see also Tolkien (II-656).

————. See "The Lord of the Legends" (II-393).

Cecil, David. See "Is There an Oxford 'School' of Writing?" (II-305).

II-92    Chambers, R. W. Review of "Beowulf: The Monsters and the Critics." *Modern Language Review*, 33 (1938), 272–73.

In this, "the finest appreciation which has yet been written of our finest Old English poem" (p. 273), JRRT has made a contribution of the utmost importance towards the study of *Beowulf* as a work of art. It is bad practice, however, to hide so many gems away in endnotes and appendixes instead of weaving them into the text. See also Kaske (II-319).

Chapman, Betsy. See Levitin (II-372).

II-93    Chedzoy, Alan. "Who Reads Tolkien—and why?" *Manchester Guardian*, 29 January 1972, p. 2.

Response to Ezard (see II-192). The young students who admire Tolkien are often "rather timid in human relationships, rather orthodox in attitude" and prefer "escapism to genuine emotional self-exploration." They usually read little else, do not like literature or "the articulation of mature experience," and frequently are "scientists or mathematicians with a preference for crossword complexities within a firm frame of traditional values." *H* and *LOTR* appeal to the state of solitary frightened adolescence, and Tolkien is "the supreme ostrich writer of our time." See Evans (II-184).

II-94    Cheney, Frances Noel. Review of West (II-715). *Wilson Library Bulletin*, 45 (January, 1971), 501.

This is a checklist, not a descriptive bibliography, useful in spite of not including fanzine articles, and enlivened by commentaries on the contents of many of the citations.

II-95    Christensen, Bonniejean. "Adventures in Manipulation."
         *English Journal*, 60 (March, 1971), 359–60.

> A freshman textbook called *Adventures in Reading* (Harcourt, Brace and
> World, 1969) quotes from *OFS* in the section on the short story. The bits
> and snippets quoted are not punctuated to indicate they are not
> consecutive; JRRT is cited as the source but it is not stated that his remarks
> were meant to apply specifically to fairy stories of any length and not just
> to any short story. Such manipulation of the learner by the teacher is
> questionable.

II-96    _____. "*Beowulf* and *The Hobbit*: Elegy Into Fantasy in
         J. R. R. Tolkien's Creative Technique." Ph.D. diss., University
         of Southern California, 1969.

> Tolkien's literary works can be understood and evaluated only in the light
> of his scholarship (which provides the matter for his work), his literary
> aesthetic (which provides the form and theme), and his religious
> commitment (which is not made explicit but provides an underlying
> metaphor). *H* is a recreation of *Beowulf* as Tolkien perceives it; the main
> plot of both concerns a series of adventures which the hero has with
> monsters, beginning with the lesser and continuing to the greater. Tolkien
> borrows details from and develops hints in *Beowulf*. His subcreation
> involves such rhetorical devices as expansion, transposition, negation,
> omission, compression, duplication, reorganization, and literal rendering of
> material. He presents a traditional Christian model of the universe to imply
> a moral order and affirm that man has the possibility of overcoming evil
> within Time. See *DAI*, 30 (1970), 4401–4402A. See also Christensen
> (II-101).

II-97    _____. "Gollum's Character Transformation in *The Hobbit*."
         In Lobdell, *A Tolkien Compass* (see II-388), pp. 9–28.

> "Tolkien's chief alterations in 'Riddles in the Dark' change the stakes in the
> riddle-game, introduce the ring as a ring of power—sentiment, malevolent,
> addictive, and independent—define the opposing forces in the universe and
> convert Gollum from a simply lost creature to a totally depraved one" (p.
> 26). The variety of rhetorical techniques (expansion, transposition,
> negation) and the amount of space devoted to the transformation in
> Gollum's character indicate that Tolkien attached great importance to
> this—more than is necessary in *H* but appropriate to Gollum's expanded
> role in *LOTR*.

II-98    _____. "J. R. R. Tolkien: A Bibliography." *Bulletin of
         Bibliography*, 27, No. 3 (July-September, 1970), 61–67.

> "This list is intended to be a record of all of Tolkien's published works,
> academic and popular, and the relevant reviews and criticism" (p. 61). See
> supplement by Hammond (II-254). See also Christensen (II-100) and West
> (II-715).

II-99      _____. "A Ready Answer." *Tolkien Journal*, 3, No. 4, Whole
No. 10 (November, 1969), 15–17.
> Review of Ready, *Tolkien Relation* (II-543). The book is pernicious
> because it is inaccurate in detail, misleading through misrepresentation, and
> inferior and obscure stylistically. Notes minor and major textual
> misreadings, giving much discussion to Tolkien's adaptations of
> Byrhtwold's speech and Canute's song in *HB*. Much of Ready's discussion
> of theme is based on an unacknowledged and inaccurate paraphrasing of
> Tolkien's article on *Beowulf*. Much of what he is trying to say, in his pretzel
> prose, is a hodgepodge of notions picked up from existentialism and myth
> criticism. His biographical information seems to have been picked up at last
> hand and then presented as if he knew the principals involved.

II-100     _____. "A Tolkien Bibliography." In Becker, *Tolkien
Scrapbook* (II-37), pp. 180–90.
> Checklist in four sections listing Tolkien's scholarly and popular works and
> then popular and scholarly works on Tolkien's fiction.

II-101     _____. "Tolkien's Creative Technique: *Beowulf* and *The
Hobbit*." *Orcrist*, No. 7 (Summer, 1973), pp. 16–20.
> A condensation of the basic argument of her dissertation (II-96). Tolkien
> "has rearranged material in *Beowulf* as he interprets it from his own
> scholarly and Christian perspective to create *The Hobbit*" (p. 20).

II-102     Christopher, Joe R. "Hwæt! We Inclinga . . ." *Fantasiae*, 7,
No. 9, Whole No. 78 (September, 1979), 1, 3.
> Review of Carpenter, *Inklings* (II-85). Though this is not without flaws
> (e.g., it does not make much of a case for its oft-repeated claim that C. S.
> Lewis was a failure as a poet, and the reductionistic chapter on the "causes"
> of the Inklings is unsatisfying), it is an excellent book, an essential
> supplement to Alice Mary Hadfield's *Introduction to Charles Williams*
> (London: Robert Hale, 1959) and a very good complement (since it is
> rather more negative than they are) to Green and Hooper's biography of
> Lewis (II-243).

II-103     _____. "An Inklings Bibliography." Part 1 in *Mythlore*, 3, No.
4, Whole No. 12 (June, 1976), 30–38; Part 2 in *Mythlore*, 4, No.
1, Whole No. 13 (September, 1976), 33–38; Part 3 in *Mythlore*,
4, No. 2, Whole No. 14 (December, 1976), 33–38; Part 4 in
*Mythlore*, 4, No. 3, Whole No. 15 (March, 1977), 33–38; Part 5
in *Mythlore*, 4, No. 4, Whole No. 16 (June, 1977), 40–46; Part 6
in *Mythlore*, 5, No. 1, Whole No. 17 (May, 1978), 40–46; Part 7
in *Mythlore*, 5, No. 2, Whole No. 18 (Autumn, 1978), 43–46;
Part 8 in *Mythlore*, 6, No. 1, Whole No. 19 (Winter, 1979),
46–47; Part 9 in *Mythlore*, 6, No. 2, Whole No. 20 (Spring,
1979), 40–46; Part 10 in *Mythlore*, 6, No. 3, Whole No. 21
(Summer, 1979), 38–45; Part 11 in *Mythlore*, 6, No. 4, Whole

No. 22 (Fall, 1979), 44–47; Part 12 in *Mythlore*, 7, No. 1, Whole No. 23 (March, 1980), 41–45; Part 13 in *Mythlore*, 7, No. 2, Whole No. 24 (Summer, 1980), 42–47.

> A continuing bibliography in each issue of *Mythlore*, devoted primarily to writings about Tolkien, C. S. Lewis, and Charles Williams but often including work about the other members of the Inklings and about related figures such as Dorothy L. Sayers. Includes fannish as well as scholarly material. The annotations of the material cited are detailed and often provide critiques. See also West (II-715).

II-104    _____. "A Note on an Unpublished (and Probably Unwritten) Collaboration." *Mythlore*, 3, No. 2, Whole No. 10 (1975), 29.

> References to Lewis and Tolkien planning to collaborate on a book on *Language and Human Nature* for the Student Christian Movement Press.

II-105    _____. "Three Letters by J. R. R. Tolkien at the University of Texas." *Mythlore*, 7, No. 2, Whole No. 24 (Summer, 1980), 5.

> Describes (but does not reprint) a letter to John Masefield dated 14 July (no year given, but Christopher dates it to 1939 on internal evidence), and two letters to Terence Tiller dated 2 November and 6 November 1956.

II-106    _____. "Who Were the Inklings?" *Tolkien Journal*, No. 15 (Summer, 1972), pp. 5, 7–10, 12–13.

> Gathers information about the activities of the group and about each member identified by C. S. Lewis. See also Carpenter (II-85).

II-107    _____. Review of West, *Tolkien Checklist* (II-715). *Choice*, 7, No. 3 (May, 1970), 360.

> Notes some omissions and makes some recommendations for improving the design. See also his longer review in Christopher (II-108).

II-108    _____. Review Of West, *Tolkien Checklist* (II-715). *Mythlore*, 3, No. 1, Whole No. 9 (1973), 26–27.

> Extended version of his review for *Choice* (II-107), with more detail.

_____. See also Becker, (II-37) and II-301.

Clarke, Robert. See Sievert (II-613).

II-109    Clausen, Christopher. "*Lord of the Rings* and *The Ballad of the White Horse*." *South Atlantic Bulletin*, 39, No. ii (May, 1974), 10–16.

> *LOTR* is heavily indebted to G. K. Chesterton's poem of 1911. This is seen in some episodes and details: e.g., Galadriel and the Virgin Mary; parallels of Dwarves, Elves, and Men with Saxons, Celts, and Romans; and placing Gandalf on the archetypal white horse. The debt is also in basic structure and conception: the major theme of both works is the war and eventual victory, despite all odds, of an alliance of good folk against vastly more powerful forces of evil, and the return of a king to his rightful state.

II-110   Cohen, John Arthur. "An Examination of Four Key Motifs Found in High Fantasy for Children." Ph.D. diss., Ohio State University, 1975.

> Contemporary "high fantasy" has deep roots in myth and folktale (though the study begins with *H*), but its concerns are very much those of the present. Examines forty-seven books by twenty-three authors for four key motifs: created worlds, time, the quest, and the combat between Good and Evil. See *DAI*, 36 (1976), 5016–17A.

II-111   Colbath, Mary Lou. "Worlds As They Should Be: Middle-earth, Narnia and Prydain." *Elementary English*, 48 (1971), 937–45.

> One unique area of fantasy writing can be identified by three distinct limitations: 1) sub-creation; 2) some degree of relation to humanity's own mythological heritage; 3) adventure, enchantment, and heroism as stimulants to the imagination. There are three great works in this area. They are not didactic, but one can learn from them: in Tolkien's Middle-earth, heroism and sacrifice in the face of despair; in C. S. Lewis's Narnia, values such as loyalty, steadfastness, and consideration for others, gained through a painful learning process; in Lloyd Alexander's Prydain, dreams of youth and the realities of growing up.

II-112   [Colby, Vineta.] "J. R. R. Tolkien." *Wilson Library Bulletin*, 31 (1957), 768. Reprinted in *Current Biography* (1957), pp. 555–56.

> Biographical sketch. For other biographical information, see especially Carpenter (II-86).

II-113   Coleman, Marigold. "Three British Bookbinders." *Crafts*, No. 1 (March, 1973), pp. 26–31.

> A discussion of the bookbinding styles of Ivor Robinson, Philip Smith, and Faith Shannon. Smith is obsessed by *LOTR* and has returned to it often. On p. 26 there is a small photograph of one of his book walls, based on a plan of Minas Tirith. See also Smith (II-632).

II-114   Colledge, Edmund. Review of *Ancrene Wisse* (I-55). *Modern Language Review*, 60 (January, 1965), 90–91.

> Thinks that many of the editorial principles for these Early English Text Society editions of the *Riwle* are inconvenient for purposes of scholarly study (e.g., the silent expansion of scribal abbreviations makes it impossible to judge what rationale was behind them). Hopes that now that these texts are available the informed studies of the *Riwle* that have been long delayed will be forthcoming. Praises the generosity and self-abnegation of the editors of the series.

II-115   Colvin, George. "An Ever-Diverse Pair." *Mythlore*, 6, No. 3, Whole No. 21 (Summer, 1979), 17, 37.

> Review of Anne McCaffrey, *Dragondrums*, and of James Allan, ed., *An Introduction to Elvish* (see II-302).

II-116   Conklin, Groff. Review of *FR* and of Poul Anderson's *Broken Sword*. *Galaxy*, 10, No. 2 (May, 1955), 115.

> *FR* "is rich, flavorsome, exhaustively detailed and almost too leisurely" while *The Broken Sword* is "a rip-snorting, bloody, imitation-Norse epic" but they are two "twigs of witching more or less off the same branch . . ." Though they are excellent in their kind, they are not to his taste.

II-117   Conrad, Peter. "The Babbit." *New Statesman*, 94 (23 September 1977), 408–09.

> Review of *Silm*. Tolkien can invent languages at will, but he can't actually write; his dialogue is poor and his syntax is flaccid. He does not provide mythology, characterization, or cosmic drama, but only dictionaries and philological quibbles. He is popular, not because he is arcane and outlandish, but because he is an unadventurous defender of mediocrity.

II-118   Coogan, Daniel. "Failing Fantasy, Tragic Fact." *America*, 137 (5 November 1977), 315–16.

> Review of *Silm*. He loved *H* and *LOTR*, but was very disappointed by *Silm*. The language is solemn and ponderous; there is little hope or humor to lighten the tragic tedium; it is hard to keep track of the characters and their aliases, their alliances and divisions, even with the help of the excellent glossary.

II-119   Cooperman, Stanley. Review of *TT*. *Nation*, 181 (17 September 1955), 251.

> Brief review. "Part two of a delightful trilogy, the fantastic story of a world as real as the imagination. Readers who enjoy provocative fantasy will want to own this handsome volume."

II-120   Cormier, Raymond J. Review of *GGKPO*. *Library Journal*, 100 (August, 1975), 1420–21.

> Brief review. Tolkien's renewal of *Sir Gawain and the Green Knight* "in alliterative blank verse is a faithful and noble, brazen yet tender rendering of the original tale of *pietas* and chivalry." This and the "inspirational and problematic" *Pearl* and *Sir Orfeo* are "outstanding examples of Middle English narrative romance" and are lovely poems clearly meant to be read aloud.

II-121   Cornwell, Charles Landrum. "From Self to the Shire: Studies in Victorian Fantasy." Ph.D. diss., University of Virginia, 1972.

> Tolkien's view, in *OFS*, of fantasy as the subcreation of believable secondary worlds, does not take into account the possibilities of fantasy for also exploring various phases of the self. Critical analysis of fantasy, and especially of Victorian fantasy, should incorporate Freud's analysis of dreamwork, Jung's theories of the unconscious and the archetypes, and the Romantic concept of the child. These concepts are used to approach selected works by George MacDonald, Lewis Carroll, Oscar Wilde, and Kenneth Grahame. See *DAI*, 33 (1972), 1163–64A.

II-122   Cosgrave, Mary Silva. Review of *Silm. Horn Book*, 54, No. 2
         (April, 1978), 196.

> Short paragraph, mostly describing contents. Tolkien "wrote poems and
> tales, invented annals and languages, with the idea, inspired in part by the
> Finnish *Kalevala*, of creating for England a mythology of its own. Into this
> life work he put his most profound thoughts and feelings. After Tolkien's
> death, his son took over the task of assembling the materials into one
> cohesive narrative. The result is a remarkable set of legends conceived with
> imaginative might and told in beautiful language."

II-123   Cox, C. B. "The World of the Hobbits." *Spectator*, 30
         December 1966, p. 844.

> Review of *LOTR*, 2nd ed. (Allen and Unwin, 1966). He suggests that *OFS*
> is the key to the virtues of *LOTR* and to Tolkien's purpose in it; see also
> Norwood (II-476), Reilly (II-549), and Roberts (II-559). He praises
> Tolkien's vivid depiction, power to relate fantasy and reality, and
> distinctive protagonists, but thinks that the simplistic role given to sex is
> the main reason for the inferiority of *LOTR* to the *Faerie Queen*.

II-124   Cox, Jeff. "Tolkien, the Man Who Created Nine Languages."
         *Quinto Lingo*, 7, No. 8–9 (August-September, 1969), 8–11.

> Tolkien is obviously in love with language, and created nine from almost
> whole cloth, with some savor of Latin, Old and Modern English, and
> German. Translates "A Elbereth Gilthoniel" as an example of Elvish (cf. I-
> 65; Blackmun, II-51; and Noel, II-469). Discusses Westron and the
> language of Rohan and the English renditions used for them. Also cites
> examples of Dwarvish, Entish, and Orcish.

II-125   Crago, Hugh. "Remarks on the Nature and Development of
         Fantasy." In Ryan, *Tolkien: Cult or Culture?* (II-580),
         Appendix D, Part I, pp. 212–20.

> An overview of the history of fantasy from *Gilgamesh* to Tolkien,
> concentrating on the last century.

II-126   _____. "Tolkien in Miniature." *Children's Libraries Newsletter*,
         4, No. 2 (May, 1968), 8–10. Reprinted in Ryan (II-580), Ch. 7,
         pp. 123–28.

> Review of *SWM*. The rightness of choosing imaginative and spiritual
> experience over everyday life is an important theme in *H*, *LBN*, and *LOTR*,
> and this is restated in *SWM*. This is not as good a work, however: partly
> because it is short and slow-paced enough that one notices stylistic
> imperfections; partly because it lacks humor; partly because human
> characters lack the glorious individuality that hobbits have; and partly
> because it is preferable only to suggest such regions as Faerie rather than
> chart them in detail.

II-127 _____. "The Way the Word-Magic Works: Style and
Archetype in *The Lord of the Rings*." In Ryan (II-580),
Appendix D, Part II, pp. 221–28.

> Tolkien's essentially simple style (the way words, phrases, images, and
> rhythms are used) is compared with the style of E. R. Eddison and that of
> Mervyn Peake.

II-128 Crist, Judith. "Why 'Frodo Lives.' " *Ladies Home Journal*, 84
(February, 1967), 58.

> She is happy that Hobbitry is the then-latest fad of American teenagers
> since "It's all far from the hot-rod, folk-rock revolt image or the drug-
> inspired sensations so many are seeking" while providing "a never-never
> world that satisfies the 20th-century mind."

II-129 Crouch, Marcus S. *Treasure Seekers and Borrowers*. London:
Library Association, 1962.

> *H* "is an exciting story of adventure, a tragedy with comic episodes, a
> picaresque romance with strands of magic in it, an historical novel about
> the remote past which, by the author's craft, becomes more real than the
> present . . ." (pp. 66–67). Notes on p. 133 that Pauline Baynes was more at
> home with the delicate mock-scholarship of *FGH* than with the robustness
> and mysticism which C. S. Lewis's Narnian chronicles sometimes
> demanded.

II-130 Cushman, Jerome. Review of Isaacs and Zimbardo, *Tolkien
and the Critics* (II-307). *Library Journal*, 93 (July, 1968), 2659.

> Serious criticism of Tolkien is made more difficult because of the
> fanaticism of enthusiasts, but this significant group of essays makes a good
> case for the permanent literary value of Tolkien's writings. The essays
> "explore many ramifications of his work—Christian values, folklore,
> language, symbolism, fairy-tale approach, his created world, poetry, and his
> work as fiction."

II-131 Dabney, Virginia. "On the Natures and Histories of the Great
Rings." *Mythcon I Proceedings* (4–7 September 1970). Ed. Glen
GoodKnight (Los Angeles: The Mythopoetic Society, 1971), pp.
8–10.

> Summarizes the information on the twenty Rings of Power of Elves,
> Dwarves, Men and Sauron, and speculates on their powers.

II-132 Dalgliesh, Alice. Review of *T&L*. *Saturday Review*, 24 April
1965, p. 44.

> She did not enjoy *H*, but admires *OFS* and thinks *LBN* is "interesting to
> any creative person, but not, in its full impact, for children."

II-133 Daunt, Marjorie. Review of "Sigelwara Land." *The Year's
Work in English Studies*, 13 (1932), 69–70.

Reviews only Part I (I-25). Tolkien, in a full and leisurely manner, tries to show why the Anglo-Saxons had a special name for the Ethiopians (the correct form is shown to be "Sigel hearwa") and what it signified.

II-134   Davenport, Guy. "J. R. R. Tolkien, R. I. P." *National Review*, 28 September 1973, pp. 1042–43.

Obituary. Tolkien was a writer of his time, who dared to resuscitate the romance. *LOTR* is a magic book, apparently beyond scholarship and criticism. Its vision of harmony and simplicity, of honor and heroism, is an articulate symbol of our inarticulate yearning. Tolkien invented nothing cynical, but transmuted into the loveliest vision the world as he knew it. Conversation with Allen Barnett, a close friend of Tolkien's at Oxford prior to World War I, shows how touches of Kentucky flavored the Shire.

II-135   _____. "The Persistence of Light." *National Review*, 20 April 1965, pp. 332, 334.

Review of *T&L* that touches on *H* and *LOTR*. The basic perception of the imagination that generates all of Tolkien's writing is "that the imagination is a metamorphosis of reality rather than an evasion of it. To find clear symbols of spiritual realities, one turns where man has always turned, to his myth-making mind, where truth can appear in a round solidity denied it in the confusing simultaneity of the mind's relentless continuum, where everything is happening at once" (p. 334).

II-136   Davidson, Avram. Review of *ATB*. *The Magazine of Fantasy and Science Fiction*, 26 (March, 1964), 83.

He finds Tom Bombadil "a sort of babbling three-quarters wit, and the poems here about him don't much enchant me." Other poems are lovely, and "Errantry" is his favorite. Anyone who has not yet read *H* or *LOTR* is advised to "Go out and begin *at once* this rich and wonderful world; and read slowly—if you can."

II-137   Davidson, Don Adrian. "Sword and Sorcery Fiction: An Annotated Book List." *English Journal*, 61 (January, 1972), 43–51.

The scope, style, and colossal depth of development of *LOTR* earn it the rightful place of honor as the ultimate standard of excellence in fantasy literature. *H* is an enjoyable novel in itself but is also an introduction to *LOTR*. He recommends Ready (II-543) and Carter (II-89). Tolkien is also mentioned in the annotations for Poul Anderson, *The Broken Sword*; E. R. Eddison, *The Worm Ouroboros*; Mervyn Peake, the Gormenghast trilogy; and Fletcher Pratt, *Well of the Unicorn*.

II-138   Davidson, E. J. Review of Kocher, *Master of Middle-earth* (II-346). *The Year's Work in English Studies*, 53 (1972), 386.

Short review, describing the contents of the book. Finds the comments on seven short pieces in the final chapter "particularly revealing," but Tolkien readers will be grateful for this critical guide as a whole.

II-139    _____. Review of Wollheim, *The Universe Makers* (II-739). *The Year's Work in English Studies*, 53 (1972), 366.

". . . a short personal assessment of science fiction as a genre, its history and its place in literature." There is "a short section on Tolkien's *The Lord of the Rings* in relation to science fiction."

II-140    Davie, Donald. "Lucky Jim and the Hobbits." Ch. 4 in his *Thomas Hardy and British Poetry* (London: Routledge and Kegan Paul, 1973), 83–104.

Most of this chapter is on Kingsley Amis, with a section on Tolkien (a revised version of Davis, II-141).

II-141    _____. "On Hobbits and Intellectuals." *Encounter*, 33 (October, 1969), 87–92.

Tolkien's prose is undistinguished, but his narrative is read avidly, this only to some degree because it answers to a hunger for the heroic, for the driving force of the book (the plot is very logical and tidy, not at all like medieval romance) is unheroic or even antiheroic. *LOTR* is a parable of authority, pointing "towards the conviction that authority in public matters, because it is always spiritually perilous to the person it is vested in, can be and ought to be resisted and refused by anyone who wants to live humanely" (p. 90). This divorce of power and authority is absurd, but is very common in the English mind and helps explain England's present political situation.

II-142    Davis, L. J. Review of *Silm. New Republic*, 177 (1 October 1977), 38–40.

By contrast with the usual hero, who has an annoying sense of destiny and higher purpose and is horribly dangerous to have around, hobbits are small and narrowminded folk who desire nothing so much as to be left alone to pursue their simple pleasures. In the hobbits, Tolkien inadvertently rediscovered one of the most potent elements of myth: that the heroism of someone who has everything to lose is the only heroism that matters. This is missing from *Silm*, where "all the characters are 37 feet tall and live for a million years and you can rest assured that if things really get out of hand, Daddy in the form of Eru-Ilúvatar will put down his pipe and lend an omnipotent hand" (p. 39; there is a direct reply to this by Brookhiser, II-72). It is also disappointing to find that the resonant legends and languages from an older time that, hinted at but never fully disclosed, give *LOTR* much of its unique texture, as presented in *Silm* sound like a cross between the *Book of Mormon* and L. Ron Hubbard as conceived by S. J. Perelman. *Silm* should be read, if at all, only as a gloss on Tolkien's later, more mature work.

II-143    Davis, Norman and C. L. Wrenn, eds. *English and Medieval Studies Presented to J. R. R. Tolkien on the Occasion of his Seventieth Birthday*. London: George Allen and Unwin, 1962.

*Festschrift*. Contents include W. H. Auden's poem, "A Short Ode to a Philologist" (pp. 11–12). The other essays deal with Old and Middle

English and Old Norse language, literature and culture. For another
*Festschrift*, see Salu and Farrell (II-590).

Davis, Tom. See Burrow (II-77).

II-144   Day, David. *A Tolkien Bestiary*. London: Mitchell Beazley,
1979; New York: Ballantine, 1979.

> This reference guide to Tolkien's fictive races, flora, and fauna is more
> limited in scope than those by Foster (II-207 and II-208) or Tyler (II-670
> and II-671), but includes maps, chronologies, and genealogies as well as "A
> Bestiary of the Beasts, Monsters, Races, Deities, and Flora." The text is
> lavishly illustrated by John Adams, Victor Ambrus, John Blanche, Jaroslav
> Braduc, Allan Curless, Michael Foreman, Linda Garland, Ian Miller, and
> Lidia Pastura. For reviews, see III-B-7.

II-145   de Camp, L. Sprague. "Merlin in Tweeds: J. R. R. Tolkien."
Ch. 9 in his *Literary Swordsmen and Sorcerers: The Makers of
Heroic Fantasy* (Sauk City, Wisc.: Arkham House, 1976), pp.
215–51 (notes on pp. 298–300).

> Appraisal of *H* and *LOTR*, with biographical information and an account
> of the author's meeting with Tolkien, and a detailed response to Edmund
> Wilson (II-729). See also de Camp (II-146).

II-146   _____. "White Wizard in Tweeds." *Fantastic Stories*, 25
(November, 1976), 69–89, 122.

> Somewhat shortened version of II-145, published after the book version.

De Cles, Diana Paxson. See II-301.

II-147   del Mastro, M. L. Review of Andrews, *Tolkien Quiz Book* (II-
11). *Library Journal*, 104 (1 February 1979), 402.

> Brief review. "Imaginative questions could have illumined the man and his
> work, but these are literal-minded in the extreme."

II-148   _____. Review of Carpenter, *The Inklings* (II-85). *Library
Journal*, 104 (1 February 1979), 403.

> Brief review. "Carpenter refuses either to read his subjects' literary work as
> disguised autobiography, or to write biography as if the life existed solely
> as a mine for the writing. His gift lies in his ability to let his subjects speak
> for themselves, while he tells their story. Effective narrative pace and
> authentic portraiture thus combine to present the people and their times as
> living realities."

II-149   _____. Review of Becker, *Tolkien Scrapbook* (II-37). *Library
Journal*, 104 (15 February 1979), 493.

> Brief review. Though there are respectable pieces by Atchity (II-14) and
> Searles (II-606), most of the criticism is banal or useless, the mini-
> biography by McClusky (II-412) is superficial and inexcusably inaccurate,
> and the other contents are uninspired or worse.

II-150  del Ray, Lester. "A Report on J. R. R. Tolkien." *Worlds of Fantasy*, 1 (October, 1968), 84–85.

> Tolkien has revolutionized modern literature and single-handedly created a demand for fantasy in soft-cover publishing. His books are "filled with such things as the love of beauty, the dignity of ordinary people, and the conflict of good and evil" (p. 85).

II-151  Dempsey, David. "The Candy Covered Copyright." *Saturday Review*, 2 October 1965, pp. 40, 45.

> Tolkien is one of numerous authors who have been denied protection because of technicalities in the International Copyright Convention. Houghton Mifflin relinquished its copyright on *LOTR* when it imported more than its quota of 1,500 copies of a foreign book written in English. See comment by Scott (II-603). See also Ace Books (II-2).

II-152  Derrick, Christopher. "And See Ye Not Yon Bonny Road?" *Tablet*, 222 (10 February 1968), 132.

> Review of *SWM*. This sad, wise book is a myth of great delicacy. Once the mad, magic gift has been handed back to its dull institutional custodian, ordinary life, which deserves a patient and positive attitude, has to continue.

II-153  _____. "From an Antique Land." *Tablet*, 216 (15 December 1962), 1227.

> Review of *ATB*. These poems should not be dismissed as high-class whimsy for nice children: they do not patronize, nor show falsely affected and irresponsible simplicity. They have music even though their rhythms are unfashionable. They display the common, appetizing, and real. They range widely, from diamond to nightmare, with much burly nourishment in between.

II-154  _____. "Talking of Dragons." *Tablet*, 204 (11 September 1954), 250.

> Review of *FR*. Though "this long fairy-story-cum-allegory by a don" may "sound like the very ecstasy of boredom" it is "in fact one of the most arresting and readable stories of our time." It is a heroic romance that is not whimsical but realistic, set in a world of varied beauty that is also harsh and desolate, a world that is quite new and yet utterly familiar. Tolkien shows an amazing fertility in devising an endless God's plenty of character and incident and place.

II-155  Despain, Jerry Lynn. "A Rhetorical View of J. R. R. Tolkien's 'The Lord of the Rings' Trilogy." *Journal of Western Speech*, 35 (1971), 88–95.

> Not seen.

II-156 Detweiler, Robert. Reviews of Reilly, *Romantic Religion* (II-547) and Urang, *Shadows of Heaven* (II-675). *Journal of Modern Literature*, 3 (1974), 405–07.

> Reilly gives an excellent exposition of Barfield, an original thinker too little known, but is weaker in his chapters on Lewis, Williams, and Tolkien. Urang's book will appeal to those already convinced of the creative significance of these latter three authors (unlike the reviewer, who sees them as minor literary-religious figures). Urang spends far too much time on plot summaries and quotations and never develops much of an argument. The concluding chapter, "Fantasy and the Motions of Grace," is his best.

Dickinson, Peter. See Malcolm (II-399).

II-157 Dockery, Carl Dee. "The Myth of the Shadow in the Fantasies of Williams, Lewis, and Tolkien." Ph.D. diss., Auburn University, 1975.

> The seven fantasies of Charles Williams, the science fiction trilogy of C. S. Lewis, and Tolkien's epic fantasy, share a symbolic form: a pattern this study labels "myths of the shadow." In this pattern, the forces of darkness initiate conflict with the positive forces, and out of the ensuing struggle the positive forces achieve renewal. Therefore, aesthetic insight, differing from an ethical perspective, discovers that the shadow is necessary as a dynamic transformative agent. See *DAI*, 36 (1975), 3727A.

II-158 Dorsch, T. S. Review of *HB*. *The Year's Work in English Studies*, 24 (1953), 22.

> A brief comment that *HB* is inspired by some passages in *The Battle of Maldon*, and that some notes on the spirit of the Anglo-Saxon poem are appended.

II-159 Dowie, William, S. J. "The Gospel of Middle Earth According to J. R. R. Tolkien." *Heythrop Journal*, 15, No. 1 (January, 1974), 37–52. Revised and reprinted in Salu and Farrell (II-590), 265–85.

> *LOTR* does not mention God or organized religion, but it is a deeply religious work because it plunges into the "sacrality" of the natural; ". . . the pervasive importance of the seasons, the great tree, the moon, the dark passage, the night and morn, the ship across the sea, and the special place makes one realize that Tolkien has indeed rooted his tale in the symbolic consciousness of naturally religious man" (p. 43 of essay, p. 274 of Salu and Farrell). Christian experience contributes much to the morals embedded in the quest of the Ring (e.g., sense of vocation, growth even in suffering, free will, compassion, humility) and to the broader ontological themes of fairy story (e.g., fellowship, kingship, providence, prophecy, prohibition, festivity, and eucatastrophe). The revision adds more footnotes and incorporates into the text what in the original was an addendum on Murray's "A Tribute to Tolkien" (II-457). See also Dowie (II-160).

II-160      _____. "Religious Fiction in a Profane Time: Charles
            Williams, C. S. Lewis, and J. R. R. Tolkien." Ph.D. diss.,
            Brandeis University, 1970.

> Tolkien eschews allegory and explicit religiosity, but he uses natural
> hierophany, the broader ontological themes of fairy story, and the morals
> embedded in the quest of the Ring to bridge the gap of natural and
> supernatural. He is more successful than either Williams or Lewis. See
> *DAI*, 31 (1970), 2911A. See also Dowie (II-159).

II-161      Drabble, Margaret. "Rebels against Iluvatar." *The Listener*, 15
            September 1977, p. 346.

> Review of *Silm*. She greatly admired *LOTR* and would have greeted *Silm*
> with passionate enthusiasm had it appeared twenty years earlier, but it
> now poses questions about the callowness of one's past self. That it is
> uneven in style and pace is due to its being assembled from different
> sources, written at different times and from different viewpoints. Its most
> serious weakness is that it is pretentious. Tolkien had a good ear, but there
> must be more to a book than sound, even for a linguist. The attempt at a
> whole imagined mythology does not offer enough in the way of story or
> description or originality to justify the length. The real tension between the
> bleak, heroic surface and the desire for a golden age, which gave such
> narrative drive to *LOTR*, is diffused and overpondered in *Silm*. The rift
> between fantasy and the real world in Tolkien, who can almost persuade
> one that the real world is false, makes one uneasy.

II-162      Duriez, Colin. "Leonardo, Tolkien, and Mr. Baggins."
            *Mythlore*, 1, No. 2 (April, 1969), 18–28.

> What Tolkien called "subcreation" can be identified with the term "exact
> fantasy" of Leonardo da Vinci. Reality is not just what can be
> mathematically described, for qualities also are real, and so what can be
> imaginatively apprehended or constructed can also be "true."

II-163      Eagen, Timothy. Review of *Silm*. *Best Sellers*, 37, No. 9
            (December, 1977), 268–69.

> *Silm* is a good job of editing. It is written as though by a learned scholar
> recounting legends, yet the telling is not dry or stale. "The beauty of it is
> rich and intense; the tragedy has the finer qualities of pathos, and the silent
> moral points are never preachy or didactic" (p. 269). The most important
> such moral point in *Silm* is the evils and penalties of appropriation; this is
> the great sin of Feänor, and it is his locking of the light of the Trees in the
> Silmarils which causes all the sorrow of the First Age.

II-164      Eakin, Mary K., compiler. *Good Books for Children*. Chicago:
            Univ. of Chicago Press, 1959.

> On p. 218 there is a brief comment on *FGH*, which is classed for the 5–7
> age group and said to be "a modern fanciful tale with much of the flavor
> and humor of the traditional tall tales." The 2nd edition (1962), revised and
> enlarged, quotes the entry in the 1st edition word for word, even to the
> misprints. The 3rd edition (1966) has no entry on any work by Tolkien.

II-165 Eaton, Anne Thaxter. *Reading With Children*. New York: Viking, 1940.

> There is an appreciation of *H* on pp. 19–22, noting its suspense and quiet humor, Bilbo's scorn for the heroic while possessing courage and resourcefulness, and the earthly quality of the fairy lands. On p. 82, *H* is called "a glorious mixture of legend, tradition, and imaginative exploits." See also Eaton (II-166).

II-166 _____. Review of *H. New York Times Book Review*, 13 March 1938, p. 12. Also printed in *Horn Book*, 14 (March, 1938), 94, 96.

> The review makes many of the same points later incorporated into her book on *Reading With Children* (II-165).

Eaton, Tom. See Piggin (II-521).

II-167 Egan, Thomas M. "Chaff and Splendor." *Mythlore*, 7, No. 2, Whole No. 24 (Summer, 1980), 36, 38.

> Review of Wyatt, *A Middle-Earth Album* (II-746).

II-168 _____. "Reflecting Wonder." *Mythlore*, 7, No. 2, Whole No. 24 (Summer, 1980), 35–36.

> Review of Day, *A Tolkien Bestiary* (II-144).

II-169 Ehling, Michael J. "The Conservatism of J. R. R. Tolkien." *Orcrist*, No. 8 (1977), pp. 17–22.

> Tolkien's type of conservatism, based on Natural Law, is distinguished from other types and discussed.

II-170 Eiseley, Loren. "Elvish Art of Enchantment." *New York Herald Tribune Book Week*, Children's Spring Book Festival issue, 9 May 1965, pp. 3, 27. Reprinted in *Horn Book*, 41 (August, 1965), 364–67.

> Review essay on *T&L*. The essential message of *T&L* is "to approach with care the interpretation of a wayward universe that despite, or because of, our learning threatens to slip away without genuine comprehension, or—and much worse—to assume unexpectedly the vanished shape of Sauron" (p. 367).

II-171 Elliott, Charles. "Can America Kick the Hobbit? The Tolkien Caper." *Life*, 62 (24 February 1967), 10. Reprinted in *Carandaith*, 1, No. 3 (July, 1969), 12–13.

> This associate editor of *Life* enjoyed *LOTR* while only a few people knew about it, but ceased to do so when it became widely popular (Searles, II-606, reports having the same reaction). "No symbolism, no sex, no double meanings, no questions about which are the Good Guys and which the Bad, just a good yarn on the level of *Tom Swift and His Electric Runabout*."

Elliott, Charles N. See Levitin (II-372).

II-172   Ellmann, Mary. "Growing Up Hobbitic." *New American Review*, No. 2 (New American Library, 1968), pp. 217–29.

> The introduction to this volume calls the article "a wry appraisal of the Tolkien cult on the campuses." *LOTR* is a book of "breathtaking puerility" (p. 218), its charm derived from its simple morality and horizontal narrative progression. Hobbits are dirty, germ-ridden, undersexed, over-shy, and apathetic; their temptation is to disappear, and, in refusing to wear the Ring, Frodo proves he has the courage to be seen. An appendix gives a tongue-in-cheek "profile of the Fellowship" as to age, species, profession, and character.

II-173   _____. Review of *Silm*. *Yale Review*, 67 (Summer, 1978), 596–97.

> Tolkien practiced and perfected the mellifluous style, but he used his source book only as background, against which his fictions might then take on more character. *Silm*, which is too slow, cramped, dry, and painfully short of dialogue and dramatic incident, might better have been left in manuscript for perusal by zealots.

II-174   Ellwood, Gracia Fay. "The Good Guys and the Bad Guys." *Tolkien Journal*, 3, No. 4, Whole No. 10 (November, 1969), 9–11.

> That, with few exceptions, the good guys are very, very good and the bad guys are horrid is one of the thoroughly satisfying things about *LOTR*. "Character development would be largely inappropriate in the *Rings* because the main characters (except the hobbits) do not represent the flesh-and-blood people we know, each participating in a complex constellation of Archtypes" [*sic*] (p. 9). She discusses the universal pattern of the Hero and his Adventure, both to defend the type-hero and to assert the universality and religious character of the epic. See also Auden (II-16).

II-175   _____. *Good News from Tolkien's Middle Earth: Two Essays on the "Applicability" of The Lord of the Rings*. Grand Rapids, Mich.: William B. Eerdmans, 1970.

> People have a deep inner need for a mythical-intuitive apprehension of wholeness in the universe. The animate world of Middle-earth is an imaginative depiction of such a view: with its places having either a good or evil "virtue"; its objects showing a semihuman kind of responsiveness; its trees and animals having personality; and the intuitions, telepathy, clairvoyance, telekinesis, retrocognitions and precognitions, and extraordinary perceptions of invisible dimensions of reality on the part of the characters. Analogues for some of these things can be found in modern studies of the paranormal. *LOTR* is a wedding of the sacred and secular, and its events and characters (notably Tom Bombadil, Gandalf, Frodo, and Aragorn) show archetypal patterns (familiar in world mythologies, including Christianity) of the Hero facing the powers of Chaos and Evil to

win new life and order for the world. A selection from the first essay (without mention of Tolkien) was published as "On Myth" in *Mythlore*, 1, No. 2 (April, 1969), 14–16. For reviews, see III-B-8.

Elston, Charles B. See Sievert (II-613).

II-176   "Elvish Mode." *New Yorker*, 41 (15 January 1966), 24–25.

Report of a meeting of the Tolkien Society of America, including a few comments on Middle-earth cosmology and languages and a very few words by W. H. Auden on "Tolkien as a Man."

II-177   Emerson, Oliver Farrar. Review of *GGK*, 1st ed. *Journal of English and Germanic Philology*, 26 (1927), 248–58.

The introduction, text, notes, and glossary are generally good, but the bibliography is much too sketchy, emendations of other scholars are adopted without crediting them, and some readings and points are insufficiently explained.

II-178   "The Epic of Westernesse." *Times Literary Supplement*, 17 December 1954, p. 817.

Review of *TT*. The reviewer is happy that "within his imagined world the author continually unveils fresh countries of the mind, convincingly imagined and delightful to dwell in" but is disturbed that "though the allegory is now plainer there is still no explanation of wherein lies the wickedness of Sauron." See the other *TLS* reviews, II-275, II-581.

II-179   Epstein, E. L. "The Novels of J. R. R. Tolkien and the Ethnology of Medieval Christendom." *Philological Quarterly*, 48 (1969), 517–25.

"The world of Middle-earth, I believe, is essentially that of medieval Europe of the period A.D. 800–1200. The languages of the various peoples, their situation (geographical and social), the position in relation to Rome, and above all the presence of a malignant southern and eastern enemy possessed of great technical powers and boundless energy, all these suggest to me that Tolkien's knowledge of medieval history reflects itself in his novels" (p. 517). He notes Old Norse meanings of Dwarf names, Welsh roots of Elvish, and Finnish words used (with new meanings) for Tengwar names. He suggests locating Rohan in Lower Brittany and Númenor in Britain. See also Allan (II-6).

II-180   Etheldreda, Sister M., R.S.M. Review of *FGH*. *Catholic Library World*, 37 (February, 1966), 380.

Brief review. *FGH* will be read by children with a flair for fantasy and subtle humor.

II-181   Etkin, Anne, ed. *Eglerio! In Praise of Tolkien*. Greencastle, Pa.: Quest Communications, 1978.

A "Land of Legend" anthology. Contents include: the title essay, on Tolkien and his work; "Letters from C. S. Lewis" to Lucy Matthews on

Narnia, fantasy, romance, and *LOTR*; "Tolkien's *Homecoming*, A Clue to His Thought and Character" (on *HB*); London *Times* obituary (see II-533); "A Chronological Biography of J. R. R. Tolkien" (compiled by Ellen Lodwick and Anne Etkin); "Tolkien and His Readers;" "Tolkien—Hobbit and Wizard" (Nan C. Scott's reminiscences of Tolkien); "Of *The Silmarillion*" (review); "Middle Earth" (poem); photographs of Tolkien and of places important in his life.

II-182    "Eucatastrophe." *Time*, 102 (17 September 1973), 101.

Obituary. Scholars and critics had at first admired Tolkien's books, while tracking down literary influences that ranged from Buchan to *Beowulf*, but when they became the objects of a cult they were denounced as escapist and jammed into allegorical straitjackets. *LOTR* is often pokey and perfervid, but it is one of the great fairy tale quests in modern literature.

II-183    Evans, Robley. *J. R. R. Tolkien*. New York: Thomas Y. Crowell, 1971. New York: Warner Paperback Library, 1972.

This book in the "Writers for the Seventies" series surveys all of Tolkien's work published to that date, with emphasis on his moral seriousness and elegiac sense of history. For reviews, see III-B-9.

II-184    Evans, W. D. Emrys. "Illusion, Tale and Epic: Susanne Langer's *Feeling and Form* and Four Books for Children." *The School Librarian*, 21 (1973), 5–11.

The four books are *H* (the main point of reference), Lewis's *Voyage of the Dawn Treader*, Ursula K. Le Guin's *A Wizard of Earthsea*, and Alan Garner's *Elidor*. Langer's criticism is supported by these books, and in turn supports their claim to be serious literature at their own level. The main points considered are the creation of a "virtual world" (more or less equivalent to Tolkien's "secondary world"); the stuff of legend, myth, and fairy tale reworked into a full "illusion of life"; and the epic as the matrix of all poetic genres. Though Evans agrees with Watson's warning (II-697) that to claim for Tolkien's work the status of "a central document of modern literature" is to take it too seriously, he also feels that Chedzoy's very negative view (II-93) in its turn takes *H* and *LOTR* too seriously.

II-185    _____. "The Lord of the Rings." *The School Librarian*, 16 (1968), 284–88.

This general discussion article deals with: the rigorously opposed but complex forces of good and evil; the ring of power as a measure of the strength of those who resist its temptation; the skillful blending of diverse strands of mythology; the beauty and power of places, things, and names.

II-186    "Ever-Ever Land." *Atlantic Monthly*, 215 (March, 1965), 194–95.

Review of *T&L*. This book is a delightful combination of the author's facets as a master of the modern fairy story and a scholar of language and literature.

II-187    Everett, Caroline Whitman. "The Imaginative Fiction of J. R.

R. Tolkien." M.A. thesis, Florida State University, 1957.

> This provides some biographical information, and discussions of *H*, *FGH*,
> and *LOTR*, and of the application of Tolkien's scholarly work to his
> writing. Appendix A prints excerpts from a letter written by Tolkien to
> Everett, containing such information as that *LOTR* had to be rewritten
> backwards and that each of the six Books had originally had its individual
> title (see I-50).

II-188   Everett, Dorothy. Review of "Ancrene Wisse and Hali
         Meidhed." *The Year's Work in English Studies*, 10 (1929),
         140–41.

> She summarizes Tolkien's linguistic argument on the localization and
> dating of *Ancrene Wisse*.

II-189   _____. Review of "Chaucer as a Philologist." *The Year's Work
         in English Studies*, 15 (1934), 98–99.

> A careful study of this essay will repay both the philologist and students of
> Chaucer who do not dare to claim that title.

II-190   _____. Review of "Some Contribution to Middle English
         Lexicography." *The Year's Work in English Studies*, 6 (1925),
         104–05.

> She discusses possible meanings and etymologies of some Middle English
> words.

II-191   Eyre, Frank. *Twentieth Century Children's Books* (London:
         Longmans, Green, 1952); revised and enlarged as *British
         Children's Books in the Twentieth Century* (London: Longman,
         1971).

> The 2nd edition has numerous references to Tolkien, particularly to *H* and
> *LOTR* (it notes that the latter was not written for children but was soon
> claimed for them); see pp. 20, 30–31, 36, 37, 53, 67, 112, 134–37, and 144.

II-192   Ezard, John. "Tolkien's World." *Manchester Guardian*, 22
         January 1972, p. 19.

> Tolkien's work is a justification for Oxford's language-based approach to
> English studies, for only with such knowledge could such a synthesis as
> *LOTR*, "in which reflections of Wagnerian myth co-exist harmoniously
> with elements of Celtic legend," be contrived. The tender part of the human
> mind which needs to create fairies is to be valued. "Tolkien's output can be
> taken, even at the barest analysis as an extended metaphor for the pact of
> friendship which needs to be struck between our considerable imaginative
> and our constricted sensory experience. Tolkien's fairyland never leeches
> the satisfactions from ordinary life. For his characters, it feeds every fibre
> of that life." *SWM* is a good example of such qualities. Notes a few facts
> from Tolkien's personal history that have a bearing on his fiction, but he
> thinks that it will be difficult to write a meaningful biography of Tolkien
> (cf. Carpenter, II-86). See reply by Chedzoy (II-93).

Farrell, Robert T. See Salu (II-590).

II-193   Fausset, Hugh l'A. Review of *RK. Manchester Guardian*, 4 November 1955, p. 4.

> On the whole, in spite of occasional concessions to the sentimental and the rather anticlimatic air of the last few chapters, Tolkien has succeeded well in combining the cosmic and heroic grandeur of his tale with the simple humours of men. His astounding inventiveness remains to the end.

II-194   Fernández, Oscar. "El Árbol y la Hoja en Tres Cuentos: J. R. R. Tolkien, O. Henry y María Luisa Bombal." *Ábside: Revista de Cultura Mejicana*, 42 (1978), 352–80.

> In Spanish. *T&L* is the work by Tolkien that is discussed.

II-195   Fifield, Merle. "Fantasy in and For the Sixties: The Lord of the Rings." *English Journal*, 55 (1966), 841–44.

> Fantasy should present an ideal which could be applied to the world as it is; in *LOTR* we have the "little man" (the hobbit) confronted by the two great twentieth-century socioeconomic evils: Sauron's combination of fascism with an industrial complex, and Saruman's totalitarian communism in the Shire. The solution to this chaos is an optimistic determinism. See also Plank (II-522).

II-196   Finder, Jan Howard. Review of *Silm. SFRA* [Science Fiction Research Association] *Newsletter*, No. 58 (September-October, 1977), pp. 1–2.

> It is disappointing that *Silm* consists of summaries rather than fully developed narratives, but it is still a joy to read.

Fisher, Janet. See II-301.

II-197   Fisher, Margery. "The Land of Faerie." Ch. 5 of her *Intent Upon Reading* (New York: Watts, 1962), pp. 69–96.

> Tolkien, whom the author remembers as bringing a bardic quality to reading *Beowulf* aloud in the classroom, drew his inspiration from Malory, Spenser, and, most of all, *Beowulf. H* and *LOTR* "are immensely exciting and compelling stories, but beyond the adventure there is the poetry of vast ideas, of appearances wonderfully visualized, of a country given form and contour, colour and weather, of people . . . perfectly realized . . . an extraordinarily varied world . . . where enchantment is at once human and supernatural" (p. 85).

II-198   _____. *Who's Who in Children's Books: A Treasury of the Familiar Characters of Childhood*. New York: Holt, Rinehart and Winston, 1975.

> On pp. 44–45 there is a description of Bilbo's character in *H*, comparing him with Gollum and with Frodo.

II-199    _____. Review of *Silm*. *Growing Point*, 16, No. 8 (March, 1978), 3257–59.

> *Silm* reflects the rise of aggression in gods, elves, and men, and the effects of greed and the lust for power on races created as generous and civilized beings. Yet it depends more on semantics than on social morality.

II-200    Fitzgerald, Edward. "The Applicability of *The Lord of the Rings*." *Tolkien Journal*, No. 15 (Summer, 1972), p. 30.

> Review of Ellwood, *Good News from Tolkien's Middle Earth* (II-175). "In these two well-written, easily read discourses she has both reinforced many ideas concerning Professor Tolkien's magnificent trilogy, and presented some exciting new ones concerning the Primary 'multi-verse' in which we (and everything else) live."

II-201    Flieger, Verlyn Brown. "Medieval Epic and Romance Motifs in J. R. R. Tolkien's *The Lord of the Rings*." Ph.D. diss., Catholic University of America, 1977.

> Tolkien did more than reuse old material from myth, epic, romance and fairytale; he also reformed and recombined traditional patterns and motifs to give them new vitality and fresh perspective. Among his borrowings and crossings of characteristic motifs we find Frodo (the fairy tale hero who, however, fights a monster and finds defeat and disillusionment), Aragorn (the epic hero who fights no monster but wins the kingdom and the fairy tale happy ending), Gollum (the monster), and Sam Gamgee (who transcends the role of comic, clever servant). He draws much from *Beowulf*, Malory, and the Grail legends, and through his work run concepts of sacrifice and rebirth, hope and renewal, light and darkness. See *DAI*, 38 (1978), 4157A; this abstract is also printed in *Olifant*, 5 (1978), 385–86.

Flinn, Charles G. See Ratliff (II-540).

II-202    Foote, Timothy. "Middle-Earth *Genesis*." *Time*, 110 (24 October 1977), 118, 120.

> Review of *Silm*. Though at times Tolkien sounds as if he were writing a parody of Edgar Rice Burroughs in the style of the Book of Revelations, at its best this posthumous revelation of his private mythology is majestic. His familiar, deep-rooted sense of the unwinnable war between good and evil is evident, and this doomed but heroic view of creation may be one reason for his popularity.

II-203    Forbes, Cheryl. "Answers about Middle-earth." *Christianity Today*, 22 (7 October 1977), 30–31.

> *Silm* summarizes events rather than developing stories, for the most part (the chapters on Beren and Lúthien and on Eärendil are exceptions), and its over-reliance on Genesis and on a pseudo-King James style become irritating; but is is interesting. Other posthumous works show Tolkien's range: the power of medieval tales in his translations in *GGKPO*; the delightful *FCL*.

II-204 _____. "For Tolkien Fans." *Christianity Today*, 21 (3 December 1976), 31.

> News item. She announces the forthcoming publication of *Silm*, *FCL*, and Carpenter's biography (II-86). She recommends Kilby's "delightful anecdotal book" on *Silm* (II-338), but does not recommend Evans (II-183) since "both style and content are relatively undistinguished." She notes three recent books that Tolkien aficionados might enjoy.

II-205 _____. "Frodo Decides—Or Does He?" *Christianity Today*, 20 (19 December 1975), 10–13.

> She explores the theme of individual free will and God's directing Providence in the "choices" and events in *LOTR*.

II-206 _____. "How to Beat the Beaten Path: An Interview With Clyde Kilby." *Christianity Today*, 21 (9 September 1977), 30–32.

> Comments on the evangelical importance of imagination and nature; the Wade Collection at Wheaton College; liberal arts education; the value of writers like Lewis and Tolkien for young people.

II-207 Foster, Robert. *The Complete Guide to Middle-earth: From The Hobbit to The Silmarillion*. New York: Ballantine Books/A Del Rey Book, 1978.

> This is a revised and updated version of his *Guide* (II-208), taking cognizance of *Silm*. This includes a tentative chronology of the First Age and a table for converting page numbers from Ballantine to Houghton Mifflin editions. For reviews, see III-B-10.

II-208 _____. *A Guide to Middle-earth*. Baltimore: Mirage Press, 1971. New York: Ballantine, 1974.

> Dictionary of everything pertaining to Middle-earth and its world in all published writings of Tolkien to that date, with supplementary information from the map by Pauline Baynes and correspondence or conversation between Tolkien and interested readers of his work, notably C. S. Kilby and Richard Plotz. He notes sources in the texts by page number, suggests meanings for words and names in Tolkien's invented languages that were not translated in the books, and includes family trees of leaders of Elves and Men. Parts of this work had appeared in earlier versions in the fanzine, *Niekas*, Nos. 16 through 20 (1966–68), under the overall title, "A Glossary of Middle Earth." The *Guide* was revised and updated in II-207. See also Day (II-144) and Tyler (II-670 and II-671). For reviews, see III-B-11.

II-209 _____. "The Heroic in Middle-earth." *Mythcon II Proceedings* (3–6 September 1971). Ed. Glen GoodKnight. Los Angeles: Mythopoeic Society, 1972, pp. 22–25.

> He discusses: the survival-hero, the destiny-hero, and the honor-hero as types and as exemplified in *H* and *LOTR*; Middle-earth as a heroic world;

and Tolkien's conception of the hero. See also Blissett (II-53), Levitin (II-370), Moorman (II-445), and Reckford (II-545).

II-210 _____. "Levels of Interpretation." *Tolkien Journal*, No. 15 (Summer, 1972), p. 22.

Tolkien's Middle-earth makes specific borrowings from many sources, but still relates to the primary world in its own way, chiefly (by linking the moral and heroic codes, as well as by other superficial cultural borrowings) as an expression of the world-view of the Christian Middle Ages.

II-211 _____. "Sindarin and Quenya Phonology." *Mythcon I Proceedings* (4–7 September 1970). Ed. Glen GoodKnight. Los Angeles: Mythopoeic Society, 1971, pp. 54–56.

A pioneering effort to describe phonemically the sound systems of Quenya and its linguistic descendent, Sindarin. See also II-302 and Stevens (II-640).

_____. See also Boardman (II-55).

II-212 Friedman, Barton R. "Fabricating History: Narrative Strategy in *The Lord of the Rings.*" *Clio: An Interdisciplinary Journal of Literature, History, and the Philosophy of History*, 2 (1973), 123–44.

By evoking the remote past of Middle-earth (through poetic interludes, old tales like that of Beren, confluence of dream and waking reality as in the house of Tom Bombadil), Tolkien establishes an all but cosmic context for Frodo's quest and implies the conflation of myth and history. The characters by their actions (freely chosen, though they dimly detect a providential design) in effect write their own epic (*LOTR* itself, but also the whole history of Middle-earth). Tom Bombadil embodies a moral consciousness in the natural world and also the power of language to enforce the dictates of that consciousness; his songs turn artifice into fact. The history that unfolds is cyclical in nature (each age sees the emergence, near triumph, and ultimate fall of the Enemy), apocalyptic in its sweep, and extends to our own age where the struggle between good and evil is renewed and the outcome remains in doubt.

Friedman, David. See Boardman (II-55).

Fromén, Björn. See II-302.

II-213 Fry, Carrol L. "Tolkien's Middle Earth and the Fantasy Frame." *Studies in the Humanities*, 7, No. i (1978), 35–42.
Not seen.

II-214 Fuller, Edmund. "The Lord of the Hobbits: J. R. R. Tolkien." In his *Books With Men Behind Them* (New York: Random, 1962), pp. 169–96. (Slightly) revised and reprinted in Isaacs and Zimbardo (II-307), pp. 17–39.

This discussion of Tolkien's work and theories of fantasy finds *LOTR* a meaningful moral fable with some Christian borrowings and an allegorical suggestiveness that connects it with the present day world. The revised version includes Tolkien's declaration that Gandalf is an incarnate angel (see *Silm*). Fuller's book also has chapters on C. S. Lewis, Charles Williams, and the Fantastic.

II-215    _____. "Of Frodo and Fantasy." *Wall Street Journal*, 4 January 1966, p. 14.

This review of the Ballantine edition of *LOTR* calls it "an immense adventure story, an adult fairy tale, a romance in the classical meaning of that word." *H* is called "a children's story—plus."

II-216    Fuller, Muriel, ed. *More Junior Authors*. New York: H. W. Wilson, 1963.

There is a biographical sketch of "J. R. R. Tolkien" on pp. 206–07.

II-217    Galbreath, Robert. "Popular Culture and Bibliography: The Serif Series." *Journal of Popular Culture*, 4 (1971), 746–51.

This review of six volumes in the Kent State University Press's Serif Series considers West's *Tolkien Checklist*, 1st ed. (II-715) a useful volume, since it records and annotates so much written on Tolkien, but advises that fanzine articles should be included. See pp. 746, 749, and 751n.

II-218    Gale, Floyd C. Review of *RK*. *Galaxy*, 12, No. 4 (August, 1956), 109.

Though *LOTR* "sounds downright silly" in synopsis, "it becomes a gripping adventure in the hands of a master like Tolkien. . . . The trance quality of the narrative is comparable to that other hypnotic masterpiece of fantasy, *The Worm Ouroboros* by E. R. Eddison—recommendation enough."

Galinsky, G. Karl. See Reckford (II-545).

II-219    Gang, T. M. "Approaches to *Beowulf*." *Review of English Studies*, NS 3 (1952), 1–12.

Cites objections both to W. P. Ker's and to Tolkien's criticism of *Beowulf* (see I-35). The dragon is not a symbol of evil as the Grendels are (see reply by Bonjour, II-56). While the poem may be a balance, it is certainly not a unity, since the events of the first part do not influence those of the second, nor produce a cumulative effect. Tolkien is neither completely historical nor completely unhistorical in his approach (cf. Rubey, II-574).

II-220    Gardner, John. "The World of Tolkien." *New York Times Book Review*, 23 October 1977, pp. 1, 39–40.

Review article on *Silm*. *LOTR* looms already as one of the truly great works of the human spirit, with rich characterization (at its heart is the individual's voluntary service of good or evil within an unfated universe), imagistic brilliance, powerfully imagined and detailed sense of place, and thrilling adventure. *Silm* also has such qualities, but they are largely undeveloped due to the compression of the narrative, the fierce thematic focus, and the stress on the meaning and coherence of newly created myth. Tolkien blends things modern (often the tawdriest of the modern, but greatly elevated by his art) with things medieval (particularly in his organizing principles, symbolism, and patterns of legends and events).

Garlick, K. J. See I-77.

II-221 Garmon, Gerald M. "J. R. R. Tolkien's Modern Fairyland." *West Georgia College Review*, 6 (1973), 10–15.

Not seen.

II-222 Garmonsway, G. N. Review of Clark Hall, *Beowulf* (I-38). *The Year's Work in English Studies*, 21 (1940), 33–34.

Tolkien and Wrenn's revision of Clark Hall's prose translation of *Beowulf* eradicates his faulty diction and has a convincing verisimilitude to the theme, tone, and temper of the Old English original. In his introduction, Tolkien has valuable things to say on the translator's dilemma, but his discussion of meter will perplex a novice.

II-223 Gasque, Thomas J. "Tolkien: The Monsters and the Critters." In Isaacs and Zimbardo (II-307), pp. 151–63.

Study of Tolkien's mythic creations. He systematized the Northern tradition for his Elves and Dwarves, and drew on the flexible tradition of the Wild Man for Gollum, the Orcs, and the Woses. Where he fails, as with Tom Bombadil, Shelob, and the Balrog, it is because these characters are not believable: they have no foundation outside the work or (as do the Hobbits and Ringwraiths) within it.

II-224 Geijerstam, Carl-Erik af. "Anteckningar om J. R. R. Tolkiens saga-epos Ringen." *Studiekamraten*, 49 (1967), 90.

In Swedish. Review of translation of *LOTR* into Swedish by Åke Ohlmarks. The reviewer relates Tolkien to the Swedish philosophy of life, notes changes in the style to fit the changing circumstances in the text, and comments that the reader is likely—or at least tempted—to read too fast to appreciate the beauties of the language, which should be savored. See also Ohlmarks (II-482).

II-225 Gerville-Réache, Joy. "Tolkien's 'Silmarillion' tests fans." *Christian Science Monitor*, 21 September 1977, p. 23.

Review of *Silm*. This book "gives us greater insight into the extraordinary world of fantasy and the rhythm of words which permeated Tolkien's life," but almost certainly it would never have become well known without *H* and *LOTR*. It is written in the heroic style of legend and ancient tale, quite unlike the easy-flowing conversational style of the Hobbit books. There is plenty of daring and adventure here, but one grows a little weary of it, and there has to be something more to explain the success of the other fantasies. Probably this is the endearing, human qualities of the hobbits, whose folksy warmth and charm is lacking in the noble but remote heroes of the prequel. *Silm* "will test the degree of ardor of Tolkien fans, and probably only those with the highest level of ardor will enthuse about it."

II-226 Gilson, Christopher. "Language and Lore: *The Silmarillion* as Trivium." *Fantasiae*, 5, No. 11–12, Whole No. 56–57 (November-December, 1977), 4–6.

> This short article discusses Elvish sentences in *Silm*, and Tolkien's creativity is demonstrated by his fabrication of Elvish with parallels in Germanic language and myth.

II-227 _____. "More Speculation on *The Silmarillion*." *Fantasiae*, 5, No. 7, Whole No. 52 (July, 1977). 10.

> Notes on the Encircling Mountains around Gondolin mentioned in Christopher Tolkien's account of *Silm* (II-656), and on the Elvish poem on p. 76 of Carpenter (II-86).

II-228 _____. "A Note on the Prelude to *The Silmarillion*." *Fantasiae*, 5, No. 3, Whole No. 48 (March, 1977), 1, 4.

> Comments on the significance of the Elvish words "Ainulindalë" and "Valaquenta" in announcements of the forthcoming publication of *Silm*.

_____. See also II-302.

Giudice, Nancy. See Levitin (II-372).

II-229 Glover, Willis B. "The Christian Character of Tolkien's Invented World." *Criticism*, 13 (1971), 39–53. Reprinted in *Mythlore*, 3, No. 2, Whole No. 10 (1975), 3–8; footnotes omitted in this reprint but later printed in *Mythlore*, 3, No. 3, Whole No. 11 (1976), 7.

> Tolkien has himself called the Third Age a monotheistic world of natural (not Christian) religion, but the presuppositions of the work are Christian, and it is monotheistic in the peculiar sense of the Biblical tradition. Evil is presented as a corruption of the good; the proper response to the good creation is to enjoy it; evil is powerful but ultimately self-defeating. "Tolkien's tale may be read as a parable of the need to adapt means to ends and of the difficulty of abiding by this when the end seems of very great importance" (p. 43). Every event and creature is part of a long, nonrecurring history which controls nature and which is acted upon by a transcendent power; yet God's sovereignty does not abrogate free will and Tolkien is successful in portraying the agony of decision. Characters who fall are treated with sympathy and a subtle understanding of temptation and the experience of moral decision. Aspects of Christian ethics are introduced unobtrusively as integral parts of the narrative.

Goodall, Sylvia. See Scriven (II-605).

II-230 GoodKnight, Glen. "A Comparison of Cosmological Geography in the Works of J. R. R. Tolkien, C. S. Lewis, and Charles Williams." *Mythlore*, 1, No. 3 (July, 1969), 18–22.

> The worlds of *LOTR*, the Chronicles of Narnia, and the Arthuriad share a pattern of Mortal Lands, and Intermediate State (Númenor and the Elf-

havens, Ramandu's island, Carbonek), and Spiritual Lands or heaven (Undying Lands, Aslan's Country, Sarras). Lewis and Tolkien made their worlds flat and mountain-encircled.

II-231    _____. "C. S. Kilby in Southern California." *Mythlore*, 1, No. 1 (January, 1969), 27–29.

Kilby gave talks on "The Oxford Christians" (the Inklings); "The Religious Experience of C. S. Lewis in the Letters of Arthur Greeves" (tracing CSL's spiritual odyssey from a very young age; Lewis's letters to Greeves have since been published; see Lewis, II-379); "Tolkien the Man" (on Kilby's meetings with JRRT and on the then unpublished *Silm*; see Kilby, II-338); "The Christian Interpretation of Tolkien" (*LOTR* is essentially Christian in its conflicts of darkness with light, the natural with the unnatural, the almost angelic with the hellish; in its emphasis on choice and free will; and in the roles of Gandalf, Frodo, and Aragorn in different aspects of Christ-figures; see also Kilby, II-336); and "Tolkien the Myth-Maker" (in his world of certainties, Tolkien contrasts being and doing, melancholy and joy, and he believes in the glory of the ordinary and in fulfillment through sacrifice).

II-232    _____. " 'Death and the Desire for Deathlessness.' " *Mythlore*, 3, No. 2, Whole No. 10 (1975), 19.

Prints a letter from Tolkien to Herbert Schiro dated 17 November 1957 (see I-76) and comments on the statement that *LOTR* deals with "Death and the desire for deathlessness."

II-233    _____. "The Social History of the Inklings, J. R. R. Tolkien, C. S. Lewis, Charles Williams, 1939–1945." *Mythlore*, 2, No. 1, Whole No. 5 [also *Tolkien Journal*, 4, No. 2, Whole No. 10] (Winter, 1970), 7–9.

Survey of the Inklings during the period of World War II, with emphasis on Williams, whom Lewis said was a principle of liveliness and cohesion in a group whose purposes were merriment, piety, and literature. See also Carpenter (II-85).

II-234    _____. "Tolkien at Eighty: An Appreciation." *Mythlore*, 2, No. 4, Whole No. 8 (Winter, 1972), 3–4.

_____. See also Sievert (II-613).

II-235    Goselin, Peter Damien. "Two Faces of Eve: Galadriel and Shelob as Anima Figures." *Mythlore*, 6, No. 3, Whole No. 21 (Summer, 1979), 3–4, 28.

The female principle of the anima appears in myth in two forms: the beautiful, benevolent, beneficent Heavenly Queen, and her opposite and perversion. The most developed use of the anima and its shadow in Tolkien's work is seen in Galadriel and Shelob in *LOTR*, and is related to the characteristics of the anima as noted by C. G. Jung and Marie-Louise von Franz.

II-236   Grant, Patrick. "Belief in Fantasy: J. R. R. Tolkien's *Lord of the Rings*." Ch. 5 in his *Six Modern Authors and Problems of Belief*. London: Macmillan, 1979; New York: Harper & Row, 1979, pp. 93–120.

> The other five authors are Owen Barfield, Robert Graves, Aldous Huxley, David Jones, and Michael Polanyi; the chapter on Tolkien also discusses Lewis Carroll and Rudyard Kipling at length.

II-237   _____. "Tolkien: Archetype and Word." *Cross Currents*, 22 (1973), 365–80.

> Not seen.

II-238   Grattan, J. H. G. Review of *GGK*, 1st ed. *Review of English Studies*, 1 (1925), 484–87.

> The editors have given us a pleasantly short discussion of date and district of origin; a sufficient account of grammar and meter; a text which is conservative, but often well emended (though in any 2nd ed. they should note the authors of the emendations they have adopted); learned, discriminating, and interesting notes; and a model glossary. It is a merit that they do not try to epitomize all the "literature" that has gathered around the poem. See also Grattan (II-239).

II-239   _____. Review of *GGK*, 1st ed. *The Year's Work in English Studies*, 6 (1925), 96–97.

> This is a learned and attractive book which respects the manuscript. There are some brilliant emendations, but none made wantonly. The Commentary is sound philology, and the Glossary is thorough. Notes some errors. (This short notice is in the "Middle English" section done by Dorothy Everett, but p. 96, n.6 credits Grattan with this particular part.)

II-240   Gray, Thomas. "Bureaucratization in *The Lord of the Rings*." *Mythlore*, 7, No. 2, Whole No. 24 (Summer, 1980), 3–5.

> Tolkien assigns bureaucracy to the evil characters, but, while the destructive effects of bureaucratization are certainly deplorable, actually it is an organizational tool which can be used to either good or ill effect.

II-241   Green, David L. "Children's Literature Periodicals on Individual Authors, Dime Novels, Fantasy." *Phaedrus*, 3 (1976), 22–24.

> Lists and annotates periodicals and fanzines on fantasy literature generally or on specific authors, including Tolkien.

II-242   Green, Roger Lancelyn. *Authors and Places: A Literary Pilgrimage*. London: B. T. Batsford, 1963. New York: G. P. Putnam's Sons, 1963.

> Brief commentary on Tolkien in the chapter on "Reluctant Dragons."

*FGH*, because it is "set in the neighborhood of Thame," is the only one of Tolkien's books with a definite geographical background (even if the Shire "is a very close neighbor of the Berkshire and Oxfordshire Downs," p. 147). In the work of Tolkien, C. S. Lewis, and Kenneth Grahame, "we catch a gleam of misty sunlight and fresh wind over Ridgeway or hear the murmur of the Thames" (p. 148).

II-243    Green, Roger Lancelyn and Walter Hooper. *C. S. Lewis: A Biography*. London and New York: Harcourt, Brace, Jovanovich, 1974.

Tolkien is mentioned frequently. This biography sees Lewis in a more admiring light than does Carpenter (II-85) and the two can be read as complementary.

II-244    Green, William H. "The Four-Part Structure of Bilbo's Education." *Children's Literature*, 8 (1980), 133–40.

Bilbo (possibly from Middle English *Bil-boie*, "sword-boy") matures through a series of hardships and tests. The structure of *H* is cyclical and Bilbo's education is in four parts (the departure from the Shire followed by adventures in the Misty Mountains, in Mirkwood, and at the Lonely Mountain) which are structurally similar in that they each begin with a well-equipped journey into the wilderness and move through want, danger, captivity, and unlikely escape to a hospitable house (whether Rivendell, the house of Beorn, or Esgaroth). Based on Ch. 2 of his dissertation (Green, II-245).

II-245    _____. "*The Hobbit* and Other Fiction by J. R. R. Tolkien: Their Roots in Medieval Heroic Literature and Language." Ph.D. diss., Louisiana State University, 1969.

Surveys medieval works in English, Norse, Irish, Welsh, French, German, and Italian to identify possible sources for names, motifs, and characters in *H* (in particular) and *LOTR*. He concludes that *H* incorporates elements from a wide range of medieval literature, but that its deepest roots are in Northern Europe and its world is essentially that of Norse heroic fiction and of *Beowulf*. See also St. Clair (II-582). See *DAI*, 30 (1970), 4944A.

II-246    _____. "Legendary and Historical Time in Tolkien's *Farmer Giles of Ham*." *Notes on Contemporary Literature*, 5, No. iii (1975), 14–15.

He disagrees with Stimpson's "complaint" that Tolkien's fiction is set in "legendary time" (see Stimpson, II-642), since most of it is set in prehistoric Europe, which is "certainly past." *FGH* is set in the real historical context of the Thames valley between A.D. 300–500. Its historical theme is the decadence of the old, over-rigid social order of the late Roman Empire, which is vulnerable to external disruptive forces such as those symbolized by the giant and the dragon, but which can be regenerated by a hobbit-like agrarian with courage, common sense, and respect for tradition.

II-247    _____. "The Ring at the Center: *Ēaca* in *The Lord of the Rings.*" *Mythlore*, 4, No. 2, Whole No. 14 (December, 1976), 17–19.

> Old English "ēaca" refers to power beyond the natural, and can be seen in the actions of various ring-bearers in *LOTR*.

II-248    Grigson, Geoffrey, ed. *The Concise Encyclopedia of Modern World Literature.* New York: Hawthorn, 1963. The entry for "Tolkien, J[ohn] R[onald] R[euel] (1892–    )" is on pp. 443–44.

> Relates Tolkien's fiction to his need to create a world for his invented languages.

II-249    Grotta, Daniel. *The Biography of J. R. R. Tolkien: Architect of Middle-Earth.* Philadelphia: Running Press, 1978.

> Revision of Grotta-Kurska (II-250), with an added commentary on *Silm*. For reviews, see III-B-12.

II-250    Grotta-Kurska, Daniel. *J. R. R. Tolkien: Architect of Middle Earth.* Philadelphia: Running Press, 1976.

> Biography written without the assistance of the Tolkien famiy. Cf. Carpenter (II-86). For reviews see III-B-13.

Guadalupi, Gianni. See Manguel and Guadalupi (II-401).

II-251    Hall, Robert A., Jr. "Tolkien's Hobbit Tetralogy as 'Anti-Nibelungen.' " *Western Humanities Review*, 32 (1978), 351–59.

> Tolkien's *H* and *LOTR*, and Wagner's Ring cycle, show basic similarities in structure and theme. Yet they are also basically different in that Wagner took the truly pessimistic view "that the only way to solve the dilemma of evil is to destroy everything and return to a primal anarchic state of Nature" (p. 355). Tolkien, in an implicit reply, took the same basic organization and content-structure and gave it an at least moderately optimistic interpretation: "although human (or hobbit) character may fail in the crucial test, Fate can step in and save the situation as a result of previous acts" (p. 358). See also Blissett (II-53) and Stein (II-637).

II-252    Halle, Louis J. "Flourishing Orcs." *Saturday Review*, 15 January 1955, pp. 17–18.

> Tongue-in-cheek review of *FR*. Even though its value as scientific history cannot be granted, since the events of the Red Book of Westmarch "have nowhere been corroborated in the chronicles of Men (let alone Elves)" (p. 17), it will survive as eminently readable literature.

II-253    _____. "History Through the Mind's Eye." *Saturday Review*, 28 January 1956, pp. 11–12.

> Review of *LOTR*. Its "meaning" is, in a word, "heroism." The two prime facts of Middle-earth are power and its consequence, suffering. "In the

historian's view, power is not a neutral element that can be used for good or evil. It is always evil, for it enables the wicked to dominate the world, or, in the hands of the good, is inescapably corrupting" (p. 12). Cf. Davie (II-141).

II-254 Hammond, Wayne G. "Addenda to 'J. R. R. Tolkien: A Bibliography.' " *Bulletin of Bibliography and Magazine Notes*, 34, No. 3 (July–September, 1977), 119–27.

Follows the format used in the first installment by Christensen (II-98) and adds much new material. See also West (II-715).

II-255 Hannabuss, C. Stuart. "Deep Down: A Thematic and Bibliographical Excursion." *Signal*, No. 6 (September, 1971), pp. 87–95.

Tolkien has vindicated the fantasy tradition and shown that the dream world is not necessarily escapist. *LOTR* concerns a quest with metaphysical and mystical overtones undertaken by an Everyman figure through a landscape of moral ambivalences.

II-256 Hardy, Gene B. *Tolkien's The Lord of the Rings and The Hobbit*. Lincoln, Neb.: Cliffs Notes, 1977.

These seventy-five pages contain a brief sketch of Tolkien's life (see Carpenter, II-86); an overview of his fictional world; plot summaries of *H* and *LOTR*; a glossary of names (see Day, II-144; Foster, II-207 and II-208; and Tyler, II-670 and II-671); a discussion of the theme of power; a short history of the First, Second, and Third Ages followed by a chronology of major events; a list of suggested research topics; and a selected bibliography of twelve critical works. Cf. Morrison (II-451) and Ready (II-542).

II-257 Harrison, M. John. "By Tennyson Out of Disney." *New Worlds Quarterly*, 2 (New York: Berkley Medallion, 1971), 185–89. Reprinted in *Anduril*, No. 3 (November, 1972), pp. 25–28.

It is not Tolkien's fault that his work is so overrated, for he has not supported the extravagant claims made for it. *LOTR* is full of poetry and action, and has a huge act of fantasy implicit in its overall structure and aims; but it takes its characters and images and components not from the beautiful chaos of reality but from other fictions; it deals with Good and Evil but avoids the riskier ethical questions; it fails to bridge the fantasy world and the real one, having a soft center of emotional abstracts and sentimentality.

II-258 Harshaw, Ruth. "When Carnival of Books Went to Europe." *A[merican] L[ibrary] A[ssociation] Bulletin*, 51 (February, 1957), 117–23.

Harshaw describes meeting the authors of children's books during a trip to Europe to tape readings for her radio program. There are two paragraphs on Tolkien on p. 120. She found she had "a language difficulty" with JRRT and "finally said in desperation, 'I do appreciate your coming up from Oxford so that I might record you, Professor Tolkien, but I can't understand a word you say.' This amused him and he said, 'A friend of mine tells me that I talk in shorthand and then smudge it.' "

II-259   Hart, Dabney Adams. "C. S. Lewis's Defense of Poesie." Ph.D. diss., University of Wisconsin, 1959.

>This study is "an analysis of the premises and the achievements of Lewis's critical and imaginative writing" (p. 4), but included are brief discussions of *H* and *LOTR*, leading to the conclusion that "Tolkien's achievement is virtually an illustration or proof of the literary principles which Lewis himself has never been able to practice as successfully as his friend" (p. 286). See *DA*, 20 (1960), 3293.

II-260   Haughton, Rosemary. *Tales from Eternity: The World of Faerie and the Spiritual Search*. London: George Allen and Unwin, 1973. U.S. ed. as *Tales from Eternity: The World of Fairytales and the Spiritual Search* (New York: Seabury, n.d.).

>This book is a philosophical essay on Christian morality rather than literary criticism. Ch. 5, "The Quest," has references to *LOTR* throughout.

II-261   Hayes, E. Nelson. "New Fiction." *Progressive* (Madison, Wis.), 19, No. 1 (January, 1955), 42–43.

>This includes a review of *FR*, which is called a prose epic and "a philosophical allegory of man's eternal questing and of the moral dangers which confront him" (p. 43). Tolkien has created a mythology that is complete, consistent, and convincing, written in a prose of great dignity and power.

II-262   Hayes, Noreen and Robert Renshaw. "Of Hobbits: *The Lord of the Rings*." *Critique*, 9 (1967), 58–66.

>This examination of the pluralistic moral nature of *LOTR* notes that no one in the work is completely good, only Sauron is completely evil, and the evil ones do not put up a monolithic front but are divided by their own antagonisms. See Auden (II-16).

Heap, George. See Becker (II-37).

II-263   Hedges, Ned Samuel. "The Fable and the Fabulous: The Use of Traditional Forms in Children's Literature." Ph.D. diss., University of Nebraska, 1968.

>Excellent literature contains meaning at a number of levels of interpretation, and one way to achieve such complexity is to work in the structural devices of traditional forms. *H*, for example, employs the devices of medieval chivalric romance in the nature of the quest, the nature of the hero (Bilbo, like the novice knight, discovers within himself the qualities necessary to the fulfillment of the quest), and the symbolic rendering of the forces of Good and Evil. The dissertation also discusses, in addition to fable and romance in *H*, fable and myth in Rudyard Kipling's *Just So Stories* and fable and epic in Kenneth Grahame's *Wind in the Willows*. See *DA*, 29 (1969), 2213A.

II-264    Heins, Ethel L. Review of *RGEO* and *PSME*. *Horn Book*, 44 (1 April 1968), 188–89.

> Describes contents briefly. On *RGEO*: "Followers of Tolkien will rejoice in his translations of two Elvish poems included in his copious notes and comments and in his own handsome Elvish script on every page of the elegantly designed book" (p. 188). On *PSME*: William Elvin "performs the songs, revealing their beautiful melodic line and the lyric romanticism that matches the mood of the texts" (p. 189).

II-265    Heiserman, A. R. Review of *GGK*, 2nd ed. *Speculum*, 44 (1969), 176–77.

> Davis's revision is careful: his new introduction describes the manuscript more fully and accurately, he updates the discussion of plot to include interlace, he replaces the stemma of lost French sources with a full and clear account of analogues, and he somewhat improves the accuracy of the text by printing *yogh* where it occurs in the manuscript. He emends freely but sometimes does not state his evidence and his notes advance his own interpretations without sufficient attention to other critics.

Helms, Marci. See Becker (II-37).

II-266    Helms, Philip. "The Evolution of Tolkien Fandom." In Becker (II-37), pp. 104–09.

> This article originally appeared in the May, 1977 issue of *Appendix*, issue "T," from the American Tolkien Society. It discusses changes in the nature of interest in Tolkien's work from the reception by the Inklings, to esoteric appreciation by a small group, to the cult, to scholarly interest by fans, to a leveling-off with the publication of *Silm*. See also Lerner (II-368).

II-267    Helms, Randel. "J. R. R. Tolkien's Territory, a World Both Familiar and Apart." *Chicago Tribune Book World*, 19 May 1974, p. 6.

> Not seen.

II-268    _____. "Orc: The Id in Blake and Tolkien." *Literature and Psychology* (University of Hartford), 20, No. i (1970), 31–35.

> William Blake gives the name of "Orc" to the fairest imaginable picture of humanity, while Tolkien gives the same name to the foulest. Both Orcs are symbols or representatives of a disruptive power that is inimical to established order and whose function is to rebel against and overturn a status quo. In Blake's radical and revolutionary vision, repressing the energies of the Id is bad, and sexual exuberance and political disorder are therapeutic. Like Blake, Tolkien opposes the life-deadening and life-denying aspects of the modern world, but his conservative and traditional vision finds it necessary to repress Orc-hood; the phallic Sauron and the fecund Orcs must be defeated, and Frodo must be symbolically castrated, in the loss of his finger, before he can rise to full heroic stature. This essay was incorporated into his book, *Tolkien's World* (II-270).

II-269    _____. "The Structure and Aesthetic of Tolkien's *Lord Of the Rings*." *Mythcon I Proceedings* (4–7 September 1970). Ed. Glen GoodKnight. Los Angeles: Mythopoeic Society, pp. 5–8.

"This paper is an attempt to show that the quality and value of the narrative in fantasy literature is dependent upon the richness and complexity of the interrelationships between the action, on the one hand, and the internal laws or structural principles of the created fantasy world on the other" (p. 5). He describes five internal laws governing Tolkien's secondary world and shows how they structure the action of each of the six books of *LOTR*. He stresses parallels in the action (cf. West, II-711). This essay was incorporated in his book, *Tolkien's World* (II-270).

II-270    _____. *Tolkien's World*. Boston: Houghton Mifflin, 1974.

The stress of this book is on Tolkien's theories of fantasy, *LOTR*, and *H* (including a Freudian reading of *H* that is not entirely serious), with some attention to *LBN*, *SWM*, and *ATB*. For reviews, see III-B-14.

II-271    Helson, Ravenna. "Fantasy and Self-Discovery." *Horn Book*, 46 (1970), 121–34.

Jungian classifications distinguish three types of fantasy written by men (I: Wish-Fulfillment and Humor; II: Heroism; III: Tender Feeling) and three types by women authors (I: Independence and Self-Expression; II: Transformation; III: Inner Mystery and Awe). *H*, which deals with Bilbo's individuation journey (see Matthews, II-411), is an example of the Heroism type. Its orientation is patriarchal and mythic. See also O'Neill (II-483).

II-272    Hennelly, Mark M., Jr. "The Dream of Fantasy: 'There and Back Again': A Hobbit's Holiday." *The Sphinx: A Magazine of Literature and Society*, 10 (1979), 29–43.

Not seen.

II-273    Henniker-Heaton, Peter J. "Tolkien Disguised as Himself." *Christian Science Monitor*, 23 May 1968, p. 7.

Review of Ready, *Tolkien Relation* (II-543). This is an "un-understandable unreadable non-introduction to Tolkien lore" but "most valuable" for that very reason: all the book's internal contradictions show that Tolkien can never be understood but must be experienced.

II-274    Hentoff, Nat and Wilson C. McWilliams. "Critics' Choices for Christmas." *Commonweal*, 83 (3 December 1965), 284, 287.

Both include *LOTR* in their recommendations, Hentoff finding it "a sweepingly plotted morality play for adults" (p. 284) and McWilliams finding it helpful for "those citizens who would recover the habit of imagination, or moral clarity, and of political vision" (p. 287).

II-275    "Heroic Endeavour." *Times Literary Supplement*, 27 August 1954, p. 541.

Review of *FR*. This is a book to be read "for sound prose and rare imagination," but the plot lacks balance because the only code is the warrior's code of courage, and what constitutes "good" is not explained. See also II-178 and II-581.

II-276    Higgins, James Edward. "Five Authors of Mystical Fancy for Children: A Critical Study." Ed.D. diss., Columbia University, 1965.

The characteristics of a story of mystical fancy are that "it appeals more to the heart than to the mind, and the truth of the story is found more through faith and feeling than through empirical knowledge; it demands an intuitively contemplative communion between book and reader; it accepts the reality of a spiritual world; it reaches for a hidden universal beyondness; it abounds with a feeling of joyful sadness." *H* is such a book, taking the reader back to a time when humanity attempted to explore the meaning of the cosmos through stories which are now called myths or legends. The other four authors considered are W. H. Hudson, George MacDonald, Antoine de Saint-Exupéry, and C. S. Lewis. See *DA*, 26 (1966), 4629–30.

Hill, Betty. See MacDonald (II-396).

Hill, Helen. See Perkins (II-514).

Hill, Joy. See II-393.

II-277    Hillegas, Mark R., ed. *Shadows of Imagination: The Fantasies of C. S. Lewis, J. R. R. Tolkien, and Charles Williams.* Carbondale: Southern Illinois Univ. Press, 1969; new ed., 1979.

Hillegas in his Introduction sees the three authors as unique in style and technique, but sharing a respect for fantasy because it is a valuable mode for presenting moral and spiritual values that could not be expressed in realistic fiction. For the essays on Tolkien, see Hughes (II-289), Kilby (II-335), Moorman (II-446), and Urang (II-676). The 2nd ed. adds a new essay on *Silm* by Kreeft (II-352). For reviews, see III-B-15.

II-278    Hillman, Aaron. "*The Lord of the Rings*: Affective Approaches to Teaching Literature." Paper presented at the 61st Annual Meeting of the National Council of Teachers of English, Las Vegas, November, 1971. DRICE (Development and Research in Confluent Education) Occasional Paper No. 10. ERIC (Educational Research Information Center) document numbers: ED 084 520; CS 200 796.

"That which we term 'fantasy' is a reflection of the inner man of the writer and is, in turn, a part of ourselves. Fantasy is what we imagine" (pp. 1–2). The paper instructs participants in an encounter session to act out themes from *LOTR* relevant to their own lives.

II-279   Hinkle, Warren. "The Oxford Fairy Tale School of Muscular
         Christianity." *Scanlan's*, 1, No. 6 (August, 1970), 36.
>    Tolkien, a Catholic convert preaching a brand of muscular Christianity, has
>    consciously used the fairy tale format as a means of propaganda for a
>    medieval social structure and ethic, reaffirming the necessity for an
>    aristocracy of the few who are endowed by God with the strength and grace
>    to lead the many.

II-280   "The Hobbit Habit" *Time*, 88 (15 July 1966), pp. 48, 51.
>    *LOTR* is this year's "in" book.

II-281   Hodgart, Matthew. "Ents, Orcs and Angels." *New Statesman*,
         85 (25 May 1973), 769.
>    Review of Kocher, *Master of Middle-earth* (II-346), and of the French
>    translation of *LOTR*.

II-282   ———. "Kicking the Hobbit." *New York Review of Books*, 8 (4
         May 1967), 10–11.
>    The cover title is "Resisting Tolkien." Notes Tolkien's sensitive descriptions
>    of landscapes and the Britishness of his hobbits. Thinks *LOTR* lacks moral
>    depth and is a simplistic Christian parable (cf. Auden, II-16). Notable for
>    the first appearance of David Levine's caricature of Tolkien with a pet
>    dragon, which can also be found in Levine's collection, *Pens and Needles*
>    (Boston: Gambit, 1969), p. 136.

II-283   Hoffman, Matthew. "*The Hobbit*: The Real Story." *Tolkien
         Journal*, 2, No. 1 (1966), 5.
>    Cites the dwarf names taken for *H* from the *Eddas*. See also Callahan (II-
>    81) and Carter (II-89).

II-284   Homberger, Eric. Review of West, *Tolkien Criticism* (II-715).
         *The Year's Work in English Studies*, 51 (1970), 353.
>    Describes contents.

II-285   Hooper, Walter. See Green and Hooper (II-243), Le Guin (II-
         365), and Lewis (II-378 and II-379).

II-286   Hope, Francis. "Welcome to Middle Earth." *New Statesman*, 72
         (11 November 1966), 701–02.
>    Review of *LOTR*. Notes its linguistic inspiration and atmosphere of Nordic
>    myth.

II-287   Horton, Sylvia Wallace. Review of *GGK*, 2nd ed. *Studia
         Neophilologia*, 41 (1969), 179–80.

II-288   Howard, Claire. Review of Stimpson, *J. R. R. Tolkien* (II-642).
         *Mythlore*, 2, No. 3, Whole No. 7 (Winter, 1971), 9–11.

         Howes, Margaret. See Becker (II-37).

Huber, Kathleen. See Berman and Nahigian (II-45).

II-289    Hughes, Daniel. "Pieties and Giant Forms in *The Lord of the Rings*." In Hillegas, *Shadows of Imagination* (II-277), 81–96.

> Although it is predicated on classical assumptions and a classical aesthetic, *LOTR* is reminiscent of Romantic poetry: Tolkien, to use Coleridge's term, is imaginative rather than fanciful. *LOTR* is basically pious, in terms of Christianity and the English countryside, and refreshes the traditions of the Heroic Age of which Tolkien had such a firm grasp. The elves are mysterious and magical, the hobbits are neither, and between these two worlds is the mediating figure of Gandalf. Frodo and Gollum together form a convincing picture of how obsession is fought and yielded to. The ordinariness of the hobbits makes the surrounding fantastic and heroic figures more acceptable (cf. Miller, II-427).

II-290    Hughes, G. I. Review of *GGK*, 2nd ed. *English Studies in Africa*, 11 (1968), 197–98.

> Not seen.

II-291    Hughes, Richard. "Books for Pre-Adults." *New Statesman and Nation*, 14 (4 December 1937), 944, 946.

> Review of thirteen children's books, of which *H* receives most space and praise. Tolkien, so saturated in Nordic mythology that it fertilizes his imagination, does not merely rehash it at second hand but adds to it himself.

II-292    _____. "The Lord of the Rings." *Spectator*, 1 October 1954, pp. 408–09.

> Review of *FR*. Tolkien's width of imagination is great and vivid, but too simplistic.

II-293    Hulbert, J. R. Review of *GGK*, 1st ed. *Modern Philology*, 23 (1925–26), 246–49.

> The editors have been able to contribute very little new material to the elucidation of the poem. Their work has been the patient collection of details, the selection of the best explanations, the decision to accept or reject emendations. They have done this well; but they fail to credit other scholars for emendations (and, though their text is conservative, some of these are unnecessary) or for the ideas or facts for their notes.

II-294    Hurwitz, K. Sue. Review of *Silm. School Library Journal*, 24 (December, 1977), 66.

> *Silm* is relentlessly grim, untouched by any vestige of the appeal of Tolkien's former works. The elves here, unlike the majestic, transcendent beings of *LOTR*, are proud, arrogant, quick to anger, and treacherous. This is not a posthumous monument to the mastery of Tolkien but only a stillborn postscript.

II-295   Hussey, S. S. Review of *Ancrene Riwle*. *Notes and Queries*, 10 (1963), 314.

II-296   _____. Review of *GGK*, 2nd ed. *Notes and Queries*, 15 (1968), 189–90.

> The revision is conscientious and successful, though the reviewer disagrees with some of the interpretations.

II-297   Huttar, Charles. "Hell and the City: Tolkien and the Traditions of Western Literature." In Lobdell, *A Tolkien Compass* (II-388), pp. 117–42.

> Tolkien has skillfully woven together a whole array of motifs traditionally associated with the images of hell (where the hero is initiated or, perhaps, triumphs) and of the city (whether heavenly or hellish), and has done so in a manner that reinforces basic structural patterns in *LOTR*.

II-298   _____. Review of Ellwood (II-175). *Reformed Review*, 25, No. 1 (Autumn, 1971), 31–33.

> Ellwood's essay on the mythic (as opposed to the "objective-analytic") way of seeing the world suffers from "gracelessness and sketchiness" resulting from compression (p. 32), but it is well worth reading, as is her essay on the Christ-figure as it is frequently symbolized by Tolkien in Tom Bombadil, Gandalf, Frodo, and Aragorn.

II-299   Huxley, Francis. "The Endless Worm." *New Statesman and Nation*, 50 (5 November 1955), 587–88.

> Review of *RK*. Discusses Mitchison's favorable review of *FR* (II-435) and Richardson's unfavorable review of *TT* (II-555). Tolkien's mythology is stupendous, but given in a flat, pretentious, Pre-Raphaelite style.

II-300   Immroth, John Phillip. Review of West, *Tolkien Criticism* (II-715). *American Reference Book Annual*, 2nd ed., 1971 (Littleton, Colo.: Libraries Unlimited, 1971), p. 463, item no. 1491.

> This has "brief but delightful annotations," but should be expanded to include fanzine articles. Nevertheless, it should prove most useful to both the fan and the scholar.

II-301   "In Tribute: What J. R. R. Tolkien Means to Some of His Admirers." *Mythlore*, 3, No. 2, Whole No. 10 (1975), 10–14, 35.

> Poems by Poul Anderson, J. R. Christopher, Diana Paxson De Cles, William Rust Norris, and Benjamin Urrutia. James Allan on "Tolkien and Recovery" and Jeanne Wardwell on "Recovery." Statements by Diana Paxson De Cles, Janet B. Fisher, and Jeanne Wardwell.

II-302   *An Introduction to Elvish and to Other Tongues and Proper Names and Writing Systems of the Third Age of the Western Lands of Middle-earth as Set Forth in the Published Writings of Professor John Ronald Reuel Tolkien.* Ed. and compiled by James Allan. Hayes, Middlesex: Bran's Head Books, 1978.

> This compilation is the result of several years of study of Tolkien's invented languages (here whimsically treated as "real" prehistoric tongues) by the Mythopoeic Linguistic Fellowship. Contributors include James Allan, Nina Carson, Björn Fromén, Christopher Gilson, Alexandra Tarasovna Kiceniuk, Laurence J. Krieg, Paula Marmor, Lise Menn, and Bill Welden. There are extensive grammars and dictionaries of Quenya and Sindarin, and linguistic discussions of these and Tolkien's other languages. The only comparable tome is that by Noel (II-469), but this work is the more scholarly of the two. For other linguistic studies, see Blackmun (II-51), Cox (II-124), Foster (II-211), and Stevens (II-640). See review by Colvin (II-115).

II-303 Irwin, W. R. *The Game of the Impossible: A Rhetoric of Fantasy.* Urbana, Chicago, London: The Univ. of Illinois Press, 1976.

> This book examines the common characteristics of fantasies written mostly between 1880–1957, including *LOTR.* Fantasy is an intellectual game; a narrative is a fantasy "if it presents the persuasive establishment and development of an impossibility, an arbitrary construct of the mind with all under the control of logic and rhetoric" (p. 9).

II-304 _____. "There and Back Again: The Romances of Williams, Lewis, and Tolkien." *Sewanee Review,* 69 (1961), 566–78.

> The romances of these three authors illustrate the compulsive movement of the soul into the unfamiliar and back again to a familiar world now informed by vision, by a larger and more precise understanding than was hitherto possible.

II-305 "Is There an Oxford 'School' of Writing?" *The Twentieth Century,* 157 (1955), 559–70.

> A discussion between Rachel Trickett and one of the Inklings, Lord David Cecil. They do not see a "school" properly speaking, but think that the religious, intellectual, and tolerant attitude at Oxford is congenial to developing writers. Cecil recalls that Lewis, Tolkien, Williams, and their friends did not form a school but shared an interest in scholarship, fantasy, and Christianity that informs their writing.

II-306 Isaacs, Neil D. "On the Possibilities of Writing Tolkien Criticism." In Isaacs and Zimbardo, *Tolkien and the Critics* (II-307), pp. 1–11.

> Possible fruitful fields of scholarly investigation are: further study of the variety of moral systems, political philosophies, and sociological patterns in the different characters and peoples; listing of folk motifs; analysis of linguistics, image patterns, time-space configurations of Middle-earth, humor, and structure. Tolkien's symbolism leads to critical dead ends because of its oblique and allusive nature.

II-307    Isaacs, Neil D., and Rose A. Zimbardo, eds. *Tolkien and the Critics*. Notre Dame and London: Univ. of Notre Dame Press, 1968.

> A collection of fifteen essays; eight of them had appeared previously, and of those, three were revised for this anthology. See Auden (II-18), Bradley (II-63), Fuller (II-214), Gasque (II-223), Isaacs (II-307), Keenan (II-321), Kelly (II-326), Lewis (II-376), Moorman (II-447), Raffel (II-537), Reilly (II-549), Sale (II-586), Spacks (II-634), Tinkler (II-653), and Zimbardo (II-752). For reviews, see III-B-16.

II-308    Jefferson, Margo. "Fool's Gold." *Newsweek*, 24 October 1977, pp. 114, 117.

> Review of *Silm*. The myriad readers who are making *Silm* a phenomenal instant best seller may well be disappointed. It is devoid of the vivid physical details and the whimsical humor that made *H* and *LOTR* so delightful; it is a pastiche that draws upon many sources but possesses no imaginative life of its own; it is cliché-ridden and written in a language that is pretentiously archaic and at times nearly incomprehensible.

II-309    Johnson, J. A. "*Farmer Giles of Ham*: What Is It?" *Orcrist*, No. 7 (Summer, 1973), pp. 21–24.

> Tolkien incorporated a variety of medieval genres into *FGH*, three (epic, romance, and fabliau) contributing in a major way, three others (fable, chronicle, and saga) in a minor way, and several others as incidental features or allusions.

II-310    Johnston, George Burke. "The Poetry of J. R. R. Tolkien." In "The Tolkien Papers" (II-663), pp. 63–75.

> Discusses Tolkien's metrical invention, alliterative verse, and major poems like *HB* and *A&I*. Quotes the early "Root of the Boot" which was revised and refined as "The Stone Troll" in *FR* and *ATB* (see I-31 and I-54). See also Kelly (II-326), Kirk (II-342), Marchesani (II-403), Raffel (II-537), and Reynolds (II-554).

Johnstone, Ted. See Becker (II-37).

II-311    Jonas, Gerald. "Triumph of the Good." *New York Times Book Review*, 31 October 1965, pp. 78–79.

> Review of *LOTR*. "The only 'escape' in Tolkien is to a world where the struggle between Good and Evil is waged more fiercely and openly than in our own, where the stakes are at least as great, and where the odds are, if anything, even more perilously balanced."

II-312    Jones, Christine. "The Rise of the Lord of the Rings: A Synopsis of the Ancient Annals." *Tolkien Journal*, 3, No. 3, Whole No. 9 (Summer, 1968), 4–10.

> A synopsis of the history of Middle-earth prior to the year 3001 of the Third Age, based on *LOTR*, *RGEO*, and published comments by Tolkien. Cf. *Silm*. See also Allan (II-9).

II-313   Jordan, Alice M. Review of *FGH*. *Horn Book*, 26 (1950), 287, 289.

> "To enjoy the book, one must have a lively imagination, an ear for wonders, a sense of absurdity and pleasure in oddly compounded words" (p. 289).

II-314   "Journeying through Middle Earth." *Economist*, 260 (7 August 1976), 78.

> Review of Tyler, *Tolkien Companion* (II-671).

II-315   "J. R. R. Tolkien." *Christianity Today*, 28 September 1973, pp. 39–40.

> Obituary. Tolkien will be remembered as a leading scholar, but even more as an outstanding fantasist and perhaps one of this century's most important authors. He wrote from a Christian perspective, but he also provides the non-Christian with new—or perhaps eternally old—images by which to view the universe.

II-316   "J. R. R. Tolkien." *Who's Who*, 1925–73.

II-317   Juhren, Marcella. "The Ecology of Middle Earth." *Mythlore*, 2, No. 1, Whole No. 5 [also *Tolkien Journal*, 4, No. 2, Whole No. 12] (Winter, 1970), 4–6, 9.

> Tolkien's close and thoughtful observation of nature underlies his description of the landmass of Middle-earth. From the hints one can see what the country would be like in primary reality, but there are impingements of the secondary world of fantasy. Tolkien's descriptions are usually of the transition from one natural community to another, and so they sustain the sense of movement throughout the story.

II-318   _____. "Mileage in Middle-Earth." *Mythlore*, 1, No. 4 (October, 1969), 22.

> Tolkien's "league" is estimated at 3.2 miles, and distances mentioned in *LOTR* are figured on this basis.

II-319   Kaske, R. E. "Beowulf." In *Critical Approaches to Six Major English Works: Beowulf through Paradise Lost*. Ed. Robert M. Lumiansky and Herschel Baker (Philadelphia: Univ. of Pennsylvania Press, 1968), pp. 3–40.

> Discusses Tolkien's essay on Beowulf (I-35) on pp. 4–5. "Despite sporadic and, in my opinion, quite unsuccessful attacks, this basic view of the poem seems to have gained for itself something like a core of general acceptance, and most subsequent interpretations will be found to rest on it in one way or another" (p. 5). See also Chambers (II-92), Gang (II-219), Kuhl (II-355), Moore (II-443), Norton (II-475), Patch (II-495), Rogers (II-568), Sisam (II-615), and Van Meurs (II-678).

II-320   Kaufmann, U. Milo. "Aspects of the Paradisiacal in Tolkien's Work." In Lobdell (II-388), pp. 143–52.

> Humanity has a complex desire for the ideal product ("sublimed finitude": the Garden) and the ideal process (infinitude: the Abyss). Niggle's Parish is such a Garden. Tom Bombadil represents all that in the Abyss is capable of renewing Nature.

II-321   Keenan, Hugh T. "The Appeal of *The Lord of the Rings*: A Struggle for Life." In Isaacs and Zimbardo (II-307), pp. 62–80.

> The appeal of *LOTR* to mature readers is rooted in its vivid, objective, and emotional presentation of the eternal conflict between, not good and evil, but life and death. The bittersweet vision of this truth is portrayed through emblematic characters (e.g., the Hobbits emphasize family and fertility; the Nazgul, death) in a world that is sentient and yet dying. Cf. GoodKnight (II-232) and Helms (II-268).

II-322   Keller, Donald G. "The Silmarillion." *Fantasiae*, 5, No. 9, Whole No. 54 (September, 1977), 1, 4.

> Review of *Silm*. This "is at times more a lengthy summary of the vast history than a true chronicle" (p. 1); it has various flaws of inconsistency, hyperbole, and "rather too much deus (and avis and canis) ex machina for modern tastes" (p. 4); and the "Akallabêth" and other final sections are too brief. But the "Ainulindalë" can stand with the great creation myths, the individual tales in the "Quenta Silmarillion" are marvelous, and all is told in "a prose that is the equal and brother of Morris, Dunsany, and Eddison"; the book is "true epic" (p. 4).

II-323   _____. "Tolkien's Music: Preliminary Remarks on Style in *The Silmarillion*." *Fantasiae*, 5, No. 11–12, Whole No. 56–57 (November-December, 1977), 8.

> It is the high style of *Silm* and parts of *LOTR*, and not the low style of *H* and other parts of *LOTR*, which is natural to Tolkien.

II-324   _____. Review of Miesel, *Myth, Symbol, and Religion in The Lord of the Rings* (II-424). *The Eildon Tree*, 1, No. 1 (1974), 27.

II-325   _____. Review of Purtill, *Lord of the Elves and Eldils* (II-536). *The Eildon Tree*, 1, No. 2 (1976), 23–24.

II-326   Kelly, Mary Quella. "The Poetry of Fantasy: Verse in *The Lord of the Rings*." In Isaacs and Zimbardo (II-307), pp. 170–200.

> Analyzes the poetry of the Hobbits, Tom Bombadil, the Elves, the Ents, Men, and some miscellaneous verses. The poetry (a natural mode of expression for Tolkien's characters, and always appropriate to the occasion) is used to expand, emphasize, and rarefy the prose, to reinforce the sense of remoteness and unreality, and to give pleasure by being charming, imaginative, and evocative in its own right. See also Johnston (II-310).

II-327   Kemball-Cook, Jessica. "There and Back Again." *Fantasiae*, 5, No. 6, Whole No. 51 (June, 1977), 1.
Review of Carpenter, *Tolkien: a biography* (II-86).

————. See also under her married name: Yates, Jessica.

II-328   Kendall, Douglas. "A Trip through Middle-earth: A Chronology of *The Hobbit* and *The Lord of the Rings*." In Becker (II-37), pp. 56–73.

II-329   Kennedy, Veronica M. S. Review of Ready, *Tolkien Relation* (II-543). *Tolkien Journal*, 3, No. 4, Whole No. 10 (November, 1969), 15.
Ready brings much sympathy and much experience to his subject, and has provided an affectionate and delightful study.

II-330   Kennedy, X. J. Review of *ATB*. *Poetry*, 105 (December, 1964), 190–93.
Singles out "Cat" for particular praise. "Tolkien's work may well reaffirm that poetry differs from prose in sounding like something special, a truth not always obvious in poetry nowadays."

Kenney, Douglas C. See Beard (II-31).

Kiceniuk, Alexandra Tarasovna. See II-302.

II-331   Kiely, Robert. "Middle Earth." *Commentary*, 43 (February, 1967), 93–96.
Review of *LOTR*. A primary source of the originality and delight of *LOTR* is language. As used by the characters and by the author, language is not merely a neutral instrument of communication or decoration, but a force which reflects personality and creates beauty or ugliness, good or evil. Tolkien invents with a mind infused by the very accents and dreams of another age and so blends history and legend with astonishing freshness and integrity.

II-332   ————. Review of Isaacs and Zimbardo, *Tolkien and the Critics* (II-307). *Thought*, 45 (1970), 134–36.

II-333   Kight, Margie. Review of *H*. *Catholic Library World*, 38 (March, 1967), 474.
"A wonderful, magical tale of dwarves and elves, goblins and trolls, dragons and treasures."

II-334   Kilby, Clyde S. "The Lost Myth." *Arts in Society*, 6, No. 2 (Summer-Fall, 1969), 155–63.
Keynote speech at Secondary Universe Conference I at University of Wisconsin-Milwaukee in 1968. Modern man feels he has tremendous power over everything but himself. Four avenues leading to human wholeness are

hierarchy, the essential mystery of nature, "coinherence" and right imagination. These are exemplified in *LOTR* and help explain its popularity.

II-335    _____. "Meaning in *The Lord of the Rings*." In Hillegas (II-277), pp. 70–80.

Middle-earth is a world of being as well as of doing, with a dependable realization of time, containing its own myths and legends from the immemorial past, catching the essential quality of many outdoor and indoor experiences, taking myth seriously and restoring to the reader a world that is whole. Tolkien also has a sense of humor for balance and a good ear for sound.

II-336    _____. "Mythic and Christian Elements in Tolkien." In Montgomery (II-439), pp. 119–43.

*LOTR* is not an allegory of Christianity, and not a "statement" or a "system": it is mythic, and so approaches truth via the imagination rather than by intellectualizing. Its leading mythic element is the religious, and moreover its meaning is Christian.

II-337    _____. "Tolkien and Coleridge." *Orcrist*, No. 3 [also *Tolkien Journal*, 4, No. 1, Whole No. 11] (Spring-Summer, 1969), pp. 16–19.

Comparison of *LOTR* with "The Rime of the Ancient Mariner."

II-338    _____. *Tolkien and The Silmarillion*. Wheaton, Ill.: Harold Shaw Publishers, 1976.

This short (89 pp.) book gives the author's reminiscences of his visits to Tolkien in 1964 and 1966, of the parts of the manuscripts of *Silm* which he read at that time and his suggestions for what needed to be included in the revision, and numerous comments by Tolkien on his work and its genesis. He sifts the evidence available on the chronology of composition of Tolkien's work, briefly describes the absorption of Christianity into the mythology of Middle-earth, and discusses Tolkien's personal and literary relationships with C. S. Lewis and Charles Williams, seeing some cross-fertilization but not a tightly knit school. For reviews, see III-B-17.

II-339    _____. "Tolkien as Scholar and Artist." *Tolkien Journal*, 3, No. 1 (1967), 9–11.

Love of fantasy and love of language form the double wellspring of Tolkien's hobbit stories. He "borrows" in the medieval fashion, not in the modern sense of "originality." His myth has its closest affinities with the Anglo-Saxon, Norse, Germanic, Finnish, and Celtic mythologies, and Greek has also had its effect; there is little use of Eastern mythology in *LOTR* or *Silm*, except for some touches of Egyptian. His pleasure in such languages as Gothic, Finnish, and Welsh led him to model invented languages on them: "for him a language, properly experienced, is capable of establishing its own full world of mythic meaning" (p. 11).

II-340    _____. "Tolkien, Lewis, & Williams." *Mythcon I Proceedings*
          (4–7 September 1970). Ed. Glen GoodKnight. Los Angeles:
          Mythopoeic Society, 1971, pp. 3–4.

> Discusses personal and literary relationships among the three authors.
> Incorporated into Ch. 5 of his *Tolkien and The Silmarillion* (II-338).

II-341    _____, and Dick Plotz. "Many Meetings with Tolkien."
          *Niekas*, No. 19 (1968), pp. 39–40.

> Edited by Ed Meskys from a transcript of remarks at the December, 1966
> meeting of the Tolkien Society of America. Kilby reported that *Silm* is long
> and unfinished, and features a beautiful creation story. Plotz said Tolkien
> feels Mordor corresponds more or less to the Mediterranean volcanic basin
> and Mount Doom to Stromboli.

          _____. See also Forbes (II-206), GoodKnight (II-231), and
          Sievert (II-613).

II-342    Kirk, Elizabeth D. " 'I Would Rather Have Written in Elvish':
          Language, Fiction and *The Lord of the Rings*." *Novel: A
          Forum on Fiction* (Brown University), 5 (1971), 5–18.

> What Tolkien has done in *LOTR* is to create a "model" (in the scientific
> sense of the term) for the relationship of language to action, to values and
> to civilization. He divorces the physical and stylistic qualities which in any
> real language are interdependent, and represents the stylistic ones by
> varieties of English, while introducing proper names and quotations of
> translatable size to give a sense of the language as a physical medium for
> thought. Thus in practice the counterpoint of "language" is primarily a
> counterpoint of stylistic levels or of genres. This strategy attempts to build
> cumulatively an awareness of human perceptions as rich and as sharp as
> that which can be achieved by the subtle development of a single style.
> Discusses his success and failure, the function of the hobbit speech, and the
> use of verse.

II-343    Knight, Richard V. "An Open Letter to Ballantine Books."
          *Tolkien Journal*, 3, No. 4, Whole No. 10 (November, 1969),
          17–18.

> Review of Carter, *Tolkien: A Look Behind The Lord of the Rings* (II-89).
> The summaries of *H* and *LOTR* contain many inexcusable errors.

II-344    Kobil, Daniel T. "The Elusive Appeal of the Fantastic."
          *Mythlore*, 4, No. 4, Whole No. 16 (June, 1977), 17–19.

> Robert Ornstein theorized that the left hemisphere of the brain governs
> rational processes while the right side controls intuition, and that these
> different aspects of consciousness should be in balance. Whether or not this
> theory is correct in all details, the appeal of fantasy such as Tolkien's or the
> idea of "monsters" such as that of Loch Ness is to our intuitive needs and
> desires.

II-345   Kocher, Paul H. "Jung in Middle Earth." *Mythlore*, 6, No. 4,
         Whole No. 22 (Fall, 1979), 25.

> Review of O'Neill (II-483). This pleasingly written book admits that
> Tolkien did not study Jung's theories carefully, but points out coincidences
> between Jungian theory and Tolkien's fiction.

II-346   _____. *Master of Middle-earth: The Fiction of J. R. R.
         Tolkien*. Boston: Houghton Mifflin, 1972. British edition as
         *Master of Middle-earth: The Achievement of J. R. R. Tolkien*
         (London: Thames and Hudson, 1972).

> This book provides commentary on all of Tolkien's fiction published up to
> 1972: primarily on *H* and *LOTR*, but including *LBN, A&I, FGH, HB,
> SWM*, "Imram," and *ATB*. Discusses the author's theory and practice of
> fantasy and the relation between the two (e.g., the interpretation of *LBN* as
> a portrait of the artist), the "inherent morality" of nondidactic story (e.g.,
> Tolkien's anticipation of later fashions such as concern with ecology), and
> the special character of Tolkien's fictive worlds (e.g., Kocher's broad
> description of Tolkien's basic technique of combining the familiar with the
> unfamiliar to make the fantasy plausible). For reviews, see III-B-18.

II-347   _____. *A Reader's Guide to The Silmarillion*. Boston:
         Houghton Mifflin, 1980.

> The first chapter, "A Mythology for England," and a three-page
> "Overview" at the end, provide general comments on *Silm*. The main body
> of the book is a close reading of *Silm*, almost entirely devoted to
> summarizing the stories, but with reference to Norse and Finnish analogues
> and the accommodation of the mythology to Christianity. See review by
> Marmor, (II-406).

II-348   _____. "The Tale of the Noldor." *Mythlore*, 4, No. 3, Whole
         No. 15 (March, 1977), 3–4, 6–7.

> A history of the wanderings of this tribe of Elves compiled from references
> in Tolkien's work prior to the publication of *Silm*. See also Allan (II-9).

II-349   Koelle, Barbara S. "Oz and Middle Earth." *The Baum Bugle*,
         15, No. 1, Whole No. 40 (Spring, 1971), 17–19.

> Reacting against Beagle's comment (in II-30) that Oz is the Great Good
> Place while Middle-earth is a world like our own, this comparison argues
> that there are many parallels between the two fictive worlds, the differences
> being in degree rather than in kind.

II-350   Kolodney, David. "Peace in Middle Earth." *Ramparts*, 9, No. 4
         (October, 1970), 35–38.

> Escape is only detrimental to social awareness if one taking pleasure in a
> charming illusion acts as if the world were at peace as well. But "When the
> enormity of evil enervates, a judicious dose of escape can revive the
> revolutionary spirit" (p. 32). Cf. Hinkle (II-279) and O'Connor (II-478).

Color photographs by Don Whittekap of four paintings by Bill Martin accompany the article, and there is a detail from one of these on the inside front cover.

II-351    Korn, Eric. "Doing things by elves." *Times Literary Supplement*, 30 September 1977, p. 1097.

Review of *Silm*. What is admirable or enjoyable in *LOTR* is absent from *Silm*, while what is bad is magnified.

II-352    Kreeft, Peter. "The Wonder of *The Silmarillion*." In Hillegas (II-277), pp. 161–78; notes on pp. 184–85.

*Silm* is a great book because it elicits the precious human experience of Wonder (including admiration, appreciation, respect, or even awe). See Patterson (II-498).

Krieg, Laurence J. See II-302 and Krieg (II-353).

II-353    Krieg, Martha and Laurence. "The Father Christmas Letters." *Mythlore*, 4, No. 2, Whole No. 14 (December, 1976), 24–25.

Review of *FCL*.

II-354    Kuhl, Rand. "Arrows From a Twisted Bow: Misunderstanding Tolkien." *Mythlore*, 1, No. 4 (October, 1969), 45–49.

Review of Ready, *Tolkien Relation* (II-543). There are numerous errors of fact and interpretation and the writing is slovenly.

II-355    _____. "Very Few Good Dragons." *Mythlore*, 1, No. 3 (July, 1969), 34–37.

Review article discussing Tolkien's essay on *Beowulf* (I-35). This uses allegory, satire, parody, and a certain romantic longing in the style, and makes reading scholarship more enjoyable. See also Kaske (II-319).

II-356    Lask, Thomas. Review of *FGH*. *New York Times Book Review*, Fall Children's Issue, 7 November 1965, p. 60.

This fetching and amusing tale ages well.

II-357    Lauritsen, Frederick Michael. Review of Ready, *Tolkien Relation* (II-543). *Library Journal*, 93 (1 May 1968), 1889.

Tolkien dislikes revelations of his private life and looks askance at criticisms of his work, so Ready instead probes the climate in which Tolkien has lived and worked. Most readers will find the book stimulating.

II-358    _____. Review of *SWM*. *Library Journal*, 92 (15 November 1967), 4175.

Unlike *FGH*, which was written purely for entertainment, *SWM* develops Tolkien's ideas concerning the land and peoples of Faerie. Both plot and characters are lacking in depth because they are used merely as media to express an idea.

II-359   Lawrence, Ralph. Review of *T&L*. *English: Magazine of the English Association, London*, 15, No. 87 (Autumn, 1964), 117.

Professor Tolkien discourses inimitably on the fairy-story, and illustrates and reinforces his argument with one of his own stories.

II-360   Léaud, Francis. "L'Épopée Religieuse de J. R. R. Tolkien." *Études Anglaises*, 20 (1967), 265–81.

In French. Tolkien's work is little known in France at this time. It is not enjoyed by positivist readers, but appeals to people of a broadly religious temperament (whether or not they have a formal creed). To provide too precise an interpretation would betray the text, but in general the mythic fantasy of *H* and *LOTR* speak, without ever naming them, of the mysteries of Providence and of grace. Tolkien's mastery of language also helps explain his appeal. The living world of Middle-earth compares favorably with the dramatized Europe of *War and Peace*.

II-361   Lee, Billy C. "The War Over Middle Earth." *Paperback Quarterly: A Journal for Paperback Collectors*, 1, No. 4 (Winter, 1978), 37–42.

This outlines the copyright controversy over paperback publication of *LOTR*, and includes much information from Donald Wollheim giving Ace Books' side in the matter. See also II-2.

II-362   Lee, Margaret L. Review of *A Middle English Vocabulary* (I-6). *The Year's Work in English Studies*, 2 (1920–21), 42–43.

Tolkien devotes much space and care to basics rather than to suggested etymologies of rare and obscure words. His vocabulary has exhaustive textual references and a value independent of the extracts to which it is appended.

II-363   Le Guin, Ursula K. *From Elfland to Poughkeepsie*. Portland: Pendragon, 1973. Reprinted in her *The Language of the Night: Essays on Fantasy and Science Fiction*. Ed. and with introductions by Susan Wood (New York: G. P. Putnam's Sons, 1979), pp. 83–96.

Text of a lecture given at the 2nd annual Science Fiction Writers' Workshop, University of Washington, 1972. ". . . when fantasy is the real thing, nothing, after all, is realer" (p. 28 of pamphlet; p. 95 of anthology), because it delves into the unconscious and has the vitality of myths. But many modern fantasies are fakes, trying, rather than live up to their responsibilities, to let the reader think he is "back at home in Poughkeepsie." This is immediately obvious in the style of a work. Tolkien is cited as one example of a master stylist; his language is simple, clear, evocative, timeless, yet his characters speak with the true accent of Elfland.

II-364    _____. "The Staring Eye." *Vector*, Nos. 67/68 (Spring, 1974), pp. 5–7. Reprinted in her *The Language of the Night* (II-363), pp. 171–74.

> Though Tolkien has a few flaws and oddities, he is an outstanding fantasist, and Le Guin is glad she did not read *LOTR*, marvelous as it is for children, until she was an adult and had already found her own voice as a writer. Notes how Tolkien upsets overly-academic critics and those who seek answers to the Problem of Evil.

II-365    _____. Review of C. S. Lewis, *The Dark Tower and Other Stories*, ed. Walter Hooper (New York and London: Harcourt Brace Jovanovich, 1977). *New Republic*, 16 April 1977, pp. 29–30.

> Lewis was a gentle, brilliant, lovable, and devout man, but he had hatred in him, and he projects evil onto women and other characters. His fiction has some brilliant effects, but he depicted evil only in terms of the Christian fighting the Enemy. This is in contrast to Tolkien who, while he was no less a Christian, depicts, not evil men, but symbols of the evil *in* men (Sauron, the Orcs), or else complementary figures (as Saruman is Gandalf's dark self, and Gollum is Frodo's shadow).

II-366    Lense, Edward. "Sauron is Watching *You*: The Role of the Great Eye in *The Lord of the Rings*." *Mythlore*, 4, No. 1, Whole No. 13 (September, 1976), 3–6.

> Balor of the Evil Eye, from Celtic myth, inspired Sauron's Eye and other evil eyes in *LOTR*. Images of evil watchfulness, whether literal or metaphoric, also appear throughout *LOTR*.

II-367    Lentricchia, Frank, Jr. "Some Coordinates of Modern Literature." *Poetry*, 108 (April, 1966), 65–67.

> Reviews several books, including *T&L*. "Tolkien's discussion of the realm of *Faerie* as an aesthetic cosmos—autonomous, but not quite autotelic—will recall the important trend in modern philosophical criticism emanating from Ernst Cassirer" (p. 67). *T&L* is important both for its work on the fairy tale and on more general literary theory.

II-368    Lerner, Fred. "On Hobbit Lore and Tolkien Criticism." *Tolkien Journal*, 3, No. 4, Whole No. 10 (November, 1969), 5.

> Keynote address at the Belknap Tolkien Conference in October, 1968. Tolkien appeals to all sorts of readers, including some who refuse to accept wholeheartedly the realization that his work was fiction (cf. Tyler, II-670 and II-671), and some delighted by parallels between *LOTR* and early Nordic literature. See also Beatie (II-34 and II-35), Helms (II-266), Thomson (II-651), Ward (II-695), and West (II-714).

Levine, David. See Hodgart (II-282) and Smith (II-631).

II-369   Levitin, Alexis. "The Genre of *The Lord of the Rings*." *Orcrist*, No. 3 [also *Tolkien Journal*, 4, No. 1, Whole No. 11] (Spring-Summer, 1969), 4–8, 23.

> *LOTR* "is basically a quest-story presented in an epic and fairy-tale medium" (p. 23), but this chapter from his M.A. thesis (see Levitin, II-371) also examines myth, romance, and parable in an attempt to show the relationship of *LOTR* "to various conventional literary genres as well as to point out the chief merits and uses of these genres" (p. 23).

II-370   _____. "The Hero in J. R. R. Tolkien's *The Lord of the Rings*." In "The Tolkien Papers" (II-663), pp. 25–37.

> Tolkien takes the two main heroic types as described by W. H. Auden (the epic hero who is noble and extraordinary, and the fairy tale hero who is humble and unprepossessing), and, in his presentation of the latter, adds a particularly Christian emphasis to satisfy his own desire to create a work strong in Christian overtones. Cf. Blissett (II-53), Foster (II-209), Moorman (II-445), Reckford (II-545).

II-371   _____. "The Lord of the Rings." M.A. thesis, Columbia University, 1964.

> Chapters on background, sources, theme of power (see Levitin, II-373), and "inherent morality" of *LOTR*.

II-372   _____. "The Lure of the Ring." *Mythcon I Proceedings* (4–7 September 1970). Ed. Glen GoodKnight. Los Angeles: Mythopoeic Society, 1971, pp. 20–21.

> Quotes letters from Betsy Chapman, Charles N. Elliott, Nancy Giudice, Mary M. Pangborn, Stephen Pangborn, and Sylvia Wendell in response to his query to the Tolkien Society of America about why *LOTR* should have such appeal. Two reasons that are given repeatedly are the satisfaction that the essential struggle between good and evil is highlighted (even though people like Hodgart, II-282, dislike the book for the same reason) and that aspects of Middle-earth are applicable to our primary reality.

II-373   _____. "Power in *The Lord of the Rings*." *Orcrist*, No. 4 [also *Tolkien Journal*, 4, No. 3, Whole No. 13] (1969–70), 11–14.

> A chapter from his M.A. thesis; see Levitin (II-371). "Tolkien demonstrates that Power is the true weapon only of evil, and that even in the hands of Good it eventually must result in corruption and suffering." The Ring is a symbol of Power, and attacks its victims through pride. See also Davie (II-140 and II-141), Halle (II-253), Hardy (II-256), Levitin (II-371), Monsman (II-437), Morrison (II-451), Osburne (II-485), Perkins and Hill (II-514), Pettit (II-516), Reinken (II-550), Ryan (II-580), Schroth (II-601), Spacks (II-633 and II-634), and West (II-711).

II-374   _____. "The Role of Gollum in J. R. R. Tolkien's *The Lord of the Rings*." *Tolkien Journal*, 2, No. 4 (1966), 2–6.

> A chapter from his M.A. thesis (II-371), on Gollum's character.

II-375 _____. "A Short—and Incomplete—Bibliography of Articles of Interest to Tolkien Fans." *Tolkien Journal*, 1, No. 2 (1965), 1.

> References to Blisset (II-53), Halle (II-252 and II-253), Irwin (II-304), Lewis (II-376 and II-377), Parker (II-492), Reilly (II-549), Spacks (II-633), Straight (II-653), and Wilson (II-729).

II-376 Lewis, C. S. "The Dethronement of Power." *Time and Tide*, 36 (22 October 1955), 1373–74. Reprinted in Isaacs and Zimbardo (II-307), pp. 12–16.

> Review of *TT* and *RK*. Dismisses the charge that the characters are simplistically good or evil. Discusses the architectonics of *LOTR* and the "moral" of heroic effort and impermanent victory.

II-377 _____. "The Gods Return to Earth." *Time and Tide*, 35 (14 August 1954), 1082–83.

> Review of *FR*. Mention of "the unforgettable Ents" shows that he already knew the later parts of the story. "Almost the central theme of the book is the contrast between the Hobbits (or 'The Shire') and the appalling destiny to which some of them are called . . ." (p. 1082). "As for escapism, what we chiefly escape is the illusions of our ordinary life. We certainly do not escape anguish" (p. 1083). To those who might not expect a great romance to be written in an age of mostly realistic literature, this work is "good beyond hope."

II-378 _____. *Selected Literary Essays.* Ed. Walter Hooper. Cambridge Univ. Press, 1969.

> The editor refers to Tolkien's unfinished and unpublished poem on "The Fall of Arthur" (p. 15, n. 2) and to the source of Lewis's fragment, "We were talking of dragons, Tolkien and I" (p. 18, n. 1).

II-379 _____. *They Stand Together: The Letters of C. S. Lewis to Arthur Greeves (1914–1963).* Ed. Walter Hooper. London and New York: Macmillan, 1979.

> Lewis frequently mentions Tolkien and his work; the references can be found in the index to this volume. See also Carpenter (II-85), Green and Hooper (II-243), and Lewis (II-381).

_____. See also Etkin (II-181), Lewis (II-381), and II-533.

II-380 Lewis, Naomi. Review of *T&L*. *New Statesman*, 67 (15 May 1964), 778.

> One sentence in a section on children's books: "A striking 60-page essay for adults on the nature of fairy-tales . . ."

II-381 Lewis, W. H., ed. *Letters of C. S. Lewis.* London: Geoffrey Bles, 1966. New York: Harcourt, Brace and World, 1966.

> This volume is not indexed. Tolkien is mentioned in letters dated 18 June

1931, 22 November 1931, 5 November 1939, 11 November 1939, 3
December 1939, 21 December 1941, 12 January 1950, 2 October 1952, 22
September 1956, 10 December 1956, 2 September 1957, and 15 May 1959.
See also Lewis (II-379).

Lindsell, Harold. See II-491.

II-382    Lloyd, Charles E. "Tolkien and the Ordinary World." *Sewanee
Review*, 86 (Winter, 1978), xi–xiv.

Reviews of Carpenter (II-86) and of *Silm*. Carpenter's biography is
thoroughly professional in scholarship and style, and, while free from
puffery, shows not only Tolkien's ordinariness and love of the ordinary, but
also his greatness as a scholar and a writer. *Silm* shows that Tolkien the
writer had been inside myth as Tolkien the philologist had been inside
language.

II-383    Lloyd, Paul M. "The Role of Warfare and Strategy in *The Lord
of the Rings*." *Mythlore*, 3, No. 3, Whole No. 11 (1976), 3–7.

Essay on the weapons, tactics, and strategy of battle in *LOTR*, with
reference to military texts of earlier periods. Sauron fails as a strategist, yet
makes mistakes that an evil being would believably make. See also Scott
(II-604).

II-384    Lobdell, Jared. "England and Always." *To the Point*, 23
December 1972, p. 65.

Review of Kocher, *Master of Middle-earth* (II-346). This is not the
definitive book on Tolkien, but it is the best that has yet been produced.
Kocher succeeds where Ready (II-543) and Carter (II-89) fail because he
has realized that Tolkien's world is the intersection of the timeless moment
and a spiritual as well as a physical state. See also his other review (II-390).

II-385    _____. "Good and Evil for Men and Hobbits." *National
Review*, 17 June 1969, p. 605.

Review of Isaacs and Zimbardo, *Tolkien and the Critics* (II-307). This is
the best volume on Tolkien to this date (cf. his opinion of Kocher in II-
384), and the essays by Sale (II-586) and Tinkler (II-653) are especially
noteworthy. However, most of this book is the data for criticism or literary
history rather than the work of practicing critics. There appear to be two
sharply divided schools of Tolkien criticism, one "pro-hobbit and anti-
Tolkien," the other not noticing sufficiently that the main concern of the
book is not the hobbits (who are "an accidental goodness"). It is the
languages, the forests, the past, the conflict of good and evil in a pre-
Christian world, that are the heart of *LOTR*.

II-386    _____. "J. R. R. Tolkien: Words That Sound Like Castles."
*Rally* (Milwaukee), 1, No. 3 (August, 1966), 24–26.

This review of *LOTR* is not the same as his review in *NR* a year later (see
II-389 below). In *LOTR* we can almost walk in the forest of the past, and
see the beauty of this and of the individuality of language.

II-387    _____. "A Medieval Proverb in *The Lord of the Rings.*"
*American Notes and Queries Supplement No. 1.* Ed. John L.
Cutler and Lawrence S. Thompson. Troy, N.Y.: Whitston,
1978, pp. 330–31.

> Although this article was not published until 1978, it had been accepted in
> 1968 and revised in 1972. This deals with the Middle English proverb,
> "Third time pays for all," and its variants, and quotes from a letter on the
> subject written by Tolkien to the author. The appearances of this proverb
> in *LOTR* attest to Tolkien's medievalism, but have other importance such
> as indicating that Gollum did indeed have a real moral choice.

II-388    _____, ed. *A Tolkien Compass.* La Salle, Ill.: Open Court
Publishing, 1975. New York: Ballantine, 1980.

> The editor discusses the various essays in his "Introduction" (pp. 1–7). The
> essays are by Christensen (II-97), Matthews (II-411), Scheps (II-597),
> Perkins and Hill (II-514), Rogers (II-564), West (II-712), Miller (II-429),
> Plank (II-522), Huttar (II-297), and Kaufmann (II-320). The *pièce de
> résistance* of this anthology is Tolkien's guide for translators of his work
> (see I-72). For reviews, see III-B-19.

II-389    _____. "Words That Sound Like Castles." *National Review*, 5
September 1967, pp. 972, 974.

> Review article on the 2nd ed. of *LOTR*, defending the book against the "at
> once perceptive and wrong-headed review" of Hodgart (II-282). It is C. S.
> Lewis who offers the best critical approach to Tolkien (see II-376 and II-
> 377). *LOTR* is a story that mediates Tolkien's "imaginative life of many
> years to those who now find that imaginative life in themselves" (p. 974),
> and this impact on the reader's consciousness helps explain its great literary
> value.

II-390    _____. Review of Kocher, *Master of Middle-Earth* (II-346).
*National Review*, 22 December 1972, p. 1417.

> Brief note. This is the best single volume published to this date on Tolkien's
> theory and practice of fantasy, partly because there is little competition for
> the honor, but chiefly because it examines all the available fiction and says
> some very good things indeed (e.g., on elven time). More work remains to
> be done, but Kocher has started well. See also Lobdell (II-384).

II-391    _____. Review of *SWM. National Review*, 7 May 1968, p. 461.

> This is that rare thing, a *new* story, and there are great moments in it. But it
> is a little *too* charming to bear rereading as well as *LBN* or *FGH*.

II-392    Lochhead, Marion. *The Renaissance of Wonder in Children's
Literature.* Edinburgh: Canongate, 1977.

> This book deals with the rebirth, after a long rationalistic period, of fantasy
> for children beginning with the work of George MacDonald. The tradition
> he founded a century ago is still alive and well, and in the best such stories
> there is holiness in the magic. There are numerous references to Tolkien,

and Chs. 12-14 (pp. 101–25) focus on his literary theory and his work, especially the Nordic, Celtic, and Christian components. Tom Bombadil is seen as a character who might have been influenced by MacDonald's work. See also Reis (II-551).

Lodwick, Ellen. See Etkin (II-181).

II-393 "The Lord of the Legends." *London Times Magazine*, 2 January 1972, pp. 24–25, 27–28.

In this tribute to Tolkien on the eve of his 80th birthday, Bill Cater (pp. 24–27) discusses the influence of Tolkien's work, Rayner Unwin (pp. 27–28) recounts his involvement with the publication of *H* and *LOTR*, and Joy Hill (p. 28) describes some of the letters and gifts sent to Tolkien by admirers.

II-394 Lucas, Mary R. Review of *H*. *Library Journal*, 63 (1 May 1938), 385.

*H* would be better read in small doses, since the adventures are too numerous for really enjoyable reading. "It will have a limited appeal unless properly introduced and even then will be best liked by those children whose imagination is alert."

II-395 Lynch, James. "The Literary Banquet and the Eucharistic Feast: Tradition in Tolkien." *Mythlore*, 5, No. 2, Whole No. 18 (Autumn, 1978), 13–14.

This paper concentrates on *FR*, but notes that the feasting ritual is used throughout *LOTR* to signify closeness and communion among humans and between humans and God.

II-396 MacDonald, Angus, and Betty Hill. Review of *Essays Presented to J. R. R. Tolkien* (II-143). *The Year's Work in English Studies*, 43 (1962), 65–67.

Describes several of the essays in this *Festschrift* and recommends particularly "The Anthropological Approach" by C. S. Lewis.

II-397 MacQueen, John. Review of *GGK*, 2nd ed. *Review of English Studies*, 20 (1969), 70–71.

Davis's new readings, emendations and repunctuation are, for the most part, convincing. His expanded introduction, notes, appendixes, and glossary are careful and excellent. The major failing is a lack of emphasis on the literary dimension of the poem in an edition which contains so much material of actual and potential literary importance.

II-398 Mahon, Robert Lee. "Elegiac Elements in *The Lord of the Rings*." *CEA Critic: An Official Journal of the College English Association*, 40, No. ii (1978), 33–36.

Elegiac perspectives in *LOTR* have a historic, social, and human (or individual) impact.

II-399   Malcolm, John. "Tolk Talk." *Punch*, 251 (16 November 1966), 755.

> Review of *LOTR*. The revisions in this new edition are aimed at adult addicts, but still this remains a children's book. There are rewards to be had from reading it, however, mostly in the extraordinary power of mythmaking. "John Malcolm" is reportedly a pseudonym for Peter Dickinson.

II-400   Mandel, Mark. "The Ring-Inscription." *Tolkien Journal*, 1, No. 2 (1965), 2.

> Analysis of elements of the grammar and vocabulary of the Black Speech.

II-401   Manguel, Alberto, and Gianni Guadalupi. *The Dictionary of Imaginary Places*. New York: Macmillan, 1980.

> A traveller's guidebook to fictional locales, including many in *H*, *LOTR*, and *Silm*, with maps. See also Day (II-144), Foster (II-207 and II-208), Post (II-526), and Tyler (II-670 and II-671).

II-402   Manlove, C. N. "J. R. R. Tolkien (1892–1973) and *The Lord of the Rings*." Ch. 5 in his *Modern Fantasy: Five Studies*. Cambridge Univ. Press, 1975, pp. 152–206 (notes on pp. 284–89).

> The other authors concentrated on are Charles Kingsley, George MacDonald, C. S. Lewis, and Mervyn Peake. He believes that all modern fantasy is of necessity flawed because of the split between science and imagination, and considers Tolkien the worst of the five authors. *LOTR* is flawed by poor style, good fortune biased toward the heroes, an absolutely happy ending when it is trying to be elegiac, and the inability to make good as fascinating as evil. For reviews, see III-B-20.

II-403   Marchesani, Diane. "Tolkien's Lore: The Songs of Middle-earth." *Mythlore*, 7, No. 1, Whole No. 23 (March, 1980), 3–5.

> There are over sixty poems and songs in *LOTR* and these serve as the folklore of Middle-earth. See also Johnston (II-310).

II-404   Marmor, Paula K. "Fair and Square With No Contradictions." *Fantasiae*, 7, No. 3, Whole No. 72 (March, 1979), 1, 8.

> Review of Andrews, *Tolkien Quiz Book* (II-11).

II-405   ———. "Wielders of the Three and Other Trees." *Mythlore*, 2, No. 4, Whole No. 8 (Winter, 1972), 5–8. Reprinted in II-302, pp. 291–99.

> A half-whimsical essay showing that the bearers of the three elven rings are archetypal figures of a Moon-Water Goddess (Galadriel), a Sky-Air-Thunder God (Gil-galad, Elrond), and a Sun-Fire God (Cirdan, Gandalf).

II-406    _____. Review of Kocher, *A Reader's Guide to The
          Silmarillion* (II-347). *Fantasiae*, 8, No. 6, Whole No. 87 (June,
          1980), 1, 5.
          > This book is mostly a summary of *Silm* with only a little critical
          > commentary, and this is a disappointment.

II-407    _____. Review of Miesel, *Myth, Symbol and Religion in The
          Lord of the Rings* (II-424). *Fantasiae*, 2, No. 1 (January, 1974),
          10–11.

          _____. See also II-302.

          Marquandt, Dorothy A. See Ward (II-696).

          Martin, Bill. See Kolodney (II-350).

II-408    Masson, Keith. "Tom Bombadil: A Critical Essay." *Mythlore*,
          2, No. 3, Whole No. 7 (Winter, 1971), 7–8.
          > The author ponders the Christian and mythic resonances of Tom's words
          > and actions, but concludes that the character remains a mystery.

II-409    Mathews, Richard. *Lightning From a Clear Sky: Tolkien, the
          Trilogy, and The Silmarillion.* San Bernardino: Borgo, 1978.
          > This monograph has brief discussions of Tolkien's fiction from *H* (1937) to
          > *Silm* (1977). See review by Patterson (II-501).

II-410    Mathewson, Joseph. "The Hobbit Habit." *Esquire*, September
          1966, pp. 130–31, 221–22.
          > He speculates that reading Tolkien was a cliquish affair at the outset; then
          > the books became the province of a clique so widely spread as to form a
          > cult. See also Bisenieks (II-47).

II-411    Matthews, Dorothy. "The Psychological Journey of Bilbo
          Baggins." In Lobdell (II-388), 29–42.
          > Bilbo's quest in *H* may be considered as a metaphor for the individuation
          > process. His quest is a search for maturity and psychic wholeness (his
          > Tookish aggressiveness and Bagginsish passivity must be wholesomely
          > balanced), and his adventures are symbolically detailed rites of maturation
          > in which he proves his self-reliance and moral and physical courage. Since
          > Bilbo represents the ordinary individual, it is natural that he should not be
          > the archetypal Hero who slays dragons and wins battles.

          Matthews, Gary. See Etkin (II-181).

II-412    McClusky, Joan. "J. R. R. Tolkien: A Short Biography." In
          Becker (II-37), pp. 9–42.
          > See also Carpenter (II-86) and Del Mastro (II-149).

II-413 McKenzie, Sister Elizabeth. " 'Above All Shadows Rides The Sun.' " *Mythlore*, 2, No. 1, Whole No. 5 [also *Tolkien Journal*, 4, No. 2, Whole No. 12] (Winter, 1970), 18.

> The central theme of *LOTR* "is that the strength of those who love, because they love, is greater than the strength of those who hate." This can be seen in: the unconcern of the Orcs for their fellows, contrasted with the community of the Ents; the unnecessary cruelty of the Orcs to Frodo, while he is magnanimous to Saruman; the desolation of Mordor, contrasted with the spendor of Lothlórien; and in the plot of the story as a whole, where the united efforts of the community are needed to overthrow Sauron.

II-414 McMenomy, Bruce. "Misconstruction." *Mythlore*, 4, No. 3, Whole No. 15 (March, 1977), 16–17.

> Review of Grotta-Kurska, *J. R. R. Tolkien: Architect of Middle Earth* (II-250).

II-415 McTurk, R. W., and D. J. Williams. Review of *GGKPO* (I-73). *The Year's Work in English Studies*, 56 (1975), 86, 94.

> Christopher Tolkien includes much introductory and subsidiary material from his father's papers that was not previously published. The translations in general read smoothly rather than colloquially and contain much useful and provocative material.

McWilliams, Wilson C. See Hentoff (II-274).

II-416 Meigs, Cornelia, et al., eds. *A Critical History of Children's Literature*. New York: Macmillan, 1953.

> *H* is discussed on pp. 467–68. Tolkien's rich store of knowledge and traditional lore comes out in this warm, noble, imaginative book.

II-417 Melmed, Susan Barbara. *John Ronald Reuel Tolkien: a bibliography*. Johannesburg: Univ. of the Witwatersrand, Department of Bibliography, Librarianship and Typography, 1972.

> This bibliography is not annotated. See also Christensen (II-98), Christopher (II-103), Hammond (II-254), and West (II-715).

Menen, Aubrey. See II-534.

Menn, Lise. See II-302.

II-418 Menner, Robert J. Review of *GGK*, 1st. ed. *Modern Language Notes*, 41 (1926), 397–400.

> The editors have admirably succeeded in their primary object of expounding the meaning of this difficult text. He questions some readings, and thinks it would have been better to have provided a more extensive bibliography.

II-419   Merla, Patrick. " 'What is REAL?' Asked the Rabbit One Day."
         *Saturday Review of the Arts*, 55 (November, 1972), 43–50.

> *LOTR* initiated a publishing trend toward adult fantasy, but it is a paradox
> that children's literature is currently turning more and more to grim
> "realism" while adults are seeking fantasy books. *LOTR*, though it has
> some successes (e.g., it shows real magic in the naming of names), is a
> failure in structure (cf. Helms, II-269 and West, II-711), extremely
> materialistic in its philosophy, leaves nothing at all to the imagination, and
> overlooks the point that Good and Evil must confront each other if they
> are to do battle. Also discusses other fantasies and realistic children's
> books, and provides a bibliography of such works.

II-420   Mesibov, Robert. "Tolkien and Spiders." *Orcrist*, No. 4 [also
         *Tolkien Journal*, 4, No. 3, Whole No. 13] (1969–70), 3–5.

> Tolkien presents spiders unfavorably, and the spider metaphors he uses also
> have unpleasant associations. But spiders do not deserve the bad press they
> receive from Tolkien and other authors.

II-421   Meskys, Edmund R. "Science Fiction Fans Salute Tolkien."
         *Tolkien Journal*, 3, No. 1 (1967), 12–13.

> Birthday greetings to Tolkien and a brief history of interest in Tolkien's
> work on the part of science fiction fandom.

II-422   Meyers, William. "Fantasy Fandom: Tolkien and
         Temperaments." *Fantastic*, August 1969, pp. 141–45.

> In this autobiographical article, written in 1962, a fantasy fan discusses the
> impact Tolkien's books had on him. "He very beautifully tied up in one
> intricate knot all the thousands of strands of imaginative lore I'd delighted
> in as a child . . . not by titillating any nostalgic, sentimentalized half-
> memories, but by yanking out by the roots what was solid and substantial
> and clothing it in . . . mature literary insight" (p. 144). He notes the
> different reactions of alien temperaments.

II-423   Miesel, Sandra. "A Cockeyed Look Behind *Lord of the Rings*."
         *Tolkien Journal*, 3, No. 4, Whole No. 10 (November, 1969), 17.

> Review of Carter, *Tolkien: A Look Behind the Lord of the Rings* (II-89).
> His character sketch of Tolkien is frankly derivative and fails to bring its
> subject to life. His chapters on ancient, medieval, and modern fantasy are
> loaded with irrelevant detail and questionable interpretations,
> disappointingly incomplete as to sources, strained in some parallels,
> ignorant of universal motifs, and outrageously padded with long
> descriptions and plot synopses.

II-424   _____. *Myth, Symbol and Religion in The Lord of the Rings*.
         Baltimore: T-K Graphics, 1973.

> This monograph identifies some elements from various histories (chiefly
> medieval Britain and Byzantium), mythologies (chiefly Norse and Celtic),
> and literatures which have been blended into *LOTR*. Incorporates material
> from her articles in *RQ*, II-425 and II-426. For reviews, see III-B-21.

II-425   _____. "Some Motifs and Sources for *Lord of the Rings*."
         *Riverside Quarterly*, 3, No. 2 (March, 1968), 125–28.

> Reference to the history of Rome and Byzantium and to Norse and Celtic
> myth.

II-426   _____. "Some Religious Aspects of *Lord of the Rings*."
         *Riverside Quarterly*, 3, No. 3 (August, 1968), 209–13.

> Tolkien's art is neither didactic nor allegorical, and the cultural framework
> of *LOTR* is religionless, but the attitudes expressed within it are traditional
> Christian ones. Moral issues cluster about the major antitheses of good and
> evil, true and false Kingship, victory and defeat.

II-427   Miller, David M. "Hobbits: Common Lens for Heroic
         Experience." *Orcrist*, No. 3 [also *Tolkien Journal*, 4, No. 1,
         Whole No. 11] (Spring-Summer, 1969), 11–15.

> The twentieth-century reader finds both the extraordinary heroes and the
> extraordinarily ordinary hobbits unbelievable, but the disbelief in the
> heroes which we share with the hobbits forces us to identify with the more
> familiar hobbits, and we come to accept what they accept.

II-428   _____. "The Moral Universe of J. R. R. Tolkien." In "The
         Tolkien Papers" (II-663), pp. 51–62.

> Examines the history of each of the Three Ages as detailed in *LOTR* and its
> appendixes, and concludes that the struggle between Good and Evil is
> becoming progressively less clear-cut.

II-429   _____. "Narrative Pattern in *The Fellowship of the Ring*." In
         Lobdell (II-388), pp. 95–106.

> Analyzes a pattern which is repeated at least nine times in Book I of
> *LOTR*: "A conference held in tranquillity (with plenty of food and drink)
> prompts a movement of the ring. The hobbits then blunder more or less
> light-heartedly into deeper danger. Unexpected aid arrives, aid that is
> exactly appropriate to the danger. Disaster is narrowly averted, and the
> feasting tranquillity is momentarily restored" (p. 101). The events of Book I
> form not so much a cycle as a spiral: stakes are constantly increased and
> the gamblers become increasingly self-aware. The journey is in a sense
> through time as well as space since the hobbits encounter the First Age in
> the Willow and the Second Age in the Barrow-wight.

II-430   _____. Review of Kocher, *Master of Middle-earth* (II-346).
         *Journal of Modern Literature*, 3 (1974), 806–07.

> There are some flaws: while Tolkien himself is no doubt profoundly
> Christian, *LOTR* is not and Kocher ignores some hints of Manicheanism;
> though Kocher has genuine successes in seeking a unifying vision, Tolkien's
> oeuvre is not, finally, of a piece (e.g., the Christian Platonism of *LBN* and
> *SWM*, the donnish humor of *FGH*, and the child's garden of *H* are all
> swervings from Tolkien's most profound vision of Middle-earth). But, on
> the whole, this is a needed and satisfying book, avoiding the pitfalls of

abstract pedantry and excess of enthusiasm that have vitiated most of what
has been written of Tolkien, and providing insightful, balanced discussions
of many aspects of Tolkien's work.

II-431   Miller, Stephen O. *Middle Earth: A World in Conflict.*
Baltimore: T-K Graphics, 1975.

Traces and analyzes the series of crucial decisions by major characters in *H*
and *LOTR*. See review by Patterson (II-496).

II-432   _____. *Mithrandir.* Baltimore: T-K Graphics, 1974.

Summarizes and comments on Gandalf's career through *LOTR*. See review
by Patterson (II-496).

II-433   Milward, Peter. "Perchance to Touch: Tolkien as Scholar."
*Mythlore*, 6, No. 4, Whole No. 22 (Fall, 1979), 31–32.

Reminiscences of studying at Oxford under Tolkien.

II-434   Mitchison, Naomi. "Maps of Middle Earth." *Books and
Bookmen*, 28, No. 1 (October, 1977), 28–30.

Reviews of Carpenter, *Tolkien, A Biography* (II-86) and of *Silm*.

II-435   _____. "One Ring to Bind Them." *New Statesman and Nation*,
48 (18 September 1954), 331.

Review of *FR*. It is not an allegory but a mythology, and "above all it is a
story magnificently told, with every kind of color and movement and
greatness." Middle-earth is a flat world, as the map proves. See Huxley (II-
299) and Richardson (II-555)

II-436   Monick, S. "The Voice of Middle Earth: Tolkien's World."
*Lantern* (Pretoria), 27, No. ii (1977), 70–74.

Not seen.

II-437   Monsman, Gerald. "The Imaginative World of J. R. R.
Tolkien." *South Atlantic Quarterly*, 69 (1970), 264–78.

Tolkien is in the Christian humanist tradition of Eliot and Auden,
presenting the same ideas as they, but from a fresh perspective. For him all
fantasy is dependent on the redemptive act, and secondary creation already
anticipates its redemption into primary reality. His reconciliation of
aesthetic and religious ideas in affirming the images of both this world and
a higher one can most clearly be seen in *LBN*, where they are allegorically
presented. The quest theme (parodied in *FGH* but taken seriously in his
other works) is involved with the theme of covetousness, while *LOTR* with
its "fleeting, tangential, and multifaceted pattern of mythic symbolism"
more complexly treats the theme of power.

II-438   Montgomery, John Warwick. "The Apologists of
Eucatastrophe." In *Myth, Allegory and Gospel* (II-439), 11–31.

Introduction to this volume. The four authors discussed all combine
ingenuousness and genius, seem to make a fetish of unoriginality, and wed

Christian apologetics with literature. Tolkien "carefully limits his imagery to the archetypal symbols of Celtic and medieval deep myth and the verities of the Christian tradition . . ." (p. 14).

II-439 _____, ed. *Myth, Allegory and Gospel: An Interpretation of J. R. R. Tolkien, C. S. Lewis, G. K. Chesterton, Charles Williams.* Minneapolis: Bethany Fellowship, Inc., 1974.

Most of the contents are somewhat revised versions of presentations given in 1969–70 in a series on Christianity and literature sponsored by the Departments of Theology and English at De Paul University. The one essay on Tolkien is by Kilby (II-336), but Chad Walsh while writing of Williams, and Edmund Fuller and Montgomery in their essays on Lewis, all refer briefly to Tolkien. For reviews, see III-B-22.

II-440 Moorcock, Michael. *Epic Pooh.* British Fantasy Society Booklet No. 4 (1978).

A chapter from his forthcoming book on epic fantasy, to be called *Heroic Dreams, Enchanted Worlds.* This paper is largely devoted to an attack on Tolkien's style and sentimentality.

II-441 Moore, Anne Carroll. Review of *H. Horn Book,* 14 (March, 1938), 92.

There is sound learning and a rich vein of humor in this refreshingly adventurous and original table. It is rooted in *Beowulf* and the old sagas, and has something in common with W. W. Tarn's *The Treasure of the Isle of Mist* and with certain tales by William Morris.

II-442 _____. Review of *H. Horn Book,* 14 (May-June, 1938), 174.

This is "A rich book, and a rare" and is good reading for anyone with imagination and a zest for adventure.

II-443 Moore, Arthur K. "Medieval English Literature and the Question of Unity." *Modern Philology,* 65 (1969), 285–300.

Discusses Tolkien's essay on *Beowulf* (I-35) on pp. 293–94. Tolkien "is general to the point of banality" (p. 293); the themes he finds in *Beowulf* (e.g., man at war with the hostile world and his inevitable overthrow in Time) are familiar in heroic literature as a class; and the contrast between youth and age said to connect the two parts and unify the poem is self-evident and also too abstract a consideration. See also Kaske (II-319).

II-444 Moorman, Charles W. *The Book of Kyng Arthur: The Unity of Malory's Morte Darthur.* Lexington: Univ. of Kentucky Press, 1965.

". . . I once told Professor J. R. R. Tolkien with great smugness that I was sure, judging from the great number of foreshadowing passages in *The Lord of the Rings,* that he had had the whole narrative in mind before he set pen to paper. Tolkien immediately informed me in no uncertain terms that he had rewritten the first sections of the work in the light of its conclusion not once but many times and that it had been a very difficult job indeed" (p. xxix).

II-445 _____. "Heroism in *The Lord of the Rings.*" *The Southern Quarterly*, 11 (1972), 29–39.

> Intended as a corrective to his article in Hillegas (II-277), where he argued that the nature of heroism in *LOTR* was pagan and Germanic (see II-446). Christian values emerge as more important when one focuses on the heart of the story (the journey of Frodo and Sam to destroy the ring) instead of the periphery (all the adventures of the rest of the Fellowship). Cf. Sale (II-585). On heroism, see also Blissett (II-53), Foster (II-209), Levitin (II-370) and Reckford (II-545).

II-446 _____. " 'Now Entertain Conjecture of a Time'—The Fictive Worlds of C. S. Lewis and J. R. R. Tolkien." In Hillegas (II-277), pp. 59–69.

> Lewis's ideas as a man and a Christian dominated him as an artist, and his world of Narnia is a deliberately didactic creation expressing the doctrines of Christianity. For Tolkien, art has no explicitly didactic purpose, and the tale and meaning of *LOTR* grew in the telling. Middle-earth is essentially pagan in nature, expressing the simple values of a heroic age (but see Moorman, II-445).

II-447 _____. "The Shire, Mordor, and Minas Tirith: J. R. R. Tolkien." Ch. 5 in his *The Precincts of Felicity: The Augustinian City of the Oxford Christians* (Gainesville: Univ. of Florida Press, 1966), pp. 86–100. Reprinted as "The Shire, Mordor, and Minas Tirith" in Isaacs and Zimbardo (II-307), pp. 201–17.

> Considers Tolkien among his fellow Inklings, Charles Williams and (especially) C. S. Lewis (see also Carpenter, II-86). One theme of *LOTR* is the establishment of a "City of God" (in the terminology of Williams) under Aragorn. Cf. Russell (II-576). For reviews of this book, see III-B-23.

II-448 Moran, Maureen. Review of Begg, *The Lord of the Rings and the Signs of the Times* (II-40). *The Year's Work in English Studies*, 56 (1975), 367.

> Begg "is more concerned with what imaginative literature tells us about our own age than with any critical assessment" of *LOTR*.

II-449 _____. Review of Manlove, *Modern Fantasy* (II-402). *The Year's Work in English Studies*, 56 (1975), 344.

> Manlove discovers that the writers "must somehow reconcile the vast gulf between the fantasy worlds they create and the reality they know exists" and he offers harsh critical appraisals, but also a useful starting place for students of this increasingly important genre.

II-450 Morris, John S. "Fantasy in a Mythless Age." *Children's Literature: The Great Excluded*, 2 (1973), 77–86.

> Some of the characteristic features of myth for archaic man (creative and sustaining power and participation by humanity in cosmic order) are

worked out in some modern fantasies, including *LOTR*.

II-451 Morrison, Louise D. *J. R. R. Tolkien's The Fellowship of the Ring: A Critical Commentary*. New York: Monarch, 1976.

This pamphlet in the Monarch Notes series includes a biographical sketch, a textual analysis that surveys each chapter of *FR*, a discussion of literary techniques and major themes (the power of evil, responsibility, love, waste lands, soil, corruption), a chapter on characterization, abstracts of eleven critical pieces on Tolkien's work, essay questions with model answers, suggested topics for research, and a selected bibliography of Tolkien's works and twenty-four critical works on Tolkien. Cf. Hardy (II-256), and Ready (II-542).

II-452 Morse, Elizabeth A. Review of *RGEO*. *Library Journal*, 93 (15 January 1968), 316.

*RGEO* "is for the enthusiastic young adults who have responded to Tolkien's books and the music of Middle Earth."

II-453 Moss, Elaine. "Pauline Baynes: Mistress of the Margin." *Signal*, No. 11 (May, 1973), 88–93.

Interview with Baynes, who talks about working with Tolkien and C. S. Lewis when illustrating their books.

II-454 Muir, Edwin. "A Boy's World." *Sunday Observer* (London), 27 November 1955, p. 11.

Review of *RK. LOTR* shows a remarkable invention, but it is not at all like the more complex Malory, since the story has the fascination only of a long and intricate game between good and evil, in which all the characters, except a few old men who are apt to be wizards, are boys masquerading as adult heroes.

II-455 _____. "The Ring." *Sunday Observer* (London), 21 November 1954, p. 9.

Review of *TT*. The crisis Tolkien describes is ageless, but now and then he does seem to glance at our age. The Ring seems to stand for evil itself, which, mysteriously, tempts the good and strengthens the bad. The involvement of everything that has a natural life in the vast struggle between good and evil makes the fable complete. *TT* is a superb story, not only for boys but for everyone (cf. his review of *RK*, Muir, II-454).

II-456 _____. "Strange Epic." *Sunday Observer* (London), 22 August 1954, p. 7.

Review of *FR*. Not seen.

II-457 Murray, Robert, S. J. "A Tribute to Tolkien." *The Tablet*, 227 (15 September 1973), 879–80.

A close personal friend reminisces about Tolkien's life, work, and faith, and quotes extensively from a letter by Tolkien on the "fundamentally religious and Catholic" nature of *LOTR*.

II-458   Myers, Doris T. "Brave New World: The Status of Women
         According to Tolkien, Lewis, and Williams." *Cimarron Review*
         (Oklahoma State University), No. 17 (October, 1971), pp.
         13–19.

> Although they shared a religious outlook, read the same medieval and
> Renaissance literature, and wrote under each other's tutelage, the worlds
> created by Lewis and Tolkien are indisputably "man's worlds" based on the
> traditional masculine-feminine stereotypes, while Williams creates worlds in
> which men and women are equally human.

II-459   "Mythbegotten." *The Economist*, 17 September 1977, p. 141.

> Review essay on *Silm*, touching briefly on Noel (II-470) and Carpenter (II-
> 86). Tolkien was not a great epic-maker with something of real importance
> to say, but "a great philologist, whose (literally) absorbing games with his
> professional material led him, ill-equipped as a prose stylist, to make
> fictions to accommodate the fruit of his games-playing." *H, LOTR*, and
> *Silm* have little of value, aside from pleasurable distractions.

Nahigian, Ken, coeditor. See Berman (II-45).

II-460   Nelson, Marie. "Non-Human Speech in the Fantasy of C. S.
         Lewis, J. R. R. Tolkien, and Richard Adams." *Mythlore*, 5, No.
         1, Whole No. 17 (May, 1978), 37–39.

> The section on Tolkien in this essay concentrates on the Ents and the
> appropriateness for trees of the Ent speech.

II-461   "A New Look at Old Books." *Young Readers Review*, 1, No. 4
         (1964), 12.

> *H* is a book of adventure with descriptive passages creating a world
> intimately known to a reader with an imaginative response to fine fantasy.
> It is a strange mixture of humor and brooding evil, and with complex and
> believable characters who, of whatever race, are all too human.

II-462   Newman, Lois. Review of Becker, *The Tolkien Scrapbook* (II-
         37). *Fantasiae*, 7, No. 2, Whole No. 71 (February, 1979), 10.

> This overpriced book has little of value.

II-463   Nicholls, Peter. "Anatomy of a Romance." *Vector*, Nos. 67/68
         (Spring, 1974), pp. 11–15.

II-464   Nichols, Lewis. "Swann in Elvish." *New York Times Book
         Review*, 22 October 1967, p. 56.

> Review of *RGEO*. Describes contents, and notes that Swann had used one
> of the songs in a tour of "At the Drop of Another Hat."

II-465   Nicol, Charles. "The Reinvented Word." *Harper's*, 255
         (November, 1977), 95–96, 99–100, 103.

> Review essay on *Silm*. Tolkien's passion for inventing languages generated
> the private, solidly based world that he shared in his books. Christopher

Tolkien's assemblage is smooth, consistent, and of high seriousness, but the works that make up *Silm* are of varying interests and styles, and, while required for serious admirers who wish to explore deeper into Middle-earth, they are not really for the general reader.

II-466    Nitzsche, Jane Chance. *Tolkien's Art: A "Mythology for England."* New York: St. Martin's, 1979.

Tolkien developed his own art and mythology from the medieval literary, religious, and cultural ideas in which he was steeped. He was intrigued by the image of kingship or lordship, and usually depicts the good lord as a healer or artist, but the evil lord as a monster or dragon. Chapters discuss Tolkien's scholarly work, the Christian fairy-stories (*H, LBN,* and *SWM*), the medieval parodies (*A&I, FGH, HB,* "Imram"), *LOTR,* and *Silm.*

II-467    Noad, Charles. *The Trees, the Jewels, and the Rings: A discursive enquiry into things little known on Middle-earth.* England: privately published, 1976.

This thirty-six-page monograph gathers information available prior to the publication of *Silm* on the light of the Two Trees, the Three Jewels or Silmarilli, and the twenty Rings of Power; their functions and history; their relation to Tolkien's characters, particularly the Valar and the Elves, and especially with regard to immortality; and implications for the story of *LOTR.* See also Allan (II-9).

II-468    Noel, Ruth S. *The Languages of Middle-earth.* Baltimore: Mirage, 1974.

See below, Noel (II-469).

II-469    _____. *The Languages of Tolkien's Middle-earth.* Boston: Houghton Mifflin, 1980.

An earlier version was published in a limited edition (see above, Noel, II-468). Discusses Tolkien as a linguist and the fourteen languages he created, providing translations of quotations from *Silm, LOTR,* and Carpenter (II-86), information on alphabets, a brief grammar of Elvish, a guide to pronunciation, an English-to-Elvish glossary, and a dictionary. This is a more popular text than *Introduction to Elvish* (II-302).

II-470    _____. *The Mythology of Middle-earth.* Boston: Houghton Mifflin, 1977.

This survey of the myths of the ancient world (mostly Norse and Celtic) that Tolkien drew on for his fantasies is divided into sections on Themes, Places, Things, and Beings. For reviews, see III-B-24.

II-471    Nordhjem, Bent. "In Quest of Tolkien's Middle-Earth: On the Interpretation and Classification of *The Lord of the Rings* by J. R. R. Tolkien (with an Old English Word-List)." In *Vølve: Scandinavian Views on Science Fiction.* Ed. Cay Dollerup. Copenhagen: Department of English, University of Copenhagen, 1978, pp. 17–42.

Not seen. This volume, which is Volume 4 in the series Anglica at Americana, consists of selected papers from the Scandinavian Science-Fiction Festival, 1977.

II-472   Nored, Gary. "The Lord of the Rings—A Textual Inquiry." *Papers of the Bibliographical Society of America*, 68 (1974), 71–74.

It can be shown that, despite the ostensible printing dates, the Ballantine paperback edition of *LOTR* of 1965 really derives from the Houghton Mifflin edition of 1966. The Allen and Unwin edition of 1966 shows further authorial changes and is actually a third, not a second, edition, and this is the latest and most definitive text of *LOTR*. Also discusses the copyright controversy over the first edition.

II-473   Norman, Philip. "Lord of the Flicks." *Show: The Magazine of Films and the Arts*, 1, No. 1 (January, 1970), 29.

Interview with Tolkien. He is reportedly content with at least the financial aspects of United Artists having the film rights to *LOTR*. He would like to make a record of *H*, doing all the voices himself (cf. I-74). Since " 'A pen is to me as a beak is to a hen,' " he is now " 'fighting the natural inertia of the lazy human being' " by working hard on *Silm*.

II-474   ———. "The Hobbit Man." *The Sunday Times Magazine* (London), 15 January 1967, pp. 34–36. Reprinted as "The Prevalence of Hobbits" in *The New York Times Magazine*, 15 January 1967, pp. 30–31, 97, 100, 102.

Interview with Tolkien discussing the cult and giving some biographical information.

Norris, William Rust. See II-301.

II-475   Norton, John. "Tolkien, Beowulf, and the Poet: A Problem in Point of View." *English Studies*, 48 (1967), 527–31.

What Tolkien in his essay on *Beowulf* (I-35) finds as mere imperfections of execution in Beowulf's last speech to his retainers are in fact important contributions to characterization which underscore the hero's resoluteness and courage. See also Kaske (II-319).

II-476   Norwood, William Durward. "Tolkien's Intention in *The Lord of the Rings*." In II-663, 18–24.

Tolkien's ideas on fantasy in *OFS* are maintained in *LOTR* (see Cox, II-123). *LOTR* is completely rational, has inner consistency, and is on a vast scale; it will induce and maintain Secondary Belief long enough to create for the reader a major experience: to image for himself and to comprehend the terrible joy that is the very essence of utter reality.

II-477   O'Connor, Gerard. "The Many Ways to Read an 'Old' Book." *Extrapolation*, 15 (1973), 72–74.

Defends his earlier article (see below, O'Connor, II-478) against criticisms by O'Hare (II-480). He "was not really attacking the popularity of the trilogy but pointing up the critical insensitivity of the Tolkien cultists which perpetuates it" (p. 72). It can be illuminating to apply sociopolitical readings to works in which social and political assumptions are unconscious. Genre classification should not be identified with evaluative and critical judgment. *LOTR* can withstand divergent critical approaches.

II-478 _____. "Why Tolkien's *The Lord of the Rings* Should *Not* Be Popular Culture." *Extrapolation*, 13 (1971), 48–55.

There are simpler explanations for the popularity of *LOTR* than the mythopoeic theory of Auden (II-18), Beatie (II-35), and Kilby (II-334), for it is a great story with wildly original and interesting characters set in a delightful world of fantasy, and it communicates, before ecology became fashionable, an extraordinary reverence for natural life. However, it is really an Establishment book, and commits six crimes against the counterculture: it glorifies age and disparages youth; it is male chauvinist (see also Myers, II-458, and Stimpson, II-642); blood supremacy is a common theme; it is authoritarian; and both a moral and a political absolutism justify a holy war where the evil enemy can be slaughtered with joy. See also O'Hare (II-480) and O'Connor's reply (II-477).

II-479 O'Hare, Colmán. "Charles Williams, C. S. Lewis and J. R. R. Tolkien: Three Approaches to Religion in Modern Fiction." Ph.D. diss., University of Toronto, 1973.

The works of the three authors are profoundly different, and show that the more a novelist attempts to fulfill the role of theologian the more his art will suffer. Religion in *LOTR* does not partake of the highly personal vision of Williams nor the ecumenical "mere Christianity" of Lewis, but is merely a necessary part of a complete secondary world. See *DAI*, 36 (1975), 1532A.

II-480 _____. "On Reading an 'Old Book.' " *Extrapolation*, 14 (1972), 59–63.

O'Connor's (II-478) sociopolitical reading of *LOTR* as thoroughly "Establishment" in outlook, aside from suffering from the use of ill-defined terminology (as in confusing respect for authority with admiration for authoritarianism), suffers worse from its disregard for the milieu in which Tolkien wrote. It is indeed a modern and not a medieval work, but it is still an "old book" that does not address itself to "now" problems. See also O'Connor's reply (II-477).

II-481 _____. "The Universe of Order: Some Aspects of the Natural Law in J. R. R. Tolkien's *The Lord of the Rings*." M.A. thesis, University of Waterloo, Ontario, 1969. Phil.M. thesis, University of Waterloo, Ontario, 1970.

Certain patterns in *LOTR* suggest that its unstated, but still binding, ethical system is analogous to (but not identical with) certain postulates of Christian moral theology and philosophy: i.e., to the Natural Law. Chapters relate the world of *LOTR* to Space, Time, and Morality; deal with that world's racial and social structures both good and evil, with the willed actions of individual characters, and with how characters join to pursue a proper or improper end; and the study concludes by considering the value of such an expression of the operations of Natural Law in a work of fiction in the light of Tolkien's criteria in *OFS*.

II-482   Ohlmarks, Åke. *Sagan om Tolkien*. Stockholm: Geber, 1972.

> Not seen. Said to be a general study of Tolkien, 245 pages in length, by the translator of *LOTR* into Swedish. See also Geijerstam (II-224).

II-483   O'Neill, Timothy R. *The Individuated Hobbit: Jung, Tolkien and the Archetypes of Middle-earth*. Boston: Houghton Mifflin, 1979.

> Summarizes Jung's psychology of Self-realization and applies this to Tolkien's work, particularly *H* and *LOTR*. See also Spice (II-636). For reviews, see III-B-25.

II-484   Orjollet, Jean-François. "J. R. R. Tolkien: Syllogistique du merveilleux." *Littérature* (University of Paris), No. 8 (décembre, 1972), pp. 41–52.

> Not seen.

II-485   [Osburne, Andrea.] "The Peril of the World." *Tolkien Journal*, No. 15 (Summer, 1972), pp. 16–17.

> That so small an object as a ring can control such power; the circular shape, which associates the ring symbolically with the sun as source of power and the circle as perfect shape; and the close association of the ring with the hand, the instrument of human mastery over the world—are reasons why the effect of *LOTR* would have been much weakened had Tolkien chosen some other type of object as the primary talisman of power.

II-486   Ottevaere-van Praag, Ganna. "Retour à l'épopée mythologique: *Le Maître des Anneaux* de J. R. R. Tolkien." *Revue des Langues Vivantes* (Brussels), 33 (1967), 237–45.

> In French. *LOTR* makes a fantasy world (one where each being, even the forces of nature, must choose sides in the struggle between good and evil) seem very real by brilliance of style. It is in the tradition of Celtic and Germanic myth, courtly romance, and Ariosto, but colored by the modern world. Gandalf and Saruman, Legolas and Gimli, Frodo and Sam (the latter is the true hero of the book) are among the series of parallelisms in the work. Tolkien's chief fault is his lack of awareness of social problems conditioned by his simple acceptance of English aristocratic traditionalism.

II-487   Pace, David Paul. "The Influence of Vergil's *Aeneid* on *The Lord of the Rings*." *Mythlore*, 6, No. 2, Whole No. 20 (Spring, 1979), 37–38.

> While there are both Homeric and Vergilian motifs in *LOTR*, the characters and events in Tolkien's work more closely resemble those in the *Aeneid* than those in the *Iliad* or *Odyssey*. See also Reckford (II-545).

II-488    Palmer, Bruce. *Of Orc-Rags, Phials, and a Far Shore: Visions of Paradise in the Lord of the Rings*. Baltimore: T-K Graphics, 1976.

> This thirty-page monograph discusses the Edenic "Blessed Realm" in *LOTR*, with Christian parallels.

Pangborn, Mary M. and Stephen. See Levitin (II-372).

II-489    Panshin, Cory Seidman. "Old Irish Influences upon the Languages and Literature of the Lord of the Rings." *Tolkien Journal*, 3, No. 4, Whole No. 10 (November, 1969), 7–8.

> Discusses the Old Irish processes of lenition and nasalization in Quenya and in Sindarin, and the use of Irish metrics in "Eärendil" and "Errantry."

————. See also under her maiden name: Seidman, Cory.

II-490    Papajewski, Helmut. "J. R. R. Tolkiens *The Hobbit* und *The Lord of the Rings*: 'Fairy Tale' und Mythos." *Literatur in Wissenschaft und Unterricht* (Kiel), 5 (1972), 46–65.

> In German. Not seen.

II-491    "The Paradox of J. R. R. Tolkien." *Christianity Today*, 9 September 1977, p. 35.

> Unsigned "Editorial" (presumably by Harold Lindsell, the editor for this issue). Although Tolkien published a great deal, gave many times more lectures than he was required to, kept up a full schedule of tutorials, and succeeded in reforming the syllabus of the English department at Oxford, curiously his friends and colleagues found him dilatory in scholarly activity. This paradox is because he was a perfectionist who was constantly revising instead of single-mindedly pursuing one project through to a speedy conclusion and going on to another, so that he frequently missed deadlines. Fortunately, Christopher Tolkien has not been dilatory in bringing out his father's work. And Carpenter's felicitously written biography (II-86), lets Tolkien's personality dominate the book; it reveals Tolkien as a brilliant, though sometimes petty and jealous, man, and subtly reminds us that much is required of one to whom much is given.

II-492    Parker, Douglass. "Hwaet We Holbytla . . ." *Hudson Review*, 9 (1956–57), 598–609.

> The meaning of *LOTR* is a re-creation of *Beowulf* as Tolkien has written about it (cf. Christensen, II-96). *LOTR* is the story of the end of an age in which the creatures of a deterministic universe face up to their various fates with heroism, since this supplies some meaning to their destinies in human terms where the universe supplies none. The human condition is tragic and must be lamented. On determinism, cf. Barber (II-23 and II-24), Fuller (II-214), Miller (II-428), and Spacks (II-633 and II-634). A long footnote explains the derivation of some of Tolkien's names (see also Ryan, II-578). The title of this essay is modelled on an Old English formula (cf. the opening line of *Beowulf*) and might be rendered into modern English as "Lo, we (have heard of) the Hobbits . . ."

II-493  Partington, Dorothy Margaret. "Tolkien, J(ohn) R(onald) R(euel)." *Britannica Book of the Year*, 1967, p. 167.

> Perhaps the cult reflected an underlying need for a positive mythology and a reassuring antidote to chaos and the machine. *LOTR* can be read on three levels: as an allegory of the eternal war between good and evil; as a political parable in which nuclear power is represented by Sauron and humanity by Frodo; or simply as an entertainment. Tolkien the scholar very much influenced Tolkien the writer.

II-494  Pasnak, James. "The Road Down From the Hill: An Image in the Work of J. R. R. Tolkien." *British Columbia Library Quarterly* (October, 1968), 14–20.

> Not seen.

II-495  Patch, Howard R. Review of *Beowulf* essay (I-35). *Modern Language Notes*, 54 (1939), 217–18.

> Tolkien is more indebted to the philologists, mythologists, and archaeologists than his comments on them might imply, and the substance of his remarks is sometimes a little thin, but the lecture covers much and its main contention is sound. More of this type of criticism is needed on medieval literature. See also Kaske (II-319).

II-496  Patterson, Nancy-Lou. "Decisions and Wizards." *Mythlore*, 3, No. 4, Whole No. 12 (June, 1976), 24–25.

> Review of Miller's two monographs (II-431 and II-432).

II-497  _____. "Evoking Wonder." *Mythlore*, 7, No. 1, Whole No. 23 (March, 1980), 24–25.

> Review of Manlove, *Modern Fantasy* (II-402).

II-498  _____. "The Hierarchy of Light." *Mythlore*, 7, No. 1, Whole No. 23 (March, 1980), 24.

> Review of reissue of Hillegas, *Shadows of Imagination* (II-277), concentrating on the essay by Kreeft (II-352).

II-499  _____. "Homo monstrosus: Lloyd Alexander's Gurgi and Other Shadow Figures of Fantastic Literature." *Mythlore*, 3, No. 3, Whole No. 11 (March, 1976), 24–28.

> Gurgi in the Prydain books (a series she compares to *LOTR*) is a Jungian Shadow figure. Literary parallels include Gollum and Grendel.

II-500  _____. "Image and Word: Tolkien Illustrates Himself." *Mythlore*, 7, No. 2, Whole No. 24 (Summer, 1980), 32, 34.

> Review of *Pictures by J. R. R. Tolkien* (I-80).

II-501  _____. "Light-weight Lightning." *Mythlore*, 6, No. 2, Whole No. 20 (Spring, 1979), 34.

> Review of Mathews, *Lightning from a Clear Sky* (II-409).

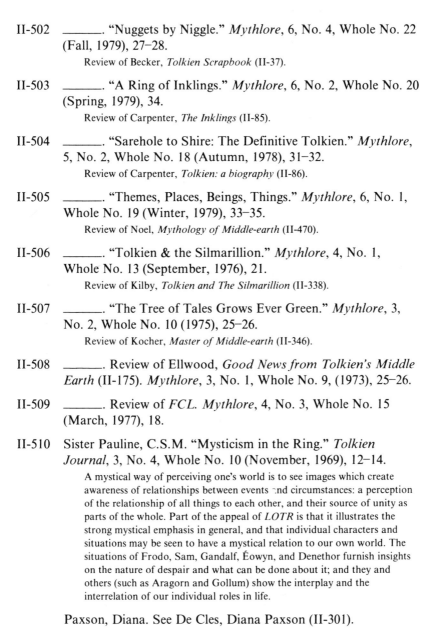

II-502 _____. "Nuggets by Niggle." *Mythlore*, 6, No. 4, Whole No. 22 (Fall, 1979), 27–28.

Review of Becker, *Tolkien Scrapbook* (II-37).

II-503 _____. "A Ring of Inklings." *Mythlore*, 6, No. 2, Whole No. 20 (Spring, 1979), 34.

Review of Carpenter, *The Inklings* (II-85).

II-504 _____. "Sarehole to Shire: The Definitive Tolkien." *Mythlore*, 5, No. 2, Whole No. 18 (Autumn, 1978), 31–32.

Review of Carpenter, *Tolkien: a biography* (II-86).

II-505 _____. "Themes, Places, Beings, Things." *Mythlore*, 6, No. 1, Whole No. 19 (Winter, 1979), 33–35.

Review of Noel, *Mythology of Middle-earth* (II-470).

II-506 _____. "Tolkien & the Silmarillion." *Mythlore*, 4, No. 1, Whole No. 13 (September, 1976), 21.

Review of Kilby, *Tolkien and The Silmarillion* (II-338).

II-507 _____. "The Tree of Tales Grows Ever Green." *Mythlore*, 3, No. 2, Whole No. 10 (1975), 25–26.

Review of Kocher, *Master of Middle-earth* (II-346).

II-508 _____. Review of Ellwood, *Good News from Tolkien's Middle Earth* (II-175). *Mythlore*, 3, No. 1, Whole No. 9, (1973), 25–26.

II-509 _____. Review of *FCL*. *Mythlore*, 4, No. 3, Whole No. 15 (March, 1977), 18.

II-510 Sister Pauline, C.S.M. "Mysticism in the Ring." *Tolkien Journal*, 3, No. 4, Whole No. 10 (November, 1969), 12–14.

A mystical way of perceiving one's world is to see images which create awareness of relationships between events and circumstances: a perception of the relationship of all things to each other, and their source of unity as parts of the whole. Part of the appeal of *LOTR* is that it illustrates the strong mystical emphasis in general, and that individual characters and situations may be seen to have a mystical relation to our own world. The situations of Frodo, Sam, Gandalf, Éowyn, and Denethor furnish insights on the nature of despair and what can be done about it; and they and others (such as Aragorn and Gollum) show the interplay and the interrelation of our individual roles in life.

Paxson, Diana. See De Cles, Diana Paxson (II-301).

II-511 Peffers, Marjorie L. Review of Kocher, *Master of Middle-earth* (II-346). *Library Journal*, 97 (1 September 1972), 2733.

This book analyzes, without technical jargon, *LOTR* in the light of Tolkien's other published writings, and impels the reader to return and reread Tolkien with new insight. The true hero of *LOTR* is Aragorn ("since he is the only member of the fellowship to withstand the lure of the ring of power") and its major theme is freedom of choice.

II-512  Pemberton, Elizabeth Leigh. "Hobbits Complete." *Spectator*, 25 November 1955, p. 744.

Review of *RK*. "The book's obsessive quality, its mysticism, its layers of incomprehensible allegory, its confusing variety of names, the tedium of much of the purely descriptive writing, would make it no more than a scholar's whimsy were it not for Professor Tolkien's inventive brilliance and narrative power."

II-513  Peoples, Galen. "The Great Beast: Imagination in Harness." *Mythlore*, 2, No. 1, Whole No. 5 [also *Tolkien Journal*, 4, No. 2, Whole No. 12] (Winter, 1970), 19–20.

The appeal of the imagination is powerful, and hence it should be expended on intentional, and moral, fantasy, not on its perverse manifestations or on a nonphilosophic confusion of fantasy with reality. The works of Tolkien, Lewis, and Williams reveal the potency of the imagination, but control it.

II-514  Perkins, Agnes and Helen Hill. "The Corruption of Power." In Lobdell (II-388), pp. 57–68.

A series of characters and incidents throughout *LOTR* explores the effects of power on characters weak and strong, good and evil, great and humble. See also Levitin (II-373).

II-515  Perret, Marion. "Rings Off Their Fingers: Hands in *The Lord of the Rings*." *Ariel: A Review of International English Literature*, 6, No. 4 (October, 1975), 52–66.

"Tolkien uses both poetic and pictorial imagery, and the reader who can respond to both will find that hand images have many uses: to differentiate characters, to further plot, to provide information, to betray emotion, to establish mood, to embody morality, to universalize" (p. 64).

II-516  Pettit, Philip. "Tolkien's Good and Evil." *Cambridge Review*, 95 (23 November 1973), 34.

For Tolkien, evil is, ontologically, not something positive, but only the absence of good. Evil has traditionally been traced to the three desires for prestige, possession, and power. In Tolkien's scheme the first two desires are relatively harmless, and the desire for power is the source of real evil in Middle-earth, and one which strengthens demonically those it enslaves. Power cannot be sought to combat evil, lest one become evil oneself. A force for good springs unprompted from the salvific power of grace. See also Auden (II-16) and Levitin (II-373).

II-517  Petty, Anne Cotton. "The Creative Mythology of J. R. R. Tolkien: A Study of the Mythic Impulse." Ph.D. diss., Florida State University, 1972.

The combined methodologies of Joseph Campbell, Vladimir Propp, and

Claude Lévi-Strauss are used to analyze the folkloristic and mythic
structure underlying *LOTR.* The book follows the three-stage hero quest
(separation, initiation, reunion), and also age-old paradigmatic patterns of
binary opposition and mediation (e.g., death and rebirth). Tolkien's
creative mythology of Middle-earth has brought about a renewal of myth
consciousness in literature. See also the book version of this dissertation
(II-518). See *DAI,* 33 (1972), 2390A.

II-518    _____. *One Ring to Rule Them All: Tolkien's Mythology.*
Univ. of Alabama Press, 1979.

Book version of her doctoral dissertation (II-517).

II-519    Pfotenhauer, Paul. "Christian Themes in Tolkien." *Cresset*
(Valparaiso University), 32, No. 3 (January, 1969), 13–15.

That Sauron's presence is always felt though always in the background may
help us see the demonic in our own midst. The more significant, yet more
hidden, presence of the One, determining the outcome of events, may help
us recognize Providence. St. Augustine's statement that predestination and
freedom are in essence the same is exemplified in the choices made by
Tolkien's characters. Recurring themes are the temptation to *hubris,* and
the Suffering Servant who is willing to die that others might live. Sam
finding Frodo light to carry exemplifies Williams's doctrine of coinherence.

II-520    Phelps, Robert. Review of *SWM. New York Times Book
Review,* 4 February 1968, p. 26.

Everything Tolkien has written is "an elegy—for the decline of our human
capacity for awe." *SWM* is a homely, haunting tale, about how access to
the invisible otherworld is a gift or a loan these days.

II-521    Piggin, Julia R. "Desirers of Dragons." *Practical English,* 42,
No. 7 (17 March 1967), 4–7.

Illustrations by Tom Eaton. Article on Tolkien's great appeal to the
"LotRians," who admire his inventiveness, trace his sources, and play
games with his invented world and languages. The cover of the magazine
cites the title as "Where Is Middle-earth."

II-522    Plank, Robert. " 'The Scouring of the Shire' ": Tolkien's View
of Fascism." In Lobdell (II-388), pp. 107–15.

The rise and character of Saruman's regime in the Shire shows the influence
of historical fascism. Tolkien opposes fascism rather as a conservative than
as a democrat.

II-523    Plimmer, Charlotte, and Denis Plimmer. "The Man Who
Understands Hobbits." *London Daily Telegraph Magazine,* 22
March 1968, pp. 31–32, 35. Reprinted as " 'In A Hole In the
Ground There Lived A Hobbit' " in *Weekend Magazine,* No. 35
(1968), pp. 6–8.

The reprint is in a weekend supplement distributed with the Saturday
editions of many newspapers in Canada. This interview with Tolkien in

Oxford gives biographical data; the story of beginning *H* on the back of an examination paper; the publisher's acceptance of *LOTR* despite its length because "It is a work of genius"; the monotheism of *LOTR* (the One is the One God); and Tolkien's refusal to be classed with Ariosto, Malory, Spenser, Cervantes, or Dante (none of these authors attract him).

II-524   Plotz, Richard. "The Ace Books Controversy." *Tolkien Journal*, 1, No. 2 (1965), 1–2.

Describes the technicality by which copyright was impossible for the U.S. edition of *LOTR*. Quotes Tolkien: " '(The law) says in effect (that) if any property is left unguarded, by inadvertance or otherwise, a person who appropriates it cannot be called a thief, even if he can be shown to have known to whom the property in justice belonged.' " Notes the advantages of the Ballantine paperback over the Ace. See also II-2.

II-525   _____. "J. R. R. Tolkien Talks About Middle-earth . . . Elvish." *Seventeen*, 26, (January, 1967), 92–93, 118.

Interview with Tolkien. Early mention of what *Silm* would contain. See also "Face-to-Face: With R. D. Plotz," *Seventeen*, 25 (April, 1966), 153, which also recounts Plotz's other interests besides the Tolkien Society of America, of which he was the first president.

II-526   Post, J. B. *An Atlas of Fantasy*. Baltimore: Mirage, 1973. Revised ed., New York: Ballantine, 1979.

Collection of maps of fantasy worlds, including Middle-earth, with introductions to each section. See also Manguel and Guadalupi (II-401).

II-527   _____. Review of Pauline Baynes, *A Map of Middle-earth*. *Luna*, No. 35–36 (April-May, 1972), pp. 60–61.

Discusses the maps by the Tolkiens (father and son), M. Blackburn (the most detailed version), "Brem" for Ballantine (barely adequate), and Baynes (the most aesthetically pleasing).

II-528   _____. Review of Ellwood, *Good News from Tolkien's Middle Earth* (II-175). *Luna*, No. 30 (November, 1971), p. 31.

The essays ramble and forget that "Christian" symbolism is often stolen from earlier mythologies.

II-529   _____. Review of Hillegas, *Shadows of Imagination* (II-277). *Luna*, No. 16 (September, 1970), p. 23.

The volume is not worth buying but some of the essays (particularly those on Williams) are informative.

II-530   _____. Review of Stimpson, *J. R. R. Tolkien* (II-642). *Luna*, No. 13 (June, 1970), p. 25.

The work is petty, pedantic, and savage.

II-531 _____. Review of West, *Tolkien Criticism* (II-715). *Luna*, No.
13 (June, 1970), p. 25.

> The listing is pretty good, though it does not include most fannish sources.

II-532 Poyet, Françoise. "Merveilleux et fantastique dans *The Lord of
the Rings*." *Caliban*, 16 (1979), 41–52.

> Not seen.

II-533 "Professor J. R. R. Tolkien: Creator of Hobbits and inventor of
a new mythology." *London Times*, 3 September 1973, p. 15,
cols. 5–8. Reprinted in Etkin (II-181), pp. 55–61. Reprinted in
Salu and Farrell (II-590), pp. 11–15.

> Obituary giving broad outline of Tolkien's life, discussing his academic
> career and literary oeuvre. C. S. Lewis is said to have written most of it.
> The reprint in Etkin adds explanatory notes.

II-534 "Professor Tolkien and the Hobbits." *Diplomat*, 18 (October,
1966), 31–43, 73–74.

> Special section on Tolkien. Cover painting, "The World of J. R. R.
> Tolkien," by Barry Geller. "Hobbitmania" (pp. 40–41) consists of letters
> from: Howard Nemerov, Richard Burton, Timothy Leary, Senator William
> Proxmire, Elizabeth Janeway (on translating Tolkien into Russian), Lynda
> Bird Johnson, Richard Plotz, Hathaway Kate Melchior, and Laurel
> Wenger (age 9½). Nancy Smith's "Pleasures of the Hobbit Table" (pp.
> 42–43, 73–74) suggests recipes for hobbit foods (cf. Becker, II-37). The only
> critical article is Aubrey Menen's "Learning to Love the Hobbits" (pp.
> 32–34, 37–38), which approves of Tolkien's wilderness and wasteland
> motifs, but dislikes his Girl Scout fairies and poverty of imagination. Also
> contains the invaluable "Tolkien on Tolkien" (I-60).

II-535 Purtill, Richard L. "Heaven and Other Perilous Realms."
*Mythlore*, 6, No. 4, Whole No. 22 (Fall, 1979), 3–6.

> Tolkien's choice, in *T&L*, of a story to accompany and illustrate *OFS* is a
> surprising one, for *LBN* is unlike his other fiction in that it is allegorical
> (with a moral, an aesthetic, and a religious "applicability," all apparent
> components of the author's intention), that it makes no mention of elves
> or Faerie, and that it is explicitly religious. The selection may have been
> at least partly a historical accident, yet *LBN* does exemplify what *OFS* calls
> the "Mystical face" of the fairy tale (whereas *SWM* shows the "Magical
> face" and *FGH* the "Mirror of scorn and pity towards Man"), and makes
> explicit what in Tolkien's other work is usually implicit.

II-536 _____. *Lord of the Elves and Eldils: Fantasy and Philosophy
in C. S. Lewis and J. R. R. Tolkien*. Grand Rapids, Mich.:
Zondervan Publishing, 1974.

> Discusses the similarities and differences between Lewis and Tolkien, and
> their ideas on literature, fantasy, language, ethics, and religion. See review
> by Keller (II-325).

II-537   Raffel, Burton. "*The Lord of the Rings* as Literature." In Isaacs
         and Zimbardo (II-307), pp. 218–46.

> While *LOTR* is a magnificent and imaginative story showing great skill in
> the narrative art, it is not, in a strict sense, literature, since stylistically
> Tolkien does not *feel* what he describes, his verse is generally poor (see
> Johnston, II-310), his characterization is adequate to the story but portrays
> only very familiar aspects of human reality, and the basic morality is a very
> simple sort of Christianity.

II-538   Randolph, Burt. "The Singular Incompetence of the Valar."
         *Tolkien Journal*, 3, No. 3, Whole No. 9 (Summer, 1968), 11–13.

> Discussion of the Valar written prior to the publication of *Silm*. The Valar
> were ineffective Guardians of the World. They were grossly inconsistent
> about the use of force, and used it only when their charges had been all but
> wiped out and then at the urging of a man who was only able to obtain a
> hearing because he carried a talisman made by an Elf they had exiled, and
> even then they omitted to deal with Sauron as well as Morgoth. Cf. Ring
> (II-557).

II-539   Rang, Jack C. "Two Servants." In "The Tolkien Papers" (II-
         663), 84–94.

> Focuses on Niggle and on Sam Gamgee, both humble and selfless
> characters. See also Rosenberg (II-570).

II-540   Ratliff, William E. and Charles G. Flinn. "The Hobbit and the
         Hippie." *Modern Age*, 12 (1968), 142–46.

> The hippies have taken up a book with a view of the universe and a
> creature's place in it which is distinctly opposed to the prevailing
> rationalist, progressive, materialist philosophies. But they have failed to
> recognize that this opposition is based on a quite different set of values
> than their own. *LOTR* is not a call to drop out of the world's struggle; the
> characters feel a present duty to struggle against evil, even without
> expectation of finally conquering it, even though the evil is not always
> clear, even by force if necessary.

II-541   Ready, William. "The Heroic Theme." *Library Review*, 21
         (1968), 283–88.

> General article on Tolkien's life and work (mostly on *LOTR*). Cf. his book
> (II-543).

II-542   _____. *The Lord of the Rings, The Hobbit Notes.* Toronto:
         Cole Publishing, 1971.

> Includes a brief introduction, short synopses of the books followed by
> chapter-by-chapter summaries, essay topics, and a selected bibliography of
> criticism. Cf. Hardy (II-256) and Morrison (II-451). See review by Allan
> (II-8).

II-543   _____. *The Tolkien Relation.* Chicago: Henry Regnery, 1968.

Reprinted as *Understanding Tolkien and The Lord of the Rings*. New York: Paperback Library, 1969.

> Tolkien's birth in South Africa, upbringing in England, boyhood conversion to Catholicism, tragic experiences in World War I, and age and class (he is in the aristocratic, academic, conservative tradition), all determined his attitudes and work. *H* can repel one, but it may draw one to *LOTR*, which is his masterpiece even though the introduction, appendixes, and verse should have been omitted, and the language of the Hobbits (reminiscent of Frank Richards's school stories) is something that must be borne. The theme of *LOTR* is the courage to persist without hope of demeaning reward, and the profound truth that humble beings like the Hobbits can act heroically. Features two letters from Tolkien and one from his son, Christopher Tolkien. For reviews, see III-B-26.

II-544 _____. "Tolkien Relation." *Canadian Library*, 25 (1968), 128–36.

> Not to be confused with his book of the same title (II-543). Tolkien's fantasy is essentially religious in character and relates man to the world around him, making of life the struggle that it really must be.

II-545 Reckford, Kenneth J. "Some Trees in Virgil and Tolkien." In *Perspectives of Roman Poetry: A Classics Symposium*. Ed. G. Karl Galinsky. Austin: Univ. of Texas Press, 1974, pp. 57–91.

> This volume is No. 1 in the series, Symposia in the Arts and the Humanities. Discusses the significance of tree references (the Golden Bough, the White Tree, etc.) in Homer, Virgil, and Tolkien. He does not try to compare *Aeneid* and *LOTR* as literature, nor to prove that Virgil influenced Tolkien (though he believes that he did, through the mediation of Tennyson), but to show "that a deep affinity exists between Virgil's mind and Tolkien's and may be observed in the way they perceive life, in their sense of the relation between heroic choice and achievement, on the one hand, and time, change, loss, sadness, uncertainty, and suffering, on the other" (pp. 57–58). Continuity through change is a major theme in Homer, Virgil, and Tolkien, each of whom takes the tradition and does something original and vital with it. We value Tolkien partly because "he affirms the old heroic values in a new guise, yet without blinking the realities of sadness, suffering, and loss" (p. 87). In all three, "The hero still strives, rejects temptations, and makes tragic choices, and is at once a responsible free agent and a man overmastered by fate" (p. 84). See also Pace (II-487). On the heroic, see also Blissett (II-53), Foster (II-209), Levitin (II-370), and Moorman (II-445).

Reed, Diane. See Burrow (II-77).

II-546 Reese, K. M. "Hobbit calendar proposed for serious consideration." *Chemical and Engineering News*, 27 March 1978, p. 52.

> The calendar used in the Shire has advantages over our actual calendar and might usefully be adopted in our primary world.

II-547    Reilly, R[obert] J. *Romantic Religion: A Study of Barfield, Lewis, Williams, and Tolkien.* Athens: Univ. of Georgia Press, 1971.

> Book version of his dissertation (see II-548), updated with reference to later criticism. For reviews, see III-B-27.

II-548    _____. "Romantic Religion in the Work of Owen Barfield, C. S. Lewis, Charles Williams, and J. R. R. Tolkien." Ph.D. diss., Michigan State University, 1960.

> The romantic experience that Tolkien is concerned with is the eucatastrophe or "good turn" of the fairy story, an experience which has religious validity. See *DA*, 21 (1961), 3461–62. See also his book version (II-547).

II-549    _____. "Tolkien and the Fairy Story." *Thought*, 38 (1963), 89–106. Reprinted in Isaacs and Zimbardo (II-307), pp. 128–50.

> He relates *OFS* to the Romantics and especially Coleridge (see also Wojcik, II-737) and to Tolkien's fiction, especially *LOTR*. He finds in *LOTR* a sense of inherent morality, an element of the numinous, a natural law that is nowhere codified but which is emotionally or imaginatively apprehended by the good and the evil alike. Cf. Scheps (II-597), and Sirridge (II-614). See also Cox (II-123), Purtill (II-535), and Roberts (II-559).

II-550    Reinken, Donald L. "J. R. R. Tolkien's *The Lord of the Rings*: A Christian Refounding of the Political Order." *Christian Perspectives: An Ecumenical Quarterly* (Winter, 1966), 16–23. Reprinted in *Tolkien Journal*, 2, No. 3 (1966), 4–10.

> Power divorced from Care or Love is evil. It should be exercised only to preserve all things unstained, in action appropriate to the nature of the actor and to his circumstances. As in Plato's myth of the ring of Gyges, "invisibility enhances power precisely insofar as it takes away responsibility for action" (p. 7). Tolkien's characters surrender human arrogance and rely upon the natural order, but the Providential workings of the plot are not contrivance but a true telling. Writing for the secular world of the twentieth century, Tolkien begins with the human things (the decent, comfortable society of the Shire with all its failings and meannesses) and ends with God. See also Levitin (II-373).

II-551    Reis, R. H. "George MacDonald: Founder of the Feast." *Tolkien Journal*, 2, No. 1 (1966), 3–5.

> Mythopoetic fiction is a genre "which is fantastic in the sense that it does *not* attempt to create a world like ours (as the novel does), but *does* attempt to cast over its created world an aura of moral and psychological truth" (p. 3). There is no continuous tradition of it before MacDonald, but he started a flowering of the genre. C. S. Lewis was strongly influenced by MacDonald, and Williams and Tolkien may have been indirectly influenced through Lewis. See also Lochhead (II-392).

Renshaw, Robert. See Hayes (II-262).

II-552   Resnick, Henry. "An Interview with Tolkien." *Niekas*, No. 18
         (Spring, 1967), pp. 37–47.

> Transcript (with some deletions) of a telephone interview with Tolkien, and
> of a tape of a Tolkien Society of America meeting at which Resnick spoke.
> Tolkien considers "fannish" activity a game, harmless if it doesn't become
> obsessive, but he feels that no one should try to research sources or meaning
> without consulting him, and doesn't approve of his work being taught in
> schools. He reads three newspapers a day. He does not feel that Williams or
> MacDonald influenced him; as a boy, *She* interested him as much as
> anything. The seed of *LOTR* is linguistic, but he was also trying to
> modernize old myths, and he tried to give *LOTR* a steady driving climax.
> He abandoned a sequel called *The New Shadow*, in which people find that
> they cannot bear peace for a hundred years.

II-553   Resnik, Henry. "The Hobbit-Forming World of J. R. R.
         Tolkien." *Saturday Evening Post*, 2 July 1966, pp. 90–92, 94.

> On the Tolkien cult. "The majority of them [Tolkien fans] are unified not
> by a need to find ethics in a hopeless modern world or a desire for escape
> or a passion for myths and language (although these may explain their
> initial attraction to the books); rather, they share the hobbit spirit—the
> pluck, the taste for adventure, the *joie de vivre*, and, above all, the total
> commitment to their goals (once they decide to have goals) that unite them
> all" (p. 92).

II-554   Reynolds, William. "Poetry as Metaphor in *The Lord of the
         Rings*." *Mythlore*, 4, No. 4, Whole No. 16 (June, 1977), 12,
         14–16.

> "By examining in detail the three poems from *The Lord of the Rings* which
> Tolkien calls 'The Old Walking Song' and 'A Walking Song' I intend to
> demonstrate that in the metaphors of these short poems Tolkien
> encapsulates the same view of History and man's role in it that he conveys
> through the larger metaphor of the trilogy itself" (p. 12). Close reading of
> these poems shows their part in the theme of eucatastrophe. See also
> Johnston (II-310).

II-555   Richardson, Maurice. "New Novels." *New Statesman and
         Nation*, 18 December 1954, pp. 835–36.

> Review of *TT*. It is a children's story that is far too long and blown up, the
> imagination is of low potential, and the characters are without
> individuality. However, some parts, such as the battle scenes, are well done.
> See Huxley (II-299) and Mitchison (II-435).

II-556   Ricks, Christopher. "Prophets." *New York Review of Books*, 24
         January 1974, pp. 44–46.

> Review of Sale, *Modern Heroism* (II-585), and of Frank Kermode, *D. H.
> Lawrence*. Tolkien, "our Ossian," receives a brief dismissal for his flaccid
> style and donnish decamping from modern life.

II-557 Ring, David. "Ad Valar Defendendi." *Tolkien Journal*, No. 15 (Summer, 1972), pp. 18, 22.

> Letter to "The Shire Post" that is a short article arguing against Randolph (II-538). The Valar did not fail in their charge; they had to allow evil in the world, since it took root by the free choice of Elves and Men, and (to a Christian like Tolkien) free will can not be abrogated. Tolkien did not create a world in which evil would always be effectively restrained because, from a storyteller's point of view, it would be too dull.

II-558 "The Ring of Romanticism." *Times Literary Supplement*, 8 June 1973, pp. 629–30.

> Review of Kocher, *Master of Middle-earth* (II-346). Kocher rightly concerns himself mostly with Tolkien's moral philosophy, but by so doing he omits, both literally and figuratively, a good deal of enchantment, including the Englishness of the Shire. He passes by a few vital properties of the Middle-earth cycle (e.g., its freeing religious imagery from the clichés of dogma into new and vivid epiphanies, and its saluting in its creatures both difference and degree), and considers Tolkien more as thinker than as artist. There is good (though sometimes superfluous) discussion of what the books are about, but little on their technique.

II-559 Roberts, Mark. "Adventure in English." *Essays in Criticism*, 6 (1956), 450–59.

> *LOTR* is just a technically competent adventure story, sprawling because it lacks a controlling vision of reality. The criteria of *OFS* fit well when applied to *LOTR*, but Tolkien's ideas are not very interesting or important. Cf. Cox (II-123), Purtill (II-535), and Reilly (II-549).

II-560 Robinson, James. "The Wizard and History: Saruman's Vision of a New Order." *Orcrist*, No. 1, (1966–67), pp. 17–23.

> Saruman represents a political philosophy, widespread today, of pragmatism and compromise with moral principle to attain a later good. *LOTR* shows that his attempt to transcend good and evil leads him to fall victim to evil.

II-561 Robson, W. W. *Modern English Literature*. Oxford Univ. Press, 1970.

> A discussion of the "Anglo-Oxford group" on pp. 146–47 notes that Tolkien's work was the most interesting in literary achievement. *LOTR* finds analogues in *Beowulf*, Malory, the sagas, folk and fairy tales, but it is relevant to the spiritual struggles of our time.

II-562 Rockow, Karen. "Funeral Customs in Tolkien's Trilogy." *Unicorn*, 2, No. 3 (Winter, 1973), 22–30. Reprinted as a monograph. Baltimore: T-K Graphics, 1973.

> Notes literary and archaeological sources (mostly from Old English and Old Norse, but also from Celtic sources) that underlay the various funeral customs in *LOTR*.

II-563       . "Voice from the Barrow." *Unicorn*, 1, No. 4 (Fall-Winter, 1969), 7–8.

> Reviews of *Bored of the Rings* (II-31), a book which shows that it is not really possible to parody Tolkien at length, and of Carter, *Tolkien: A Look Behind The Lord of the Rings* (II-89), which finds it joyous indeed, but also rambling, condescending, and sometimes inaccurate.

II-564 Rogers, Deborah Champion Webster. "Everyclod and Everyhero: The Image of Man in Tolkien." In Lobdell (II-388), pp. 69–76.

> Hobbits are "normal people" par excellence, but the heroic sleeps within them. Aragorn is a hero already, but what sleeps within him is kingship. Individually, we humans are hobbits; collectively, we are Aragorn.

II-565       . "The Fictitious Characters of C. S. Lewis and J. R. R. Tolkien in Relation to Their Medieval Sources." Ph.D. diss., University of Wisconsin, 1972.

> There are seven sections: The Hero, the Lady, the Companion, the Villain, the Magician, Non-Human Beings, and Man in general. Though Tolkien's way of characterizing appears more medieval, Lewis's "image of Man" is more in harmony with the Middle Ages and Tolkien's with the twentieth century. See *DAI*, 34 (1973), 334A. See also Rogers (II-567).

II-566       , and Ivor A. Rogers. *J. R. R. Tolkien*. Boston: Twayne Publishers, A Division of G. K. Hall and Co., 1980. Twayne's English Authors Series, TEAS 304.

> "The purpose of this book is to introduce briefly and clearly Tolkien's life (chapter 1), some of his mental furniture of a literary kind (chapter 2), and his major short works [*ATB, FGH, LBN, SWM*] and his long fiction [*H, LOTR, Silm*] (chapters 3–6). The concluding chapter shows how Tolkien's art and values jointly contradict those most conspicuous in the Europe of his adulthood" (quoted from preface). An appendix prints a letter from Tolkien to the first author dated 25 October 1958 (see I-83). A Selected Bibliography (pp. 151–58) of primary and secondary sources and of phonorecords includes short annotations.

II-567       . "A Proposal for a Doctoral Dissertation." *Orcrist*, No. 4 [also *Tolkien Journal*, 4, No. 3, Whole No. 13] (1969–70), 21–23.

> The original proposal for her dissertation (II-565).

      . See also under her maiden name: Webster, Deborah.

II-568 Rogers, H. L. "Beowulf's Three Great Fights." *Review of English Studies*, New Series, 6 (1955), 339–55.

> He argues that the three battles against Grendel, Grendel's mother, and the dragon form a progression, and hence he doesn't agree with Tolkien's view (I-35) that the structure of the poem is a balance of youth and age, endings and beginnings. See also Kaske (II-319).

Rogers, Ivor A. See Rogers (II-566).

II-569   Roos, Richard, S. J. "Middle Earth in the Classroom: Studying J. R. R. Tolkien." *English Journal*, 58 (1969), 1175–80.

> Tolkien successfully plays four roles in his writing. As novelist, he welds his fantastic geography and history, characterization, and complex plot to work toward a unified effect. As linguist, he plays cleverly with language, shows himself a student of denotation and connotation, and his Appendixes E and F are useful for teaching the generative principles of language. He is also a sensitive and expressive poet, and examples of ballads, pastorals, songs of war, prophecy, lament, and protest, and parallels to Greek choral odes, can be shown to students in his work. As mythologist, he is familiar with classical, Germanic, and Eastern myth, and has created a myth of the beginning of an era. *LOTR* is thematically unified and meaningful through issues like the war against the power of evil in the world, the search for the transcendent, and the ascendency of Man in the person of Aragorn. It is not feasible to work with all of *H* and *LOTR* because of time and expense, so *FR*, with its rich content, might serve as the center of concentration. Cf. Taylor (II-647).

Rosen, Mel. See Becker (II-37).

II-570   Rosenberg, Jerome. "The Humanity of Sam Gamgee." *Mythlore*, 5, No. 1, Whole No. 17 (May, 1978), 10–11.

> Sam's commonplace nature is an important aspect of *LOTR*. See also Rang (II-539).

II-571   Rossi, Lee Donald. "The Politics of Fantasy: C. S. Lewis and J. R. R. Tolkien." Ph.D. diss., Cornell University, 1972.

> These authors have been among the most sensitive registers of the moral crisis in modern capitalist society. Unhappy with present reality and seeing no possibility of any kind of radical improvement by the unaided action of the human will, they produced complementary fictions. Lewis concentrated on a search for alternate realities and values, while Tolkien focused on the dangers of political reality. See *DAI*, 33 (1973), 5195–96A.

II-572   Rossi, Sergio. Review of *GGK*, 2nd ed. (I-17). *Studi Medievali* (Spoleto), series 3, IX, i (1968), 444–45.

> In Italian. The edition is exemplary with regard to the text, notes, and glossary, but Davis's intentional omission of critical interpretation is a weakness.

II-573   Rottensteiner, Franz. *The Fantasy Book: An Illustrated History from Dracula to Tolkien.* London: Thames and Hudson, 1978. New York: Macmillan, 1978.

> Tolkien's type of "alternative world" creation is only one aspect of fantastic literature, but a very important one.

II-574   Rubey, Daniel. "Identity and Alterity in the Criticism of

J. R. R. Tolkien and D. W. Robertson, Jr." *The Literary Review*, 23 (1980), 577–611.

> When seeking to explicate the literature of an earlier period, a critic may look at its "identity," or those features of a work which speak to his or her own experience in the present, or at its "alterity," its alien character. Tolkien's work, both as critic and as artist, reflects his own experience.

II-575   Ruskin, Laura A. "Three Good Mothers: Galadriel, Psyche, and Sybil Coningsby." *Mythcon I Proceedings* (4–7 September 1970). Ed. Glen GoodKnight. Los Angeles: Mythopoeic Society, 1971, pp. 12–14.

> These three characters are archetypes of the ideal Mother. Galadriel in *LOTR* "personifies the fundamental Mother Moon of the primitive man, from whom flow blessings and good gifts" (p. 14).

II-576   Russell, Mariann Barbara. "The Idea of the City of God." Ph.D. diss., Columbia University, 1965.

> Emphasis on the myth of the City that figures prominently in the work of Charles Williams, but with reference to Lewis and to Tolkien. Cf. Moorman (II-447). See *DA*, 26 (1965), 3350–51.

II-577   _____. " 'The Northern Literature' and the Ring Trilogy." *Mythlore*, 5, No. 2, Whole No. 18 (Autumn, 1978), 41–42.

> Tolkien saw the tradition of English chivalry as centering on the northern virtue of indomitable will. This is found in a purer form in a loyal subordinate than in the Hero himself, since he tends to have also a desire for personal glory. *LOTR* illustrates this.

II-578   Ryan, J[ohn] S[prott]. "German Mythology Applied—The Extension of the Literary Folk Memory." *Folklore*, 77 (Spring, 1966), 45-59. Reprinted in Ryan (II-580), Ch. 8, pp. 129–40.

> Discusses the evocations of some of Tolkien's special words and names, in relation to philological meaning and Germanic myth. See also Parker (II-492).

II-579   _____. "Modern English Myth-Makers, An Examination of the Imaginative Writings of Charles Williams, C. S. Lewis, and J. R. R. Tolkien." Doctoral diss., Cambridge University (U.K.), 1967.

> Not seen.

II-580   _____. *Tolkien: Cult or Culture?* Armidale, New South Wales, Australia: Univ. of New England, 1969.

> Lectures presented at a seminar held in Armidale from 23–25 May 1969 under the auspices of the Department of University Extension of the University of New England. The prefatory matter, thirteen chapters, and five appendixes provide a detailed account of Tolkien's life and academic career; discuss the intellectual and spiritual context of the Christian

viewpoints of the Inklings; examine the heroic and medieval literatures on which Tolkien draws for so much of his imaginary world; and treat the style and themes (including the nature of power, recovery, determinism, archetypes, and time) in all of Tolkien's work published to that date. Reprints "Goblin Feet" (I-3), p. 209. See also Crago (II-125, II-126 and II-127) and Ryan (II-578).

II-581    "The Saga of Middle Earth." *Times Literary Supplement*, 25 November 1955, p. 704.

Review of *RK*, with reference to the complete book of *LOTR*. The fantasy is massive and energetic, with a power of conviction coming from the detailed history of the invented world. The good do not seem to be outstandingly virtuous nor the evil outstandingly wicked (cf. Auden, II-16). There is no consistent allegorical attack on mechanism; even the idyllic agriculture of the Shire is already a complex product of an advanced civilization (cf. Brown, II-73). For the *TLS* reviews of the two earlier volumes, see II-178 and II-275.

II-582    St. Clair, Gloria Ann Strange Slaughter. "Studies in the Sources of J. R. R. Tolkien's *The Lord of the Rings*." Ph.D. diss., University of Oklahoma, 1970.

*LOTR* is basically a saga, working with Northern materials, and the Old Norse civilization provides a closer pattern for that of Gondor than any other civilization does. See also Green (II-245). See *DAI*, 30 (1970), 5001A.

II-583    ———. *"The Lord of the Rings* as Saga." *Mythlore*, 6, No. 2, Whole No. 20 (Spring, 1979), 11-16.

*LOTR* has been assigned by different critics to such genres as fairy story (see Barber, II-23, Reilly, II-549, and Roberts, II-559), the traditional epic (see Beatie, II-32), the romance (see Blissett, II-53 and Thomson, II-649), and the novel, but it should be classed as a saga, a genre which more thoroughly explains its structure, style, and orientation. Cf. Ch. 2 of her dissertation (II-582).

II-584    Sale, Roger. "England's Parnassus: C. S. Lewis, Charles Williams, and J. R. R. Tolkien." *Hudson Review*, 17 (1964), 203-25.

The others get short shrift, but Tolkien earns praise for his wasteland motif and his gift for storytelling. The section on Tolkien is expanded in Sale (II-585 and II-586).

II-585    ———. *Modern Heroism: Essays on D. H. Lawrence, William Empson, and J. R. R. Tolkien*. Berkeley and Los Angeles: Univ. of California Press, 1973.

The main part of the discussion on Tolkien is in Ch. 4, "Tolkien and Frodo Baggins" (pp. 193–240), a revision of his earlier essay of the same title (II-586), but Tolkien is also mentioned passim in the "Introduction" (pp. 1–15) and the "Afterword" (pp. 241–56). For reviews, see III-B-28.

II-586 _____. "Tolkien and Frodo Baggins." In Isaacs and Zimbardo (II-307), pp. 247–88.

> Reworking of Sale (II-584), excising the treatment of Williams and Lewis and greatly expanding the treatment of Tolkien. What fires Tolkien's imagination is not the traditional heroism of warriors borrowed from old books, but the lonely heroism of Frodo. Frodo understands and rejects the Ring, which is a symbol of "the final possessiveness, the ultimate in power that binds things apart from ourselves to ourselves" (p. 264). See also his further revision of this essay in II-585.

II-587 _____. "Tolkien as Translator." *Parnassus: Poetry in Review*, 4 (1976), 183–91.

> Review article on *GGKPO* (I-73). It is a solid, respectable book, which could be popular as a classroom text. If one wanted to read just *GGK*, there are smoother translations available, but Tolkien's is a better "pony" because he is good at building bridges between fourteenth-century English and our own. His translations are also revealing about his own fiction. See also Sale (II-589).

II-588 _____. "Tolkien's private lifetime companion finally comes to life." *Chicago Tribune Book World*, 11 September 1977, p. 1.

> Review of *Silm*. Though Tolkien tries to achieve a tragic sense of loss, this outline only manages a feeling of sadness undercut by its delight in splendid names. This lacks the narrative detail and interest of *LOTR*, and will appeal mostly to cultists.

II-589 _____. "Wonderful to relate." *Times Literary Supplement* (London), 12 March 1976, p. 289.

> Reviews of *GGKPO* (I-73) and of Manlove, *Modern Fantasy* (II-402). Manlove's book could have been useful, but fails because it has no sense of story. Tolkien translations are welcome, especially since *Pearl* and *Orfeo* are so seldom made available to non-specialists (see also his longer review in II-587).

II-590 Salu, Mary, and Robert T. Farrell, eds. *J. R. R. Tolkien, Scholar and Storyteller: Essays In Memoriam*. Ithaca and London: Cornell Univ. Press, 1979.

> *Festschrift.* This features ten essays on Old and Middle English and Old Norse literature, the London *Times* obituary (II-534), Tolkien's valedictory address (I-81), a reminiscence by d'Ardenne (II-13), essays by Brewer (II-70), Dowie (II-159), and Shippey (II-610), and a "Handlist" of Tolkien's published work by Carpenter (II-84). For another *Festschrift*, see Davis (II-143).

II-591 Sanders, Joseph Lee. "Fantasy in the Twentieth Century British Novel." Ph.D. diss., Indiana University, 1972.

> Fantasy is a literary form that utilizes basic fears and desires in concrete form and that is based on the belief that people are incapable of

understanding or controlling themselves or their environment. Contemporary fantasy novels accommodate a wide range of viewpoints, as in the work of William Golding, Mervyn Peake, and Tolkien. *LOTR* is based on a Christian view of existence in which people are able to ally themselves with supernatural power in the struggle against the forces that would debase and destroy them. See *DAI*, 33 (1972), 764A.

II-592    Sapiro, Leland. Review of Hillegas, *Shadows of Imagination* (II-277). *Riverside Quarterly*, 4, No. 3 (June, 1970), 210-11.

The divergent views given in different essays often correct or complement one another. The most successful essay is that by Hughes (II-289).

II-593    Sardello, Robert J. "An Empirical-Phenomenological Study of Fantasy, with a note on J. R. R. Tolkien and C. S. Lewis." *Psychocultural Review*, 2 (1978), 203–20.

Not seen.

II-594    Savage, Henry L. Review of *GGK*, 2nd ed. (I-17). *Medium Aevum*, 39 (1970), 218–23.

Lengthy comments on the excellence of the first edition. Davis has performed well in absorbing and adding to what his predecessors had done, but there are numerous lines where the reviewer prefers other readings than those adopted by Davis.

II-595    Sayer, George. Notes on the record jackets of *J. R. R. Tolkien reads and sings his "The Hobbit" and "The Fellowship of the Ring"* (Caedmon Record TC 1477) and *J. R. R. Tolkien reads and sings his "The Lord of the Rings": "The Two Towers," "The Return of the King"* (Caedmon Record TC 1478). New York: Caedmon Records, 1975.

The first eight paragraphs on each jacket are the same on both, and tell of the visit by Tolkien during which he taped the passages. The remainder describes and comments on the selections. See also I-74 and I-75.

II-596    Schaumberger, Joe. Review of Carter, *Tolkien: A Look Behind The Lord of the Rings* (II-89). *Luna*, No. 8 (January, 1970), 26.

This is a lively and entertaining study of the plot, sources, and literary effects of *LOTR* and *H*.

II-597    Scheps, Walter. "The Fairy-Tale Morality of *The Lord of the Rings*." In Lobdell (II-388), pp. 43–56.

Good and evil in *LOTR* are almost always generically defined, and we can usually judge a character according to geography, ancestry, diction, and color imagery. If we attempt to transfer the moral values inherent in *LOTR* to the "real world" we find that they are paternalistic, fascistic, and even irrelevant. The so-called fairy tale is the other form of literature in which such moral values are inherent. Tolkien was aware of this difficulty and in his foreword to *LOTR* warned against any "allegorical" reading of his self-contained fictive world. Cf. Reilly (II-549) and Sirridge (II-614).

II-598  Schlau, Stacey. "Modern Romance: A Study of Techniques and Themes." Ph.D. diss., The City University of New York, 1975.

William Morris, Lord Dunsany, Mervyn Peake, and Tolkien are four representative authors whose works are used to analyze and describe the genre of romance as written in modern times. Chapters discuss the characteristics of the quest, landscape, character, structure and language, and a final chapter places romance in the larger family of modern antirealistic fiction (comparing it primarily to science fiction and the suspense-romance). See *DAI*, 36 (1976), 4480A.

II-599  Schlobin, Roger C. *The Literature of Fantasy: A Comprehensive, Annotated Bibliography of Modern Fantasy Fiction.* New York: Garland, 1979.

Frequent mention of Tolkien's work and influence. See pp. 242–45 for descriptions of *FGH, T&L, Silm, SWM, TR, H* and *LOTR*. Cf. Tymn (II-672) and Waggoner (II-683).

II-600  Schmidt, Sandra. "Taking fairy tales seriously." *Christian Science Monitor*, 15 April 1965, p. 11.

Review of *T&L. LBN*, though charmingly written, is disappointing because it is also sententious and sentimental. *LOTR* is a better investigation of the fairy tale; there, the conflict between Good and Evil develops from the simple black and white of unalloyed good versus pure evil into the more complex patterns of grey that color actual moral decisions.

II-601  Schroth, Raymond A. "Lord of the Rings." *America*, 116 (18 February 1967), 254.

Though he finds *LOTR* "too long, too cluttered, too much," and the appendixes merely a treasure-trove of trivia for pseudo-scholarly investigation, he does not think that Tolkien's work has only the dubious value of a psychologically refreshing escape to a simplistic view of reality. Rather, the work is a myth, inviting man to witness with new eyes the secrets of the earth, at the same time warning us against the spiritual idolatry of making power the object of our ultimate concern.

II-602  Schultz, Elizabeth. "Do Elves Live in Those Woods?" *Fantasiae*, 6, No. 5, Whole No. 62 (May, 1978), 1, 3.

Middle-earth provides an accurate reflection of life because, for all its troubles, it is all of what we most deeply believe in and love.

II-603  Scott, Nan C. "No 'Intermediary.' " *Saturday Review*, 23 October 1965, p. 56.

Letter. The article by Dempsey (II-151) implies that Ace Books sent a "polite note" to Tolkien via Mrs. Scott, which she denies. She considers Ace's conduct unethical. Donald A. Wollheim has a letter on the same page defending Ace Books. See also II-2.

II-604  _____. "War and Pacifism in *The Lord of the Rings.*" *Tolkien Journal*, No. 15 (Summer, 1972), pp. 23–25, 27–30.

A paper given at the Tolkien Conference at Belknap College in 1968. Tolkien, in *H* and *LOTR*, carefully balances the ugliness and attractiveness of war. He seems to be pessimistic about the prospects for a long-term peace among mankind (if not among Hobbits), but to prefer other arts to the martial. Frodo becomes a complete pacifist, but, unable to harm any creature even to defend others, he can only depart for a more perfect world. There is comfort in the circumstance that none of the victories in war would have preserved Middle-earth but for the four separate acts of mercy in which Gollum is spared by Bilbo, Frodo, Faramir, and Sam. See her letter of 10 November 1972 commenting on this essay in *Orcrist*, No. 8 (1977), p. 25. On the nature of war in Middle-earth, see also Lloyd (II-383).

————. See Etkin (II-181).

II-605   Scriven, R. C. "Hobbit's Apotheosis: The World of Professor Tolkien." *Tablet*, 207 (11 February 1956) 129–30.

Review of *RK*, but makes reference to all of *LOTR*. Tolkien had drawn on his specialized knowledge of myth and legend, yet *LOTR* is original in treatment, style and characterization, and all of these elements blend to make this epic fairy tale a work for adults rather than for children. Also refers to radio dramatizations by Terence Tiller and Sylvia Goodall.

II-606   Searles, Baird. "Confessions of a Tolkien Fiend." In Becker (II-37), pp. 110–13, 116–19.

He discusses his enthusiasm for Tolkien's work from childhood on, his dismay at the cult, various editions of *H* and *LOTR*, illustrating and animating Tolkien's stories, and other fantasies which have some of the same qualities as Tolkien's work.

II-607   Seidman, Cory. "A Uniform System of Tengwar for English." *Tolkien Journal*, 2, No. 1 (1966), 8–9.

She uses the Tehtar for phonemic notation, based on the method of Trager and Smith.

————. See also under her married name: Panshin, Cory.

II-608   Serjeantson, Mary S. Review of "Sigelwara Land" (I-25 and I-29). *The Year's Work in English Studies*, 15 (1934), 81.

She calls the essay "interesting and suggestive."

II-609   Shaw, Greg. "People Who Read J. R. R. Tolkien's *Lord of the Rings*: Some Thoughts." *Unicorn*, 1, No. 1 (1967), 18–19.

Three types of people comprise the ranks of organized Tolkien fandom: the science fiction-fantasy freak; the neurotic youngster who withdraws into the book and often develops a compulsive fixation on it; and the college student, who finds parallels between his own field of interest and Tolkien's books. Shaw edited the "fanzine" *Entmoot*, but many of its readers were offended when he took it to a "psychedelic" orientation. He sees as "the primary event, or trend of this century, the coming-together and

intercombination of all forms of thought and art and life" (p. 19), and
hopes to apply the beauty of *LOTR* to the mundane world. See also Helms
(II-266) and Lerner (II-368).

II-610  Shippey, T. A. "Creation from Philology in *The Lord of the
Rings*." In Salu and Farrell (II-590), pp. 286–316.

Though the linguistic basis of Tolkien's art is often dismissed as trivial or a
mere philological game, it is highly significant. Tolkien corrects
contemporary dictionary definitions of "dwarf" and "elf," develops old
meanings of "ent" and "orc," makes good use of Welsh and Old Norse and
Middle and Old English (especially *Beowulf*) and of proverbs. Even a
reader unaware of the specific linguistic source (who may not know, for
example, of King Froda the peacemaker standing in back of Frodo) feels
the appropriateness of the sounds and the depth lent by the languages.

II-611  _____. "The Foolhardy Philologist." *Times Literary
Supplement*, 13 May 1977, p. 583.

Review article on Carpenter, *Tolkien: a biography* (II-86). The cover calls
this article "Tolkien and the Norman Conquest," and Shippey notes that
*LOTR* purposely avoids words of Latin and especially French origin in an
attempt "to re-establish the mythological creatures and heroes of England
as they would have been if only the French had let them alone." Tolkien
believed that he could see into antiquity through language and ancestral
memory, and that his mythology, though it came from his own head,
reflected truth which he did not originate. Carpenter's achievement is to
have taken reminiscences, confusion, and unordered manuscripts and
written a clear and coherent account.

II-612  Sibley, Brian. "History for Hobbits." *The Listener*, 2 October
1980, pp. 443–44.

Review of *UT*. Not everything here is a "tale," but everything is
"unfinished" in some sense (sometimes lacking an ending, sometimes
unpolished, sometimes little more than scraps held together by CT's
commentaries). Some of the later fragments are of interest to readers who
know and admire *LOTR*, but who are this side of slavish adulation. The
book adds little to Tolkien's reputation or to the appreciation of his other
work, but neither does it take anything from them.

II-613  Sievert, William A. "A Mania for Middle-earth." *Chronicle of
Higher Education*, 6 February 1978, pp. 3–5.

Comments from Ann N. Barrett, Humphrey Carpenter, Robert Clarke,
Charles B. Elston, Glen GoodKnight, and C. S. Kilby are included in a
description of the growth of a campus cult into a widespread passion for
the writings of Tolkien.

II-614  Sirridge, Mary. "J. R. R. Tolkien and Fairy Tale Truth." *British
Journal of Aesthetics*, 15 (1975), 81–92.

Language is used for other purposes than making statements. The creation
of a fairy-tale world is a "thought-experiment" and is not even an indirect

statement about this world. Questions about moral worth may still be asked, however, and actions weighed against roughly similar actions in the real world. *LOTR* is morally quite complex. Cf. Reilly (II-549) and Scheps (II-597).

II-615    Sisam, Kenneth. *The Structure of Beowulf*. Oxford: Clarendon, 1965.

He argues for a tripartite structure in *Beowulf* instead of the two-part structure discerned by Tolkien. See also I-35 and Kaske (II-319).

II-616    Sklar, Robert. "Tolkien and Hesse: Top of the Pops." *Nation*, 204 (8 May 1967), 598–601.

These are the two authors who speak most intimately to and for the present generation of youth. *LOTR* provides "a most dramatic and mythic analogy for the rite of passage to maturity" and "a paradigm for action" since it "simply states: this is the task; are you willing to carry it through?" (p. 600).

II-617    Slater, Ian Myles. "By elf messenger." *Fantasiae*, 4, No. 10, Whole No. 43 (October, 1976), 1, 3.

Review of *FCL*.

II-618    _____. "A Long and Secret Labour: The Forging of The Silmarillion: Songs of Light." *Fantasiae*, 6, No. 3, Whole No. 60 (March, 1978), 6–11.

He discusses Tolkien's acquaintance with Finnish and the possible influence of that language on Quenya, notes parallels between *The Kalevala* and *Silm*, and briefly recounts the history of Elias Lönnrot and his compilation and composition of *The Kalevala*.

II-619    _____. "Notes & Comments." *Fantasiae*, 5, No. 6, Whole No. 51 (June, 1977), 1, 9.

Review of Carpenter, *Tolkien* (II-86). This book "shows how an accurate account of a writer's life can contribute to literary *history*" which is different from criticism but is also important.

II-620    _____. "Why?" *Fantasiae*, 5, Nos. 11–12, Whole Nos. 56–57 (November-December, 1977), 6–8.

He speculates on why Tolkien felt there was not already "a mythology for England" and so needed to create one in *Silm*.

II-621    _____. Review of Carter, *Imaginary Worlds* (II-88). Part I in *Fantasiae*, 1, No. 4 (July, 1973), 8. Part II in *Fantasiae*, 1, No. 5 (August, 1973), 9.

". . . the haste, clumsiness, misinformation, and sheer confusion demonstrated in this volume undermine any possible value of the criticism" (p. 8 of Part I). Part I demonstrates failure to carry out thorough research of ancient and medieval literature; Part II notes errors in the bibliography.

II-622    _____. Review of Day, *A Tolkien Bestiary* (II-144). *Fantasiae*, 8, No. 6, Whole No. 87 (June, 1980), 5–6.

Review of the text, published jointly with Zuber's review of the illustrations (II-755). This is not a reference book, but is valuable chiefly for the illustrations.

II-623 _____. Review of Helms, *Tolkien's World* (II-270). *Fantasiae*, 2, No. 6 (June, 1974), 8.

This compact, very readable volume sets Tolkien in the mainstream of European literature and critical tradition; is good on the structure and aesthetics of *LOTR*; demonstrates the relationships of *H* with *OFS* and with the essay on *Beowulf* (I-35); shows the structural similarities of *H* and *LOTR*, and the parallel structures of Books I and II of *FR*; and has a funny and sometimes thought-provoking "reply" to William Empson's "Freudian" reading of *Alice in Wonderland*.

II-624 _____. Review of Kilby, *Tolkien and The Silmarillion* (II-338). *Fantasiae*, 4, No. 6, Whole No. 39 (June, 1976), 6.

II-625 _____. Review of Lobdell, *A Tolkien Compass* (II-388). *Fantasiae*, 3, No. 4, Whole No. 25 (April, 1975), 5–6.

He cites Christensen (II-97) and West (II-712) as the two best essays and Scheps (II-597) as the worst, while Tolkien's "Guide" (I-72) is the most important single feature.

II-626 _____. Review of *GGKPO* (I-73). *Fantasiae*, 8, No. 4, Whole No. 85 (April, 1980), 6–11.

He provides considerable detail on the Middle English background of the works translated.

II-627 Slattery, Sister Mary Francis. Review of Reilly, *Romantic Religion* (II-547). *Journal of Aesthetics and Art Criticism*, 30 (1972), 406–07.

The "religion" of the book's title seems to belong more properly to the realm of aesthetics, and "Christian" refers more to the historical epoch of the four authors than to the character of their religion. The treatment is essentially historical, but the last chapter sprawls with weak theoretical comment and an unspoken assumption that literature is the handmaiden of religion and philosophy.

II-628 Slavin, Jan. Review of *SWM and FGH* (Ballantine, March, 1969). *Luna*, No. 8 (January, 1970), p. 27.

These are spun sugar delights, containing only wholesome, nourishing characters, lacking the contrast and complexity of *LOTR*, enjoyable but shallow.

II-629 Slethaug, Gordon E. "Tolkien, Tom Bombadil, and the Creative Imagination." *English Studies in Canada*, 4 (1978), 341–50.
Not seen.

Sloman, Peter. See Boardman (II-55).

II-630   Smith, Irene. "The People's Hero." *New York Times Book Review*, 26 November 1950, p. 50.

> Review of *FGH* in two short paragraphs, mostly plot summary.

II-631   Smith, Janet Adam. "Does Frodo Live?" *The New York Review of Books*, (14 December 1972), 19–21.

> Review article on Kocher, *Master of Middle-earth* (II-346). She agrees with Kocher's general estimate of Tolkien's worth, with some reservations. The device of the hobbits—small, sensible, humdrum folk—is excellent, a necessary counterpoint to the magical and heroic happenings around them; still, the world of the Shire is made of thinner stuff (Chesterton, Merrie England, the villagers of British detective stories) than is the world outside it (with its echoes of romance and saga, *Beowulf* and *Maldon*, Malory, Morris, Browning). Tolkien uses many styles, fitting each to the scene, but not always to equally good effect. *LOTR* can be read as a parable of power, the environment, anti-imperialism, or many another preoccupation of the reader. David Levine contributes a caricature of Tolkien with his pipe.

Smith, Nancy. See II-534.

II-632   Smith, Philip. *The Lord of the Rings and Other Bookbindings.* Redhill, Surrey, England: C. P. Smith, 1970.

> He describes his "book-wall" of *LOTR* and his intentions in making it. See also Coleman (II-113).

II-633   Spacks, Patricia Meyer. "Ethical Pattern in *Lord of the Rings*." *Critique*, 3, No. 1 (Spring-Fall, 1959), 30–42.

> The "force and complexity of its moral and theological scheme provides the fundamental power of" *LOTR* (p. 30). See also Spacks (II-634).

II-634   _____. "Power and Meaning in *The Lord of the Rings*." In Isaacs and Zimbardo (II-307), pp. 81–99.

> Revision of Spacks (II-633). The expanded conclusion sees *LOTR* as stylistically derivative and often impoverished and pretentious, and suggests that the mass of detail at times obscures the imaginative energy and meaning of the action.

II-635   Spaulding, Martha. Review of *Silm.* *Atlantic*, 240 (October, 1977), 105.

> *Silm* is of scholarly interest as background material for those who approach Tolkien's other work in all seriousness, but it has neither the charm of *H* nor the magic of *LOTR*. It is probably a faithful indication of the scope of Tolkien's imagination, but his attention to detail makes it dull going. The bits of enchantment (the memorably grotesque Ungoliant, the love story of Beren and Lúthien) are imprisoned in a morass of multiple-named battles, characters, and places, so that one rapidly loses track of—and interest in—who has gone where and why.

II-636   Spice, Wilma Helen. "A Jungian View of Tolkien's 'Gandalf': An Investigation of Enabling and Exploitative Power in

Counseling and Psychotherapy from the Viewpoint of
Analytical Psychology." Ph.D. diss., University of Pittsburgh,
1976.

> Gandalf, whose functions in *LOTR* parallel the Jungian archetype of the
> Wise Old Man, is a valuable role-model for a psychotherapist. He
> demonstrates beneficial and enabling uses of power (uses which foster the
> individual fulfillment of the client and his potential) as contrasted to
> exploitative uses of power (uses through which the therapist satisfies his
> own needs at the expense of the client). See *DAI*, 37 (1976), 1417B. See also
> O'Neill (II-483).

II-637    Stein, Ruth M. "The Changing Styles in Dragons—from Fáfnir
          to Smaug." *Elementary English*, 45 (February, 1968), 179–83,
          189.

> Traces the evolution of the dragon from the stories of Sigurd, Beowulf, and
> St. George to "The Reluctant Dragon" and the beginning of the "literary
> fluff" tradition of modern dragons. Smaug, being in the old Northern
> tradition, answers our need for gutsy fictional dragons to toughen our
> hearts. Chrysophylax, however, "is no match for Smaug, either in
> wickedness, slyness, humor, or literary quality" (p. 182). Notes correlation
> between *H* and *Beowulf* (see also Christensen, II-96 and II-101) and
> between *LOTR* and Wagner's Ring cycle (see also Blissett, II-53, and Hall,
> II-251).

————. See also Taylor (II-647).

II-638    Sternlicht, Dorothy. Review of Helms, *Tolkien's World* (II-
          270). *Library Journal*, 99 (1 May 1974), 1303.

> This is a "masterstudy of a masterwork" which "adequately and creatively
> deals with and explicates the Ring epic." Helms "innovatively deals in
> depth with the totality of the Tolkien canon, using the scholarly, critical,
> and minor fiction writings to illuminate" *LOTR*.

II-639    Stevens, C. D. "High Fantasy versus Low Comedy: Humor in
          J. R. R. Tolkien." *Extrapolation*, 21 (1980), 122–29.

> Laughter-producing humor is found in *H* and, to a lesser extent, in the first
> three chapters of *LOTR*. The comic (in the regenerative and reintegrating
> sense of Northrop Frye) is also found in both works. (There is little of
> either in *Silm*, with its recurrent motif of death and loss.) There is tension
> inherent in Tolkien's attempt to combine and reconcile Christian
> "commedia" with the elegiac and epic, and in the world of high fantasy
> humor is an inadequate means of lifting the spirit from sorrow or of healing
> the wounds of loss.

II-640    Stevens, Cj. "Sound Systems of the Third Age of Middle-
          Earth." *Quarterly Journal of Speech*, 54 (October, 1968),
          232–40.

> "This present study . . . seeks to present a more compact and systematic
> overview of one aspect of the language of the Third Age: the sound
> systems. Consideration is given especially to the dialects of Eldarin" (p.
> 232). See also Foster (II-211) and II-302.

II-641   Stewart, Douglas J. "The Hobbit War." *Nation*, 9 October
1967, pp. 332–35.

> "Tolkien's endless tale of the Ring, like the Vietnamese War, depends for its
> movement and rationale upon a thoroughly muddled concept of causality"
> (p. 332), since both assume that "Good" and "Evil" are substantive things,
> apart from the good or evil moral condition of individuals, and that they
> are in themselves the causes of events. Those who consider themselves
> "Good" mindlessly and simplistically do what they are told in order to
> annihilate "Evil," overcoming not by intelligence or skill but by sheer
> determination. Hence the popularity of Tolkien's myth among the South
> Vietnamese army. The article includes a parody of the map of
> Middle-earth.

II-642   Stimpson, Catherine R. *J. R. R. Tolkien.* Columbia Essays on
Modern Writers No. 41. New York: Columbia Univ. Press,
1969.

> This monograph manages, in its forty-two pages, to give some discussion to
> all of Tolkien's fiction published to that date. While Tolkien's stories and
> style are superficially pleasing, really his prose rhythms are often bad, his
> imagery banal, his politics conservative, his morality perverse and its
> symbolic representation rigid and simplistic. He has rummaged through
> most of Western culture for his substance and style (especially Norse
> mythology, the Anglo-Saxon ethos, Celtic sources, and the English
> bourgeois pastoral idyll, all glued together with Christian ethics and
> cosmology), but lacks the Joycean energy to forge borrowed elements into
> a transcendent whole. The journey of Frodo, Sam, and Gollum to Mordor
> perhaps shows him at his best (cf. Sale, II-585). He can burlesque his
> sources and his scholarship, as in *FGH*. His verse is mild, delighting in
> strange words and metrical play, using hackneyed symbols, showing plastic
> religiosity and wistful romanticism. He is irritatingly, blandly, traditionally
> masculine. Like Hesse and Golding, he offers the seductive charm of moral
> didacticism, cloaked in remote and exotic settings. However (and here cf.
> Ellwood, II-175 and Kilby, II-334), "We need genuine myths and rich
> fantasy to minister to the profound needs he is now thought to gratify" (p.
> 45). For reviews, see III-B-29.

II-643   Straight, Michael. "Fantastic World of Professor Tolkien." *New
Republic*, 134 (16 January 1956), 24–26.

> Tolkien has added his scholar's perception and humanist's faith to his elvish
> craft to produce a gripping and meaningful fantasy in *LOTR*, which is one
> of the few works of genius in recent literature.

II-644   Strong, L. A. G. "The Pick of the Bunch." *Spectator*, 3
December 1937, p. 1024.

> Brief mention of *H* in a general review of children's books; it "should
> become a classic."

II-645   Strothman, Janet. Review of Ready, *Tolkien Relation* (II-543).
*Library Journal*, 93 (July, 1968), 2742.

The book gives biographical information and considers the deeper levels of meaning in Tolkien's work.

Studebaker, Don. See Becker (II-37).

II-646    Tabbert, Reinbert. "Bedurfnis nach Mythen: Zur Produktion der Hobbit Presse." *Merkur: Deutsche Zeitschrift für Europäisches Denken*, 32 (1978), 1034–46.
Not seen.

II-647    Taylor, William L. "Frodo Lives: J. R. R. Tolkien's The Lord of the Rings." *English Journal*, 56 (1967), 818–21.
*LOTR* is a useful pedagogical tool for helping the high school student grasp difficult concepts and values he or she meets with in other literature (e.g., the significance of fantasy and of heroic literature, the concept of fate, a sense of evil, character "types"). Cf. Roos (II-569). In a letter to the editor published in *English Journal*, 57 (1968), 252–53, Ruth M. Stein objects that using *LOTR* as a pedagogical tool will be a disaster for all concerned, since children will not read receptively any book assigned, recommended, or called a "classic" by adults.

II-648    Tedhams, Richard Warren. "An Annotated Glossary of the Proper Names in the Mythopoeic Fiction of J. R. R. Tolkien." M.A. thesis, University of Oklahoma, 1966.
Not seen.

II-649    Thompson, Kirk L. "Who Is Eldest?" *Tolkien Journal*, No. 15 (Summer, 1972), p. 19.
He quotes the relevant passages from *LOTR* and concludes that, though not all statements can be resolved with complete satisfaction, "the genesis of the races in Middle-earth occurred in the following order: Tom Bombadil, who is unique as well as eldest; then . . . Elves, Dwarves, Ents, Hobbits, and Men."

II-650    Thomson, George H. "*The Lord of the Rings*: The Novel as Traditional Romance." *Wisconsin Studies in Contemporary Literature*, 8 (1967), 43–59.
"Tolkien has been able to combine a very nearly complete catalogue of romance themes (many of them extraordinary in the highest degree) with an elaborate, capacious, immensely flexible plot structure and make of the whole a coherent and convincing modern prose narrative" (p. 50). See also Blissett (II-53) and Brewer (II-70).

II-651    _____. "Tolkien Criticism." *Tolkien Journal*, 3, No. 4, Whole No. 10 (November, 1969), 6.
This survey of reactions to *LOTR* considers the early and later reviewers, the scholars (with their emphasis on Tolkien's association with the Christian Inklings, and on language, myth, epic, and medieval narrative), and the journalists (reporting straightforwardly and with reasonable

accuracy, but routinely, Tolkien's character, sales figures, and cult status with the young). See also Beatie (II-34 and II-35), Lerner (II-368), Ward (II-695), and West (II-714).

Tiller, Terence. See Scriven (II-605).

II-652   Timmerman, John. "Tolkien's Crucible of Faith: The Sub-Creation." *Christian Century*, 91 (5 June 1974), 608–11.

Tolkien has created an accessible world by simplicity and unpretentiousness of diction, by appropriate naming of places, people, and things, by skill in evoking mood and emphasis upon human concerns. Through the enchantment of subcreation we recover the optics of insight into the human spirit and rediscover that childlike wonder at the glory of being that artists like Dickens, Hardy, and Schiller feared was irretrievably lost.

II-653   Tinkler, John. "Old English In Rohan." In Isaacs and Zimbardo (II-307), pp. 164–69.

He explains the Old English meaning of some of the names given to people, places, and things in Rohan and occasional words of the language of the Rohirrim.

II-654   Tolkien, Baillie. "Introduction" to *Drawings by Tolkien* (I-77).

II-655   ———. "Introduction" to *FCL* (I-78).

II-656   Tolkien, Christopher. *The Silmarillion by J. R. R. Tolkien: A Brief Account of the Book and Its Making*. Boston: Houghton Mifflin, 1977. Reprinted in *Mallorn*, No. 14 (1980), pp. 3–5, 7–8.

II-657   "Tolkien, J. R. R." *International Who's Who*, 34th edition. 1970–71, p. 1611.

Biographical sketch and list of publications.

II-658   "Tolkien, John Ronald Reuel." *Britannica Book of the Year*, 1974, p. 527.

Obituary. Brief summary of Tolkien's career and major publications.

II-659   Tolkien, J(ohn) R(onald) R(euel). *Encyclopedia Britannica*, 15th edition, 1974. Micropedia, Vol. X, p. 32. Macropedia, Vol. 10, p. 1222; Vol. 13, p. 279.

II-660   "Tolkien, J(ohn) R(onald) R(euel) 1892–    ." *Contemporary Authors: A Bio-Bibliographical Guide to Current Authors and Their Works*. Ed. James M. Ethridge and Barbara Kopala. Detroit: Gale Research Co., 1967, Vol. 17–18, pp. 394–96.

Outlines Tolkien's personal life and professional career, and provides a checklist of his writings and of criticism of his work. Discusses the reactions of critics, Tolkien's comments on fantasy and on his own work, and the Tolkien cult.

II-661   "Tolkien, John Ronald Reuel (1892–       )." *Guide to Catholic Literature, 1880–1940* (Detroit: Walter Romig and Co., 1940), 1141.

Notes date and place of birth, education, service in World War I, positions held at Leeds and Oxford. Lists four of his works: the essay on *Beowulf* (I-35), *H*, the Middle English vocabulary (I-6), and *GGK (I-17)*.

II-662   "Tolkien, J(ohn) R(onald) R(euel) (tôl′kēn)." *Current Biography Yearbook*, 1967, pp. 415–18. *Ibid.*, 1973, p. 462.

II-663   "The Tolkien Papers." *Mankato Studies in English*, No. 2. *Mankato State College Studies*, Vol. 2 (February, 1967).

Publishes the papers that were read at the Tolkien Symposium at Mankato on 28–29 October 1966, plus a few additional papers. See Barber (II-23), Beatie (II-32), Bisieniks (II-49), Blackmun (II-50 and II-51), Johnston (II-310), Levitin (II-370), Miller (II-428), Norwood (II-476), and Rang (II-539). Reprinted by the American Tolkien Society.

II-664   "Tolkien Notes." *Tolkien Journal*, 2, No. 1 (1966), 2, 8.

On the pronunciation of "Meriadoc" and "Michel," and Tolkien's literal translation of "A Elbereth Gilthoniel" (cf. *RGEO*).

II-665   "Tolkien Notes." *Tolkien Journal*, 2, No. 2 (1966), 2.

East of Rhun are Asia and Japan, south of Harad is Africa, and Middle-earth is Europe.

II-666   Torrens, James. "With Tolkien in Middle-earth." *Good Work*, 31 (Winter, 1968), 17–23.

Not seen.

II-667   Traversi, Derek A. "The Realm of Gondor." *Month*, 15 (June, 1956), 370–71.

Review of *RK*. The verisimilitude of Tolkien's imaginary world and the fitting tone of dignity and remoteness caught by the writing are praiseworthy. But this achievement cannot be reproduced, and so cannot serve as a model for future literary creations.

Trickett, Rachel. See II-305.

II-668   Tunick, Barry. "Social Philosophy in *The Lord of the Rings*." *Tolkien Journal*, 2, No. 2 (1966), 9.

Though the author is a liberal, democratic, would-be pacifist, he enjoyed *LOTR* in spite of its being conservative, and authoritarian, and its glorifying of violence and showing of a romantic idealism. Tolkien was writing escape fantasy, not socialist realism, and has marvelous abilities as a storyteller. See also O'Connor (II-478) and Scott (II-604).

II-669   Turner, Alice K. Obituary. *Publishers Weekly*, 17 September
         1973, p. 32.

II-670   Tyler, J. E. A. *The New Tolkien Companion*. London:
         Macmillan, 1979. New York: St. Martin's, 1979.
> Revised and updated version of II-671, taking cognizance of *Silm*.

II-671   _____. *The Tolkien Companion*. London: Macmillan, 1976,
         New York: St. Martin's, 1976.
> This dictionary covering all of Tolkien's published work to that date takes
> the whimsical view that the fiction was really translation of ancient texts.
> This book does not refer to page numbers in Tolkien's books, except in a
> few instances. There is some speculation, labelled as such. Translations are
> suggested for non-English words left untranslated by Tolkien. Revised and
> updated in II-670. See also Day (II-144), and Foster (II-207 and II-208).
> For reviews, see III-B-30.

II-672   Tymn, Marshall, Kenneth Zahorski, and Robert Boyer, eds.
         *Fantasy Literature: A Core Collection and Reference Guide*.
         New York and London: R. R. Bowker, 1979.
> Frequent mention of Tolkien's work and influence. See pp. 162–68 for
> annotations of *H*, *LOTR*, *FGH*, *SWM*, *FCL*, and *Silm*. Cf. Schlobin (II-
> 599) and Waggoner (II-683).

II-673   Ugolnik, Anthony J. "*Wordhord Onleac*: The Mediaeval
         Sources of J. R R. Tolkien's Linguistic Aesthetic." *Mosaic: A
         Journal for the Comparative Study of Literature and Ideas*, 10,
         No. 2 (Winter, 1977), 15–31.
> Tolkien, a modern defender of Ingeld against Alcuin's strictures, drew his
> aesthetic of language from such medieval sources as Isidore of Seville and
> Anglo-Saxon oral-formulaic poetry. Linguistic analysis of Quenya and the
> Black Speech shows what makes one language beautiful and "good" and
> the other ugly and "evil"; and the other languages of Middle-earth are also
> appropriate to their speakers. Tolkien's linguistic aesthetic is fundamental
> to his literary art.

         Unwin, Rayner. See II-3 and II-393.

II-674   Unwin, Sir Stanley. *The Truth About a Publisher: An
         Autobiographical Record*. London: George Allen and Unwin,
         1960.
> Ch. 13, "The Nineteen-Thirties," discusses *H* on p. 233, and Ch. 16, "Post-
> War Years," discusses *LOTR* on pp. 300–01. For more information on the
> background of the publication of these books, see Carpenter (II-86).

II-675   Urang, Gunnar. *Shadows of Heaven: Religion and Fantasy in
         the Writing of C. S. Lewis, Charles Williams, and J. R. R.
         Tolkien*. Philadelphia: United Church Press, 1971.
> For reviews, see III-B-31.

II-676    _____. "Tolkien's Fantasy: The Phenomenology of Hope." In
          Hillegas (II-277), pp. 97–110.

> Tolkien's conviction that fantasy satisfies certain primordial human desires
> gives his work a dimension of wonder; the thrust of mythical allegory gives
> *LOTR* a dimension of import and perhaps of incipient belief. Tolkien's
> fantasy speaks of the nature of the struggle against evil, the inescapability
> of involvement, the qualities of heroism, the possibilities of real loss in
> that encounter, and the viability of hope. Our point of view within the work
> is that of the hobbits—the ordinary coming to know the heroic, the
> everyday encountering the supernatural, the uninvolved becoming
> committed, and the weak and fearful wondering about their chances (cf.
> Miller, II-427). But we also see a providential pattern in the history of
> Middle-earth, a series of minor eucatastrophes leading up to the major one.
> Part of what Tolkien has done is to provide a "re-paganized" imaginative
> framework for the Christian experience of hope, aimed specifically at the
> despair of the modern world.

Urrutia, Benjamin. See II-301.

II-677    Van de Bogart, Doris. "Some Comments on the *Lord of the
          Rings* by J. R. R. Tolkien." *Dialogue* (University of Pittsburgh
          at Bradford, Pa.), 1 (1973), 33–42.

> Not seen.

II-678    Van Meurs, J. C. "*Beowulf* and Literary Criticism."
          *Neophilologus*, 39 (1955), 114–30.

> Tolkien's lecture on *Beowulf* (I-35) was the first serious attempt at a literary
> evaluation of the poem. It is a brilliant and important contribution, but it is
> not the ultimate truth; there are serious objections to Tolkien's
> interpretation of the theme and structure of *Beowulf*, and it appears
> doubtful whether such a perfect unity of structure and so much symbolism
> underlie the poem as Tolkien discovers in it. Some modern critics who have
> based their work on Tolkien's theory have been led into oversubtle analysis,
> and thus to treat *Beowulf* as a contemporary work of art, while neglecting
> in it elements determined by its historical period. Cf. Kaske (II-319).

II-679    Vaughan, Belinda. Review of *GGK*, 2nd ed. *AUMLA: Journal
          of the Australasian Universities Language and Literature
          Association*, No. 30 (November, 1968), pp. 237–38.

> Not seen.

II-680    Vigures, R. H. Review of *SWM*. *Horn Book*, 44 (February,
          1968), 63.

> This paragraph describes the contents of *SWM*, a book that is graceful,
> joyous, and beautiful.

II-681    Wade, David. "Mighty Midget." *New Statesman*, 74 (29
          December 1967), 908.

> Review of *SWM*. Where *LOTR* hangs in the mind like a huge mural in

which all creation is locked in cosmic war, good against evil, *SWM* may be compared to a most delicate miniature, but one with an overwhelming density of meaning. The swallowing of the star is akin to the coming of grace: it is lent, it has nothing to do with merit, although it must fall onto ground where it will not be extinguished. People like Nokes play their part in spiritual designs even by their malice or sheer cussedness. To those who have not yet negotiated the lower rungs of the fairy ladder, its upper levels are usually invisible, or if visible, then exceedingly dangerous.

II-682    Wagenknecht, Edward. "Proving Imagination is Not Yet Dead." *Chicago Sunday Tribune Magazine of Books*, 15 January 1956, p. 4.

> Review of *RK*. Tolkien is more like E. R. Eddison than like James Branch Cabell, since he has none of the latter's sly wit. *LOTR* is a work of insight and imagination.

II-683    Waggoner, Diana. *The Hills of Faraway: A Guide to Fantasy.* New York: Atheneum, 1978.

> *OFS* and the work of Northrop Frye serve as the basis for a description of fantasy as a literary form and of its subgenres. Most of the book is an annotated bibliography of 996 works of fantasy or of critical studies of fantasy, including *ATB, FGH, H, LOTR, RGEO, SWM, TR, T&L,* and several works about Tolkien. Cf. Schlobin (II-599) and Tymn (II-672).

II-684    Wain, John. *Sprightly Running: Part of an Autobiography.* London: Macmillan, 1963.

> Includes an account of the Inklings.

II-685    Wakeman, John, ed. *World Authors 1950–1970: A Companion Volume to Twentieth Century Authors.* New York: H. W. Wilson, 1975.

> There is a biographical sketch of "Tolkien, J(ohn) R(onald) R(euel) (January 3, 1892–September 2, 1973)" on pp. 1430–32. This includes a bibliography of Tolkien's works and of writings about him.

II-686    Walbridge, Earle F. Review of *TT. Library Journal*, 80 (15 May 1955), 1219.

> "Quite pagan, unlike the ethical C. S. Lewis, this literally outlandish narrative casts a spell of its own. An astonishing feat of the imagination, the book also suddenly surprises with a haunting lyric . . ." (the Song of the Ents and the Entwives).

II-687    Walker, Paul. Review of *Silm. Galaxy*, 39, (December, 1977-January, 1978), 138–42.

> *Silm* is "not a novel, but a mythology" (p. 139) and, though the reviewer loves the book, it shows that Tolkien, while a good writer, was "imitating pre-Christian literature with the intellect and imagination of a middle-class Victorian, and what is most poignant, most dramatic, and most profound in the former is utterly lacking in the latter" (p. 140).

II-688   Walker, Stephen L. "The *War of the Rings* Treelogy: An Elegy for Lost Innocence and Wonder." *Mythlore*, 5, No. 1, Whole No. 17 (May, 1978), 3–5.

"Trees are axiological to the aesthetic, ethic and metaphysic of Tolkien's Middle-earth" (p. 3).

II-689   Walker, Steven Charles. "Narrative Technique in the Fiction of J. R. R. Tolkien." M.A. thesis, Harvard University, 1973.

Not seen.

II-690   _____. "Super Natural Supernatural: Tolkien as Realist." *Proceedings of the Fifth Annual Conference of the Children's Literature Association, Harvard University, March, 1978* (Villanova, Pa.: Children's Literature Association, 1979), pp. 100–05.

Tolkien, the world's greatest fantasist, is essentially a realist. There is much external accuracy to Middle-earth—details of weather and topography, for example, are compellingly tangible—but even more important are incidental glimpses of psychological rightness. There are implicit but realistic motivations for characters (e.g., Denethor's paranoia or Théoden's manic depression) and they act appropriately in any given situation (e.g., the riddle-game in *H* grows in strict naturalness out of the immediate psychological environment). Tolkien gives a mundane appearance to the magical and discovers the marvelous in the ordinary. Art at its best incarnates unseen truth, in Tolkien's view; and we come to accept Middle-earth not just as a clever fiction but as a vision of a larger reality in which the world we thought we knew represents only an aspect of the total truth.

II-691   Wallace, James P. "Riastradh" (column). *Fantasiae*, 7, No. 2, Whole No. 71 (February, 1979), 4.

Discusses the textual evidence that the Glorfindel who dies in *Silm* is identical with the Elf of the same name in *LOTR*. See letter by Alexei Kondratiev and comment by Ian Myles Slater in *Fantasiae*, 7, No. 6, Whole No. 75 (June, 1979), 10 and letter by Christopher Gilson in *Fantasiae*, 7, No. 8, Whole No. 77 (August, 1979), 9. See also Cater (II-91).

II-692   _____. "Riastradh" (column). *Fantasiae*, 7, No. 3, Whole No. 72 (March, 1979), 2.

Speculates on inter-species marriage in Middle-earth. Cf. .Boardman (II-55).

II-693   Walsh, Chad. "In the 'As-If' World." *New York Times Book Review*, 14 March 1965, pp. 4–5.

Review of *T&L*. Like Charles Williams and C. S. Lewis, Tolkien has "renewed the sense of magic and enchantment and assimilated it into the contemporary Christian sensibility" (p. 4). *OFS* provides an illuminating view of the fairy tale and its function by one of the most successful modern practicioners of this difficult art, though it is controversial in its assertion that tales of faerie are more profound than realism and strive to regain the lost unity of religion and mythology. *LBN*, whose fairyland purgatory and heaven may have provided Lewis with the germ of *The Great Divorce*, has sweetness combined with sober moral rigor and a world curiously familiar and yet transformed, making it a haunting and successful demonstration of the qualities of faerie.

II-694    Walton, Evangeline. "Celtic Myth in the Twentieth Century." *Mythlore*, 3, No. 3, Whole No. 11 (1976), 19–22.

There is a brief mention of Tolkien. The journey into Moria is the only part of *LOTR* which suggests Celtic influence.

II-695    Ward, Dederick C. Review of West, *Tolkien Criticism* (II-715). *College and Research Libraries*, 31 (1970), 422–23.

There were stages in Tolkien criticism: book reviews up to 1956; general criticism from 1957–64; widespread popularity from 1965–68; and intense criticism from 1965 to date (see also Beatie, II-35). He would have preferred a chronological arrangement for Section B to reflect this; but this is a minor quibble and the Tolkien enthusiast will find this a most welcome symposium.

II-696    Ward, Martha E., and Dorothy A. Marquandt. *Authors of Books for Young People*. New York and London: Scarecrow Press, 1964.

There is a short (four sentences) biographical sketch of Tolkien on p. 245.

Wardwell, Jeanne. See II-301.

II-697    Watson, J. R. "The Hobbits and the Critics." *Critical Quarterly*, 13 (1971), 252–58.

Review essay on Isaacs and Zimbardo, *Tolkien and the Critics* (II-307). The essays are mixed in quality, with some going overboard with enthusiasm, and some showing naïveté or sheer oddity; but many are thoughtful and perceptive. The collection is ultimately unsatisfactory, however, because the pursuit of single lines of enquiry allows so much of *LOTR* to escape. Critics should not be misled by the size and popularity of *LOTR* into treating it with more seriousness than it seeks or deserves (see also Evans, II-184).

II-698    Weber, Karl. "List of Translations and Publishers of J. R. R. Tolkien's Books from Geo. Allen & Unwin Ltd." *Tolkien Journal*, 3, No. 2 (1967), 15.

Lists three translations of *FGH* (Hebrew, Polish, Swedish), three of *LOTR* (Dutch, Polish, Swedish), and seven of *H* (Dutch, German, Japanese, Polish, Portuguese, Spanish, Swedish).

II-699    Weber, Rosemary. "Folklore and Fantasy—Mix or Match?" ERIC (Educational Resources Information Center). Document numbers: ED 154 424; CS 204 161.

Paper (eleven pages) presented at the Pennsylvania School Librarians

Conference (Seven Springs, Pa., 28–29 April 1978). Folktales codified and reinforced the ways in which people thought, felt, believed and behaved. Much modern fantasy repeats folklore themes; *H*, for example, abounds in such motifs as the dragon and his treasure, the journey, the wizard, rings of power, elves, and talking animals.

II-700  Webster, Deborah C., Jr. "Good Guys, Bad Guys: A Clarification on Tolkien." *Orcrist*, No. 2 (1967–68), pp. 18–23.

An examination of the moral complexity of *LOTR* shows that Tolkien does not present simplistic characters. See also Auden (II-16), Ellwood (II-174), Hayes (II-262), and Hodgart (II-282).

———. See also under her married name: Rogers, Deborah Champion Webster.

II-701  Weinig, Sister Mary Anthony. "Images of Affirmation: Perspectives of the Fiction of Charles Williams, C. S. Lewis, J. R. R. Tolkien." *University of Portland Review*, 20, No. 1 (1968), 43–46.

"Bedrock reality of human values and spiritual truth comes to light under the probing of rays beyond the ordinary spectrum of the naturalistic novel, and a vision emerges whose depth and wholeness stagger an imagination fed on fragments" in "the symbolic situation of Charles Williams, the allegorical narrative of C. S. Lewis, and the mythic rendering of J. R. R. Tolkien" (p. 43).

II-702  Weir, Arthur. "No Monroe in Lothlorien." *Triode*, No. 17 (January, 1960) and No. 18 (May, 1960). Reprinted in Becker (II-37), pp. 120–23.

Discusses possible casting for a hypothetical movie of *LOTR*, and actual settings that might be used.

II-703  "Weirdies." *Time*, 22 November 1954, pp. 106, 108, 110.

Review of *FR* and of *The Visionary Novels of George MacDonald*, ed. Anne Fremantle. Both Tolkien and MacDonald fashioned fairy tales for adults, fueled by strong and unorthodox imaginations, but Tolkien is the more disciplined storyteller. Frodo and his friends best the dangers that beset them in the modern manner, more by muddling through than by measuring up. *FR* is obscure in allegorical meaning but apocalyptic in tone, and sometimes is too ordinary and plausible to maintain fairy tale magic.

II-704  Weisbord, Jane. Review of *LOTR*. *Publishers Weekly*, 26 December 1966, p. 95.

Tolkien's revised edition has a number of textual changes, a new foreword, new appendixes, and an index. *LOTR* is not light reading, but once into the adventure, it is not easy to put down.

Welden, Bill. See II-302.

Wendell, Sylvia. See Levitin (II-372).

II-705    Wenzel, David. *Middle Earth: The World of Tolkien Illustrated*. New York: Centaur, 1977.

> Illustrations for *H*, with an accompanying summary of the story by Lin Carter.

II-706    West, Paul. "Nondiwasty Snep-Vungthangil." *Book Week* (*Washington Post*), 26 February 1967, pp. 1–2.

> Review of *LOTR*. The hobbit books are a harmless family game, but have been made a "bogus lotus." These philologist's doodles are not good fantasy, having no bearing on humanity and dealing only with a virtue that triumphs untested and an evil that dies uninvestigated (cf. Bisenieks, II-47).

II-707    West, Richard C. "An Annotated Bibliography of Tolkien Criticism." *Orcrist*, No. 1 (1966–67), pp. 52–91. Supplement One in *Orcrist*, No. 2 (1967–68), pp. 40–54. Supplement Two in *Orcrist*, No. 3 [also *Tolkien Journal*, 4, No. 1, Whole No. 11] (1969), pp. 22–23. Supplement Three in *Orcrist*, No. 5 [also *Tolkien Journal*, 4, No. 3, Whole No. 14] (1970-71), pp. 14–31.

> Bibliography of Tolkien criticism, arranged alphabetically, with annotations describing the contents of the studies. Also includes a list of Tolkien's own writings, a separate list of reviews of individual books, and an index of titles. See below, West (II-708 and II-715).

II-708    _____. "An Annotated Bibliography of Tolkien Criticism." *Extrapolation*, 10, No. 1 (December, 1968), 17–45.

> A somewhat revised and expanded version of Section B only (critical works about Tolkien's oeuvre) of the bibliography from basically the first two issues of *Orcrist* (see West, II-707).

II-709    _____. "Contemporary Medieval Authors." *Orcrist*, No. 3 [also *Tolkien Journal*, 4, No. 1, Whole No. 11] (1969) pp. 9–10, 15.

> T. H. White, C. S. Lewis, and Tolkien were inspired by their reading of medieval literature to reshape and rewrite medieval material and conventions for the pleasure and profit of a contemporary audience.

II-710    _____. "The Critics, and Tolkien, and C. S. Lewis." *Orcrist*, No. 5 [also *Tolkien Journal*, 4, No. 3, Whole No. 14] (1970–71), pp. 4–9.

> Reviews of Ready, *Tolkien Relation* (II-543); Carter, *Tolkien: A Look Behind The Lord of the Rings* (II-89), Ellwood, *Good News from Tolkien's Middle Earth* (II-175), Isaacs and Zimbardo, *Tolkien and the Critics* (II-307), Hillegas, *Shadows of Imagination* (II-277), Stimpson, *J. R. R. Tolkien* (II-642) and of a number of studies of C. S. Lewis.

II-711    _____. "The Interlace and Professor Tolkien: Medieval Narrative Technique in *The Lord of the Rings*." *Orcrist*, No. 1 (1966–67), pp. 26–49.

> The medieval interlace (interweaving separate themes and stories to cohere meaningfully in a theoretically infinite series of echoes and anticipations)

was reinvented by Tolkien as the proper form to express the narrative and vision of *LOTR*. Two appendixes discuss the theme of power and the imagery of white and black. See West (II-712).

II-712    _____. "The Interlace Structure of *The Lord of the Rings*." In Lobdell (II-388), 77–94.

Revised version of II-711, without the appendixes.

II-713    _____. "Progress Report on the Variorum Tolkien." *Orcrist*, No. 4 [also *Tolkien Journal*, 4, No. 3, Whole No. 13] (1969–70), pp. 6–7.

Details the aims and methods of a group of scholars attempting to edit the Tolkien manuscripts at Marquette University. Notes Tolkien's original titles for the six books of *LOTR* (see I-50).

II-714    _____. "The Status of Tolkien Scholarship." *Tolkien Journal*, No. 15 (Summer, 1972), p. 21.

Analyzes the published writing on Tolkien into types (that disapproving of fantasy and escapism; neo-Gothic enthusiasm; pretending Middle-earth is the primary world; myth criticism; the Christian approach; genre criticism; the medieval/modern approach; the anti-Establishment approach). Most of these tacks can be valuable, though each has limitations and many articles using them haven't been well-handled. See also Beatie (II-35).

II-715    _____. *Tolkien Criticism: An Annotated Checklist*. Kent, Ohio: Kent State Univ. Press, 1970. The Serif Series, No. 11.

The basic contents appeared earlier in *Orcrist* Nos. 1–3 (see West, II-707) but there are numerous additions. First version of the present work. For other bibliographies, see Christensen (II-98), Christopher (II-103), Hammond (II-254), Levitin (II-375), and Melmed (II-417). For reviews, see III-B-32.

II-716    _____. "Tolkien in the Letters of C. S. Lewis." *Orcrist*, No. 1 (1966–67), pp. 2–16.

Discusses references to Tolkien in letters by Lewis (see Lewis, II-381), the Inklings (see especially Carpenter, II-85), *LBN*, *Perelandra*, and differences between the two authors.

II-717    _____. Review of Kilby, *Tolkien and The Silmarillion* (II-338). *Christian Scholar's Review*, 6 (1977), 352–53.

II-718    Wheen, Natalie. "Ring-a-Ding." *Tablet*, 222 (6 April 1968), 343.

Review of *RGEO*. The work has travel and movement as a connecting theme. Musically, the songs are simple and pleasant, but they do not hold together to form a cycle, since the attempt to achieve unity by quoting the opening music in the middle and at the end of the work fails (this because the first reintroduction of the theme does not blend into the character of the song).

II-719   White, William. "Notes on Hemingway, West, Tolkien and Wise." *American Book Collector*, 18 (January-February, 1968), 30–31.

> Notes paperback books by and/or about Ernest Hemingway, Nathanael West, Tolkien, and the notorious literary forger, Thomas J. Wise. *LOTR* is a highly imaginative heroic romance that is popular on college campuses for good reason. Refers to Mathewson (II-410) and to *Tolkien Journal* (though the date of the birthday issue is misprinted as "1957" instead of 1967).

II-720   Whitmore, Harry E. Review of West, *Tolkien Criticism* (II-715). *Library Journal*, 95 (1 June 1970), 2134.

> Welcomes the volume ("The title is misleadingly modest") and describes the contents.

Whittekep, Don. See Kolodney (II-350).

II-721   Wickenden, Dan. "Heroic Tale of Tiny Folk." *New York Herald Tribune Book Review*, 14 November 1954, Part I, p. 5.

> Review of *FR*. Praises its sustained imaginative exuberance, its simple but wonderfully graphic and often eloquent style, and the complicated, eventful, and exciting narrative.

II-722   _____. "Humor, Drama, Suspense In a Unique, Romantic Epic." *New York Herald Tribune Book Review*, 8 May 1955, p. 5.

> Review of *TT*. The heroic and poetic rhythms of the writing are reminiscent of Malory and of the great Nordic sagas. "It is clear by now that the Tolkien trilogy is an imaginative accomplishment of a very high order."

II-723   _____. "Notable Allegorical Trilogy Comes To a Triumphant End." *New York Herald Tribune Book Review*, 5 February 1956, p. 3.

> Review of *RK*. Allegorical meanings can be read into *LOTR*, but it is basically an engrossing and dramatic fairy tale for adults, intended seriously, and one of extraordinary scope, power, and beauty.

II-724   Willard, Derek. "Literature and the New Community." *American Scholar*, 42 (Fall, 1973), 684–86.

> Review of Sale, *Modern Heroism* (II-585).

Williams, D. J. See McTurk (II-415).

II-725   Willis, Katherine Tappert. Review of *T&L*. *Library Journal*, 90 (1 February 1965), 651.

> *OFS* should be read by all lovers of fantasy. *LBN* is a beautiful, delicate, and penetrating allegory.

II-726  Willy, Margaret. Review of Moorman, *Precincts of Felicity* (II-447). *The Year's Work in English Studies*, 47 (1966), 309.

> Moorman attempts to show that the image of the City formulated by St. Augustine largely shapes and regulates the tone and form of the work of Williams, Lewis, Tolkien, T. S. Eliot, and Dorothy L. Sayers. It is surprising to find Eliot bracketed with the others in the group.

II-727  Wilson, Colin. "The Power of Darkness: J. R. R. Tolkien," in his *The Strength to Dream: Literature and the Imagination.* London: Victor Gollancz, 1962; Boston: Houghton Mifflin, 1962, pp. 130–32.

> There are similarities between Tolkien's fantasy and the work of H. P. Lovecraft, E. T. A. Hoffmann, and Nikolai Gogol, but other forebears are the adventure novels of John Buchan and R. L. Stevenson. *LOTR* is basically a straightforward adventure story set in a mythological land, but it owes its power and its fascination to its sense of evil: Sauron broods over the book, and the reader is left with a strong impression of the old, simple dualism between good and evil of the Eastern mythologies (cf. Blair, II-52).

II-728  _____. *Tree by Tolkien.* London: Covent Garden Press, 1973. Santa Barbara: Capra Press, 1974. Abridged version reprinted in Becker (II-37), pp. 74–88.

> He replies to a number of points in E. Wilson's review (II-729), and mentions Auden and the essay by Beagle (II-30), but thinks there has been very little written about Tolkien otherwise. Tolkien's work is flawed by sentimentality, but *LOTR* is still a masterpiece, far better written than most science fiction, and splendid just as an imaginary travel book. The core of *LOTR* is Frodo's journey, and this remains exciting even after several readings, even if other parts, such as the battles, do not wear so well (cf. Sale, II-584). Tolkien's medievalism (which is literary and idealistic rather than precise and detailed) is less important an influence than his late Victorian and Edwardian upbringing. *LOTR* is a criticism of the modern world and of the values of technological civilization, and a manifesto for the values embodied in the visionary artist.

II-729  Wilson, Edmund. "Oo, those Awful Orcs!" *Nation*, 182 (14 April 1956), 312–13. Reprinted in his *The Bit Between My Teeth: A Literary Chronicle of 1950–65* (New York: Farrar, Straus and Giroux, 1965), pp. 326–32. Reprinted in Becker (II-37), pp. 50–55.

> Though this is called by Parker (II-492) a "sarcastic piece of wrong-headedness," it should still be read, as it is the most important attack on *LOTR*. Wilson argues that *LOTR* is an overgrown children's story (it could not have been written for adults because there are only a few details that are even a little unpleasant); that the conflict between Good and Evil is turned into a showdown between Good Guys and Goblins; that Tolkien's prose and verse, since he has little skill at narrative and no instinct for

literary form, are on the same level of professorial amateurishness; and that the book's admirers (except Auden, who is excused because he has a taste for Quest stories) must have a lifelong appetite for juvenile trash. See also De Camp (II-145) and Wilson (II-728).

II-730    Wilson, R. M. Review of "English and Welsh" (I-56). *The Year's Work in English Studies*, 44 (1963), 61.

Tolkien "describes the possible effects of the two languages on each other, and notes some English forms on which a new light is thrown by Celtic evidence."

II-731    _____. Review of *GGK*, 2nd ed. (I-17). *Modern Language Review*, 64 (1969), 854.

Davis is responsible for a large amount of fresh material in this model edition, which makes good and critical use of all the available work on the poem.

II-732    _____. Review of *HB* (I-46). *The Year's Work in English Studies*, 24 (1953), 50.

Summarizes Tolkien's critique of *Battle of Maldon*.

II-733    _____. Review of Nicholson, *An Anthology of Beowulf Criticism* (see I-35). *The Year's Work in English Studies*, 44 (1963), 71.

Tolkien's "influential" essay on *Beowulf* (I-35) deals "with the meaning and value of the poem as a whole."

II-734    _____. Review of Davis and Wrenn, *Essays Presented to J. R. R. Tolkien* (II-143). *Modern Language Review*, 58 (1963), 397–98.

Though this collection is more homogeneous than some *Festschriften*, it does not entirely avoid the hazards of undue compression in some places, and undue expansion in others. There are some good factual essays, and two particularly stimulating essays by Ursula Dronke and by C. S. Lewis (though there is more to be said for the "anthropological approach" to literature than he allows).

II-735    Winter, Karen Corlett. "Grendel, Gollum, and the Un-man: The Death of the Monster as an Archetype." *Orcrist*, No. 2 (1967–68), pp. 28–37.

Lewis in *Perelandra* and Tolkien in *LOTR* use archetypal elements also present in *Beowulf*.

II-736    Wojcik, Jan. S. J. "Samwise—Halfwise? or, Who Is the Hero of *The Lord of the Rings?*" *Tolkien Journal*, 3, No. 2 (1967), 16–18.

It is Sam Gamgee who is responsible for many heroic deeds, and he returns to live meaningfully in the normal world while Frodo passes beyond mortal ken. Two of the main motifs, friendship and gifts, focus in Sam. But really this work does not have a central character.

II-737 ———. "Tolkien and Coleridge: Remaking of the 'Green Earth.' " *Renascence*, 20, No. 3 (Spring, 1968), 134–39, 146.

Tolkien's disagreement with Coleridge in *OFS* is over words rather than meaning, since actually their thought on the function of the imagination in art, the nature of the artistic product, and the motives behind creation are quite similar.

II-738 Wolfe, Gene. "On the Tolkien Toll-Free Fifties Freeway." *Vector*, Nos. 67/68 (Spring, 1974), pp. 7–11.

II-739 Wollheim, Donald A. "Why Frodo Lives." Ch. 25 in his *The Universe Makers: Science Fiction Today*. New York: Harper and Row, 1971, pp. 107–11.

On pp. 13–14 he notes that, while some rewriting could have made Middle-earth a parallel world and therefore enabled *LOTR* to be considered a science-fiction novel, as it stands the work is fantasy. The clear-cut division between Good and Evil in *LOTR* does much to explain the popularity of the work; moreover its young admirers are not cynics or victims of despair, and this gives hope for the future of humanity. See review by Davidson (II-139).

———. See also Lee (II-361) and Scott (II-603).

II-740 Wood, Michael. "Tolkien's Fictions." *New Society*, 13 (27 March 1969), 492–93.

When Tolkien called *Beowulf* a heroic-elegiac poem by a learned man writing of old times, he might almost have been setting the program for his own work. His "old times" are partly a magical Arthurian past, partly a preindustrial England. The theology of his work is an extraordinary synthesis of heroic Northern myth and Christian promise, with the journey motif so central because it is a type of death, the happy release, the blessed departure. He is a born storyteller, good when the action is moving and embarrassing when it stops. He borrows widely, but this is saved from becoming just a mishmash because of the extent and variety of his work and because he manages to sustain a complex moral fable. He is not good at creating individuals, but his types are fascinating. His opposition to the modern world, without compromise and without resort to the engines of the enemy, is not an attractive or realistic position but it is a powerful and coherent one. He turns to fantasy as the enemy of a narrow rationalism.

Wood, Susan. See Le Guin (II-363).

II-741 Woods, Frederick. "*Poems and Songs of Middle-earth*: A review." The *Gramophone* (May, 1968), 607. Reprinted in *Carandaith*, 1, No. 1 (July, 1968), p. 7.

There is something structurally unsound in a song cycle blending so many different and disparate languages and cultures as Hobbit, Elvish, and Entish, and Swann's musical styles are not in themselves consistent, but the songs are engaging and eminently hummable, and it is a delight to hear authentic Elvish spoken by Tolkien. The handsome accompanying volume, *RGEO*, not only prints the poems and musical settings but includes a new exposition of Elvish syntax by Tolkien.

II-742    Woods, Samuel, Jr. "J. R. R. Tolkien and the Hobbits." *Cimarron Review*, 1, No. 1 (September, 1967), 44–52.

Review article on *LOTR*. There are two principal reasons for the appeal of this very long fantasy-romance: "First, his [Tolkien's] narrative gift, particularly his skillful management of suspense; and second, his fertility of imagination in creating a world unique in its charm and attraction, yet sufficiently like our own experience that we readily see similarities between the two" (p. 45). He demonstrates this by plot summaries and by discussions of Middle-earth and its creatures. He also gives a brief biographical sketch of Tolkien.

II-743    "A World for Children." *Times Literary Supplement*, 2 October 1937, p. 714.

Review of *H*. This is a children's book only in that people will first read it during childhood, but in later readings will realize "what deft scholarship and profound reflection have gone to make anything in it so ripe, so friendly, and in its own way so true."

II-744    Wright, Marjorie Evelyn. "The Cosmic Kingdom of Myth: A Study in the Myth-Philosophy of Charles Williams, C. S. Lewis, and J. R. R. Tolkien." Ph.D. diss., University of Illinois, 1960.

Each of these mythmakers creates his own cosmology. See *DA*, 21 (1961), 3464–65.

II-745    ———. "The Vision of Cosmic Order in the Oxford Myth-makers." In *Imagination and the Spirit: Essays in Literature and the Christian Faith*. Ed. Charles A. Huttar. Grand Rapids, Mich.: William B. Eerdmans, 1971), pp. 259–76.

"The myths of cosmic order [in Lewis, Williams, and Tolkien] are not dull and dreary police states. They are kingdoms full of life, movement, ceremony, courtesy. They are ordered in changing equalities, in exchanges of love and obedience. The members of the hierarchy are all, depending on how one looks at it, superfluous or significant, for the whole system coinheres in each" (p. 276).

II-746    Wyatt, Joan. *A Middle-Earth Album: Paintings by Joan Wyatt Inspired by J. R. R. Tolkien's The Lord of the Rings*. London: Thames and Hudson, 1979. New York: Simon and Schuster, 1979.

There is an introduction by Jessica Yates, who also provides commentaries on each painting and summarizes *LOTR*. See review by Egan (II-167).

II-747   Yamamoto, Judith T. Review of *Silm*. *Library Journal*, 102 (August, 1977), 1680.

> *Silm* provides plenty of background material for those who love to unravel the complicated threads of the myth and legend of Middle-earth, but those who want fun and adventure would be better advised to start with *LOTR*. There is high adventure here, but no hobbits. The reviewer was predisposed to love the book, and did, despite occasional inconsistencies and more hard-to-remember names than a Russian novel.

II-748   Yates, Jessica. Review of Lochhead, *The Renaissance of Wonder in Children's Literature* (II-392). *Fantasiae*, 6, No. 9, Whole No. 66 (September, 1978), 5–6.

> That a fantasy has both Celtic and Christian elements is enough for Lochhead to judge it good. She ignores the common attacks on children's fantasy as escapist, didactic, and simplistic, and so only preaches to the converted.

_____. See also Wyatt (II-746).

_____. See also under her maiden name: Kemball-Cook, Jessica.

II-749   Yolton, John. "In the Soup." *Kenyon Review*, 27 (1965), 565–67.

> This review of *T&L* discusses Tolkien's ideas on sub-creation, "the merging of story with reality" (p. 565).

II-750   Zettersten, Arne. Review of *Ancrene Wisse* (I-55). *English Studies*, 47 (1966), 290–92.

> This is a good edition, but there are some misprints.

II-751   Zgorzelski, Andrzej. "Time Setting in J. R. R. Tolkien's *The Lord of the Rings*." *Zagadnienia Rodzajów Literackich*, 13, No. ii, Whole No. 25 (1971), 91–100.

> In English. There are present in *LOTR* three time layers (fairy story time or timelessness, chronicle or pseudo-historical time, and epic time), and these influence the creation of a "fable time" which is a hybrid of the conventions of fairy story and heroic epic. See also Barbour (II-25).

II-752   Zimbardo, Rose A. "Moral Vision in *The Lord of the Rings*." In Isaacs and Zimbardo (II-307), pp. 100–08.

> In the moral vision of romance, the "All" is a chain of being and good is the cooperation of the individual "selves" within it, while evil is the service only of self (a perversion of will which causes a perversion of nature both human and cosmic). She notes the place of each good being and of its perverted counterpart on the scale of creatures in *LOTR*.

_____. See also Isaacs and Zimbardo (II-307).

II-753   Zipes, Jack. "The Utopian Function of Fairy Tales and
         Fantasy: Ernst Bloch the Marxist and J. R. R. Tolkien the
         Catholic." Ch. 5 in his *Breaking the Magic Spell: Radical
         Theories of Folk and Fairy Tales*. London: Heinemann, 1979;
         Austin: Univ. of Texas Press, 1979, pp. 129–59.

II-754   Zuber, Bernie. Review of Carter, *Tolkien: A Look Behind The
         Lord of the Rings* (II-89). *Mythlore*, 1, No. 3 (July, 1969), 5.
         > "This informative book not only tells about Tolkien's life but also about his
         > inspirational sources and the origins of fantasy. While reading it I learned
         > of Greek, Roman and Medieval writers I had never heard of before."

II-755   _____. Review of Day, *A Tolkien Bestiary* (II-144). *Fantasiae*,
         8, No. 6, Whole No. 87 (June, 1980), 6–9.
         > Notes on the illustrations and background of the artists. See also Slater
         > (II-622).

         _____. See also Andrews (II-11).

# III.   Book Reviews

## A.   Reviews of Tolkien's Writings

III-A-1        *The Adventures of Tom Bombadil*
     a.   Davidson, II-136.
     b.   Derrick, II-153.
     c.   Kennedy, II-330.
     d.   Waggoner, II-683.
     e.   *Booklist*, 60 (15 December 1963), 366.

III-A-2        *Ancrene Wisse: The English Text of the Ancrene Riwle*
     a.   Colledge, II-114.
     b.   Hussey, II-295.
     c.   Zettersten, II-750.

III-A-3        *Farmer Giles of Ham*
     a.   Adams, II-4.
     b.   Bechtel, II-36.
     c.   "Before King Arthur," II-39.
     d.   Brady, II-64.
     e.   Etheldreda, II-180.
     f.   Jordan, II-313.
     g.   Lask, II-356.
     h.   Schlobin, II-599.
     i.   Slavin, II-628.
     j.   Smith, II-630.
     k.   *Christian Science Monitor*, 13 November 1950, p. 11
        (A. T. Eaton).
     l.   *Junior Bookshelf*, 14 (January, 1950), 14–15
        (M. S. Crouch).
     m.   *Saturday Review of Literature*, 11 November 1950, p. 41.
     n.   *Spectator*, 18 November 1949, p. 718
        (Gwendolen Freeman).

III-A-4        *The Father Christmas Letters*
     a.   Brewer, II-69.
     b.   Forbes, II-203.
     c.   Krieg, II-353.
     d.   Patterson, II-509.
     e.   Slater, II-617.
     f.   Tymn, II-672.
     g.   *Choice*, 13 (February, 1977), 1600.
     h.   *Economist*, 261 (25 December 1976), 93.

III-A-5        *The Hobbit*

- a.   Becker, II-38.
- b.   Binsse, II-46.
- c.-d.   Eaton, II-165, II-166.
- e.   Hughes, II-291.
- f.   Kight, II-333.
- g.   Lucas, II-394.
- h.-i.   Moore, II-441, II-442.
- j.   Schlobin, II-599.
- k.   Strong, II-644.
- l.   Tymn, II-672.
- m.   Waggoner, II-683.
- n.   "A World for Children," II-743.
- o.   *Booklist*, 34 (15 April 1938), 304.
- p.   *Books and Bookmen*, 18 (1973), 137.
- q.   *Catholic World*, 147 (1938), 507.
- r.   *Junior Bookshelf*, 14 (March, 1950), 50–53 (M. S. Crouch, "Another Don in Wonderland").
- s.   *Saturday Review of Literature*, 2 April 1938, p. 28.

III-A-6        *The Lord of the Rings*

- a.-c.   Auden, II-15, II-17, II-19.
- d.   Bailey, II-20.
- e.   Barr, II-27.
- f.   Blair, II-52.
- g.-i.   Boucher, II-60, II-61, II-62.
- j.   Conklin, II-116.
- k.   Cooperman, II-119.
- l.   Cox, II-123.
- m.   Derrick, II-154.
- n.   Elliott, II-171.
- o.   "The Epic of Westernesse," II-178.
- p.   Fausset, II-193.
- q.   Fuller, II-215.
- r.   Gale, II-218.
- s.   Glendinning, II-252.
- t.   Halle, II-253.
- u.   Hayes, II-261.
- v.   "Heroic Endeavour," II-275.
- w.   Hodgart, II-282.
- x.   Hope, II-286.
- y.   Hughes, II-292.

z.      Huxley, II-299.
aa.     Jonas, II-311.
bb.     Kiely, II-331.
cc.-dd.  Lewis, II-376, II-377.
ee.-ff.  Lobdell, II-386, II-389.
gg.     Malcolm, II-399.
hh.     Mitchison, II-435.
ii.-kk.  Muir, II-454, II-455, II-456.
ll.     Pemberton, II-512.
mm.     Richardson, II-555.
nn.     Roberts, II-559.
oo.     "The Saga of Middle Earth," II-581.
pp.     Schlobin, II-599.
qq.     Schroth, II-601.
rr.     Scriven, II-605.
ss.     Traversi, II-667.
tt.     Tymn, II-672.
uu.     Wagenknecht, II-682.
vv.     Waggoner, II-683.
ww.     Walbridge, II-686.
xx.     "Weirdies," II-703.
yy.     Weisbord, II-704.
zz.     West, II-706.
aaa.-ccc.  Wickenden, II-721, II-722, II-723.
ddd.    Wilson, II-729.
eee.    Woods, II-742.
fff.    *Best Sellers*, 15 (1 May 1955), 25. (R. Grady, S.J.
        Review of *TT*).
ggg.    *Best Sellers*, 15 (1 February 1956), 327. (Review of *RK*).
hhh.    *Booklist*, 51 (1 January 1955), 204. (Review of *FR*).
iii.    *Booklist*, 51 (1 May 1955), 368. (Review of *TT*).
jjj.    *Booklist*, 52 (15 February 1956), 252. (Review of *RK*).
kkk.    *Books and Bookmen*, 12 (December, 1966), 72–73.
lll.    *Books on Trial*, 13 (February, 1955), 169. (R. Flood,
        C.S.B. Review of *FR*).
mmm.    *Choice*, 4 (July-August, 1967), 535.
nnn.    *Christian Century*, 91 (1974), 617–18, 620.
        (Dainis Bisenieks).
ooo.    *The Economist*, 251 (13 April 1974), 69–70, 72. ("Quests
        and tranquillities.")
ppp.    *Manchester Guardian*, 20 August 1954, p. 3.
        (Review of *FR*).

qqq.  *Manchester Guardian*, 26 November 1954, p. 9.
(Review of *TT*).
rrr.  *New Yorker*, 30 (13 November 1954), 202–03.
(Review of *FR*).
sss.  *New Yorker*, 31 (14 May 1955), 154, 157. (Review of *TT*).
ttt.  *Publishers Weekly*, 3 August 1970, p. 62.
uuu.  *Time*, 22 November 1954, pp. 106, 108. (Review of *FR*).

III-A-7        *Poems and Songs of Middle Earth*
a.  Heins, II-264.
b.  Woods, II-741.

III-A-8        *The Road Goes Ever On*
a.  Heins, II-264.
b.  Morse, II-452.
c.  Nichols, II-464.
d.  Wheen, II-718.
e.  *Best Sellers*, 27 (1 December 1967), 358.
f.  *Booklist*, 64 (15 February 1968), 672.
g.  *Choice*, 4 (February, 1968), 1390.
h.  *Punch*, 254 (13 March 1968), 402.

III-A-9        *The Silmarillion*
a.  Adams, II-5.
b.  Brookhiser, II-72.
c.  Conrad, II-117.
d.  Coogan, II-118.
e.  Cosgrave, II-122.
f.  Davis, II-142.
g.  Drabble, II-161.
h.  Eagen, II-163.
i.  Ellmann, II-173.
j.  Etkin, II-181.
k.  Fisher, II-199.
l.  Foote, II-202.
m.  Forbes, II-203.
n.  Gardner, II-220.
o.  Gerville-Réache, II-225.
p.  Hurwitz, II-294.
q.  Jefferson, II-308.
r.  Keller, II-322.
s.  Korn, II-351.
t.  Lloyd, II-382.
u.  Mitchison, II-434.

   v.   "Mythbegotten," II-459.
   w.   Nicol, II-465.
   x.   Sale, II-588.
   y.   Schlobin, II-599.
   z.   Spaulding, II-635.
 aa.   Walker, II-687.
 bb.   Yamamoto, II-747.
 cc.   *Booklist*, 74 (15 September 1977), 142.
 dd.   *Bookviews*, 1, No. 2 (October, 1977), 36.
 ee.   *Choice*, 14 (February, 1978), 1650.
 ff.   *Isaac Asimov's Science Fiction Magazine*, 2, No. 2
       (March-April, 1978), 14 (Charles N. Brown).
 gg.   *Kirkus Reviews*, 45 (15 July 1977), 749.
 hh.   *Publishers Weekly*, 18 July 1977, p. 127.
 ii.   *Virginia Quarterly Review*, 54, No. 1 (Winter, 1978),
       23 ("Notes on Current Books").

III-A-10     *Sir Gawain and the Green Knight*, 1st ed.
   a.   Brett, II-68.
   b.   Emerson, II-177.
   c.   Grattan, II-238.
   d.   Hulbert, II-293.
   e.   Menner, II-418.

III-A-11     *Sir Gawain and the Green Knight*, 2nd ed.
   a.   Caluwé-Dor, II-83.
   b.   Heiserman, II-265.
   c.   Horton, II-287.
   d.   Hughes, II-290.
   e.   Hussey, II-296.
   f.   MacQueen, II-397.
   g.   Rossi, II-572.
   h.   Savage, II-594.
   i.   Vaughan, II-679.
   j.   Wilson, II-731.

III-A-12     *Sir Gawain and the Green Knight, Pearl and Sir Orfeo*
   a.   Cormier, II-120.
   b.   Forbes, II-203.
   c.   McTurk and Williams, II-515.
 d.-e.   Sale, II-587, II-589.
   f.   *Choice*, 12 (January, 1976), 1443–44.
   g.   *Kirkus Reviews*, 43 (1975), 988–89.

III-A-13          *Smith of Wootton Major*
    a.  Crago, II-126.
    b.  Derrick, II-152.
    c.  Lauritsen, II-358.
    d.  Lobdell, II-391.
    e.  Phelps, II-520.
    f.  Schlobin, II-599.
    g.  Slavin, II-628.
    h.  Tymn, II-672.
    i.  Vigures, II-680.
    j.  Wade, II-681.
    k.  Waggoner, II-683.
    l.  *Best Sellers*, 27 (1 December 1967), 358.
    m.  *Books and Bookmen*, 21, No. 2 (1975), 62–64 (Sally Emerson, "Children's Books Noticed").
    n.  *Junior Bookshelf*, 32, No. 1 (February, 1968), 54.
    o.  *Kirkus*, 35 (15 September 1967), 1164–65.
    p.  *Publishers Weekly*, 18 September 1967, p. 62.
    q.  *Times Literary Supplement*, 30 November 1967, p. 1153.

III-A-14          *The Tolkien Reader*
    a.  Schlobin, II-599.
    b.  Waggoner, II-683.
    c.  *Publishers Weekly*, 8 August 1966, p. 61.

III-A-15          *Tree and Leaf*
    a.  Dalgliesh, II-132.
    b.  Davenport, II-135.
    c.  Eiseley, II-170.
    d.  "Ever-Ever Land," II-186.
    e.  Lawrence, II-359.
    f.  Lentricchia, II-367.
    g.  Lewis, II-380.
    h.  Schlobin, II-599.
    i.  Schmidt, II-600.
    j.  Waggoner, II-683.
    k.  Walsh, II-693.
    l.  Willis, II-725.
    m.  Yolton, II-749.
    n.  *Best Sellers*, 24 (15 March 1965), 488 (Mother Anthony).
    o.  *Booklist*, 61 (1 March 1965), 643.
    p.  *Choice*, 3 (May, 1966), 204.
    q.  *Christian Century*, 82 (3 March 1965), 280.

r.  *New York Herald Tribune*, 4 March 1965, p. 21
        (A. Pryce-Jones).
s.  *Virginia Kirkus' Service*, 33 (1 January 1965), 40.
t.  *Young Readers Review*, 1 (June, 1965), 9 (R. Hamilton).

III-A-16        *Unfinished Tales*
a.  Buechner, II-75.
b.  Sibley, II-612.
c.  *Fantasiae*, 8, No. 9, Whole No. 90 (September, 1980),
        9 (Paula Marmor).
d.  *Fantasiae*, 8, No. 10, Whole No. 91 (October, 1980),
        1, 3–5 (Ian M. Slater, "Rough Magic").

**B.   Reviews of Critical Works on Tolkien**

III-B-1            Bart Andrews, *The Tolkien Quiz Book*
         a.   Del Mastro, II-147.
         b.   Marmor, II-404.

III-B-2            Alida Becker, ed., *The Tolkien Scrapbook*
         a.   Del Mastro, II-149.
         b.   Patterson, II-502.

III-B-3            Humphrey Carpenter, *The Inklings*
         a.   Christopher, II-102.
         b.   Del Mastro, II-148.
         c.   Patterson, II-503.
         d.   *Best Sellers*, 39 (May, 1979), 65.
         e.   *Booklist*, 75 (15 February 1979), 902.
         f.   *Books and Bookmen*, 24 (January, 1979), 10.
         g.   *Christian Century*, 96 (16 May 1979), 573.
         h.   *Guardian Weekly*, 119 (5 November 1978), 22.
         i.   *Kirkus Reviews*, 47 (1 January 1979), 40.
         j.   *New Statesman*, 96 (20 October 1978), 510.
         k.   *New York Times Book Review*, 8 April 1979, p. 3.
         l.   *Observer* (London), 5 November 1978, p. 31.
         m.   *Publishers Weekly*, 8 January 1979, p. 65.
         n.   *Times Educational Supplement* (London), 10 November
              1978, p. 24.

III-B-4            Humphrey Carpenter, *Tolkien: a biography*
         a.   Kemball-Cook, II-86.
         b.   Lloyd, II-382.
         c.   Mitchison, II-434.
         d.   Patterson, II-504.
         e.   Shippey, II-611.
         f.   Slater, II-619.
         g.   *Analog*, 97, No. 11 (November, 1977), 174
              (Lester del Rey).
         h.   *Atlantic Monthly*, 240 (July, 1977), 87.
         i.   *Booklist*, 73 (15 June 1977), 1549.
         j.   *Books and Bookmen*, 23 (January, 1978), 54.
         k.   *Changing Times*, 32 (December, 1978), 40.
         l.   *Choice*, 14 (October, 1977), 1046.
         m.   *Criticism*, 36 (Spring, 1978), 74.
         n.   *Economist*, 264 (17 September 1977), 141.

o.  *Galileo*, No. 5 (October, 1977), p. 85.
p.  *Growing Point*, 16 (July, 1977), 3135.
q.  *Guardian Weekly*, 116 (22 May 1977), 22.
r.  *Horn Book*, 53 (December, 1977), 697 (Mary Silva Cosgrave).
s.  *Isaac Asimov's Science Fiction Magazine*, 2, No. 1 (January-February, 1978), 129 (Charles N. Brown).
t.  *Kirkus Reviews*, 45 (15 April 1977), 458.
u.  *Kliatt Paperback Book Guide*, 13 (Winter, 1979), 29.
v.  *Library Journal*, 102 (1 June 1977), 1269.
w.  *Listener*, 97 (12 May 1977), 631.
x.  *National Observer*, 16 (27 June 1977), 21.
y.  *New Statesman*, 93 (13 May 1977), 642 (J. Fenton).
z.  *New Statesman*, 94 (20 October 1978), 510 (Kingsley Amis).
aa. *New York Times Book Review*, 14 August 1977, p. 20.
bb. *Newsweek*, 4 July 1977, p. 74.
cc. *Observer* (London), 8 May 1977, p. 26.
dd. *Observer* (London), 26 June 1977, p. 29.
ee. *Observer* (London), 18 December 1977, p. 25.
ff. *Observer* (London), 23 July 1978, p. 21.
gg. *Publishers Weekly*, 25 April 1977, p. 68.
hh. *Publishers Weekly*, 24 July 1978, p. 98.
ii. *Saturday Review*, 4 (25 June 1977), 31.
jj. *School Library Journal*, 24 (January, 1978), 100.
kk. *Spectator*, 14 May 1977, p. 21.
ll. *Times Educational Supplement* (London), 29 September 1978, p. 29.
mm. *Washington Post Book World*, 26 June 1977, p. E1.
nn. *Washington Post Book World*, 4 December 1977, p. E4.

III-B-5     Lin Carter, *Imaginary Worlds*
a.  Slater, II-621.
b.  *Algol*, No. 22 (May, 1974), pp. 32–33 (Richard Lupoff).
c.  *Amazing*, 49, No. 1 (July, 1975), 118–20 (Cy Chauvin).
d.  *Fantastic*, 24, No. 3 (April, 1975), 113–15 (D. Leiber).
e.  *Kliatt Paperback Book Guide*, 7 (November, 1973), 93 (P. Mattern).
f.  *Library Journal*, 98 (August, 1973), 2295 (Dorothy Sternlicht).
g.  *Luna Monthly*, 60 (December, 1975), 23 (B. Fredstrom).

III-B-6          Lin Carter, *Tolkien: A Look Behind The Lord
                 of the Rings*
        a.       Knight, II-343.
        b.       Miesel, II-423.
        c.       Rockow, II-563.
        d.       West, II-710.
        e.       Zuber, II-754.

III-B-7          David Day, *A Tolkien Bestiary*
        a.       Egan, II-168.
        b.       Slater, II-622.
        c.       Zuber, II-755.

III-B-8          Gracia Fay Ellwood, *Good News from Tolkien's
                 Middle Earth*
        a.       Fitzgerald, II-200.
        b.       Patterson, II-508.
        c.       Post, II-528.
        d.       West, II-710.
        e.       *Choice*, 7 (February, 1971), 1662 (J. R. Christopher).

III-B-9          Robley Evans, *J. R. R. Tolkien*
        a.       Forbes, II-204.
        b.       *Kliatt Paperback Book Guide*, 7 (April, 1973),
                 85 (M. Griffin).
        c.       *Library Journal*, 101 (15 May 1976), 1212.
        d.       *SFRA [Science Fiction Research Association]
                 Newsletter*, No. 38 (March, 1975), pp. 2–4
                 (Deborah Rogers).

III-B-10         Robert Foster, *The Complete Guide to Middle-earth*
        a.       *Booklist*, 75 (15 April 1979), 1316.
        b.       *Isaac Asimov's Science Fiction Magazine*, 2, No. 5
                 (September-October, 1978), 18 (Charles N. Brown).
        c.       *Times Literary Supplement*, 24 November 1978, p. 1365.

III-B-11         Robert Foster, *A Guide to Middle-earth*
        a.       *Booklist*, 68 (1 January 1972), 377.
        b.       *Booklist*, 68 (15 June 1972), 429–30.
        c.       *Luna Monthly*, No. 28 (September, 1971), p. 28
                 (Paul Walker).
        d.       *Orcrist*, No. 7 (1973), p. 29 (Deborah Rogers, "Solid
                 Gold Guide").
        e.       *Vertex*, 2, No. 5 (December, 1974), 11.
        f.       *Worlds of If*, 22, No. 7 (September-October, 1974),
                 132–33 (Lester del Rey).

III-B-12              Daniel Grotta, *The Biography of J. R. R. Tolkien: Archi- tect of Middle earth*
- a.   *Booklist*, 75 (1 September 1978), 24.
- b.   *Modern Fiction Studies*, 24 (Winter, 1978–79), 602.

III-B-13              Daniel Grotta-Kurska, *J. R. R. Tolkien: Architect of Middle-earth*
- a.   McMenomy, II-414.
- b.   *Best Sellers*, 36 (December, 1976), 295.
- c.   *Booklist*, 73 (15 September 1976), 109.
- d.   *Choice*, 13 (November, 1976), 1134.
- e.   *Library Journal*, 101 (July, 1976), 1520.
- f.   *Publishers Weekly*, 10 May 1976, p. 81.
- g.   *SFRA [Science Fiction Research Association] News- letter*, No. 57 (July-August, 1977), p. 2 (Marvin E. Mengeling).

III-B-14              Randel Helms, *Tolkien's World*
- a.   Allen, II-10.
- b.   Slater, II-623.
- c.   Sternlicht, II-638.
- d.   *American Libraries*, 6 (March, 1975), 169.
- e.   *Booklist*, 70 (15 June 1974), 1125.
- f.   *Kirkus Reviews*, 42 (1 March 1974), 279.
- g.   *Kirkus Reviews*, 42 (15 March 1974), 375.
- h.   *Publishers Weekly*, 11 March 1974, p. 48.
- i.   *SFRA [Science Fiction Research Association] News- letter*, No. 35 (December, 1974), p. 4 (Deborah Rogers).

III-B-15              Mark Hillegas, ed., *Shadows of Imagination*
- a.   Patterson, II-498.
- b.   Post, II-529.
- c.   Sapiro, II-592.
- d.   West, II-710.
- e.   *Booklist*, 66 (15 April 1970), 1016.

III-B-16              Neil D. Isaacs and Rose A. Zimbardo, eds., *Tolkien and the Critics*
- a.   Callahan, II-82.
- b.   Cushman, II-130.
- c.   Kiely, II-332.
- d.   Lobdell, II-385.
- e.   Watson, II-697.
- f.   West, II-710.

g. *Choice*, 5 (November, 1968), 1132.

h. *Kirkus Reviews*, 36 (1 May 1968), 536.

i. *Notes and Queries*, NS 19 (1972), 353–54 (Katherine Duncan-Jones).

j. *The Year's Work in English Studies*, 49 (1968) (H. C. Castein and Margaret Willy).

III-B-17   Clyde S. Kilby, *Tolkien and The Silmarillion*

a. Forbes, II-204.

b. Patterson, II-506.

c. Slater, II-624.

d. West, II-717.

III-B-18   Paul H. Kocher, *Master of Middle-earth*

a. Davidson, II-138.

b. Hodgart, II-281.

c.-d. Lobdell, II-384, II-390.

e. Miller, II-430.

f. Patterson, II-507.

g. Peffers, II-511.

h. "The Ring of Romanticism," II-558.

i. Smith, II-631.

j. *Booklist*, 69 (1 March 1973), 616.

k. *Books and Bookmen*, 18 (July, 1973), 124–26 (Piers Brendon).

l. *Choice*, 9 (February, 1973). 1590.

m. *Economist*, 247 (14 April 1973), 123.

n. *Extrapolation*, 14 (August, 1973), 165–66 (Veronica Kennedy).

o. *Guardian Weekly*, 108 (21 April 1973), 21.

p. *Instructor*, 82 (June, 1973), 62.

q. *Kirkus Reviews*, 40 (15 August 1972), 999. Reprinted in ibid., 40 (15 October 1972), 1212.

r. *Psychology Today*, 6 (April, 1973), 103.

s. *Publishers Weekly*, 21 August 1972, p. 79.

t. *Publishers Weekly*, 5 September 1977, p. 71.

u. *SFRA [Science Fiction Research Association] Newsletter*, Nos. 17–18 (November-December, 1972), p. 3 (Deborah Rogers).

v. *Times Literary Supplement*, 8 June 1973, p. 629.

III-B-19   Jared Lobdell, ed., *A Tolkien Compass*

a. Slater, II-625.

b. *Booklist*, 71 (15 May 1975), 937.

  c.  *Choice*, 12 (July-August, 1975), 682.
  d.  *Library Journal*, 100 (1 May 1975), 855.
  e.  *Psychology Today*, 9 (August, 1975), 94.
  f.  *Publishers Weekly*, 23 September 1974, p. 157.

III-B-20      C. N. Manlove, *Modern Fantasy: Five Studies*
  a.  Moran, II-449.
  b.  Patterson, II-497.
  c.  Sale, II-589.
  d.  *Choice*, 13 (March, 1976), 71.
  e.  *Extrapolation*, 17 (December, 1975), 53 (Thomas Clareson).
  f.  *Extrapolation*, 18 (May, 1977), 142–44 (Jane Mobley).
  g.  *Library Journal*, 100 (15 October 1975), 1926 (M. Hounion).
  h.  *New Republic*, 27 November 1976, p. 30.
  i.  *Sewanee Review*, 86 (January, 1978), 121.
  j.  *Times Literary Supplement*, 12 March 1976, p. 289.

III-B-21      Sandra Miesel, *Myth, Symbol and Religion in The Lord of the Rings*
  a.  Keller, II-324.
  b.  Marmor, II-407.

III-B-22      John Warwick Montgomery, ed., *Myth, Allegory and Gospel*
  a.  *Fantasiae*, 3, No. 8, Whole No. 29 (August, 1975), 4, 11 (Ian Slater).
  b.  *National Review*, 22 November 1974, p. 1359.

III-B-23      Charles Moorman, *The Precincts of Felicity*
  a.  Willy, II-726.
  b.  *Catholic Library World*, 38 (February, 1967), 407.
  c.  *Choice*, 4 (April, 1967), 152.
  d.  *Journal of English and Germanic Philology*, 66 (October, 1967), 614.

III-B-24      Ruth S. Noel, *The Mythology of Middle-earth*
  a.  Patterson, II-505.
  b.  *Best Sellers*, 37 (May, 1977), 59.
  c.  *Booklist*, 73 (15 February 1977), 871.
  d.  *Choice*, 14 (July-August, 1977), 683.
  e.  *Economist*, 264 (17 September 1977), 141.
  f.  *Horn Book*, 53 (August, 1977), 469 (Mary Silva Cosgrave).

g. *Kirkus Reviews*, 44 (1 December 1976), 1294.
h. *Kliatt Paperback Book Guide*, 13 (Winter, 1979), 23.
i. *Library Journal*, 102 (1 February 1977), 386 (Dorothy Sternlicht).
j. *Publishers Weekly*, 27 December 1976, p. 49.
k. *Publishers Weekly*, 3 July 1978, p. 64.
l. *School Library Journal*, 24 (September, 1977), 155 (C. Johnson).
m. *Spectator*, 17 September 1977, p. 17.

III-B-25    Timothy R. O'Neill, *The Individuated Hobbit*
a. Kocher, II-345.
b. *Publishers Weekly*, 13 August 1979, p. 56.

III-B-26    William Ready, *The Tolkien Relation*
a. Callahan, II-82.
b. Christensen, II-99.
c. Henniker-Heaton, II-273.
d. Kennedy, II-329.
e. Kuhl, II-354.
f. Lauritsen, II-357.
g. Strothman, II-645.
h. West, II-710.
i. *Choice*, 5 (December, 1968), 1310–11.
j. *Library Journal*, 93 (1 May 1968), 1889.
k. *Library Journal*, 93 (July, 1968), 2742.
l. *National Review*, 14 January 1969, p. 44.

III-B-27    Robert Reilly, *Romantic Religion*
a. Detweiler, II-156.
b. Slattery, II-627.
c. *America*, 25 September 1971, pp. 215–16 (Edwin D. Cuffe).
d. *Catholic World*, 214 (December, 1971), 140.
e. *Choice*, 8 (December, 1971), 1330.
f. *Christian Century*, 88 (June 9, 1971), 727.
g. *Commonweal*, 95 (29 October 1971), 116–18 (Sallie TeSalle).
h. *Library Journal*, 96 (August, 1971), 2510.
i. *National Review*, 17 March 1972, p. 292.
j. *Virginia Quarterly Review*, 48 (Spring, 1972), lxxvi.

III-B-28    Roger Sale, *Modern Heroism*
a. Ricks, II-556.

b. Willard, II-724.

c. *Choice*, 10 (November, 1973), 1389.

d. *Journal of Modern Literature*, 4, No. 2 (November, 1974), 221.

e. *The Key Reporter*, 39, No. 1 (Autumn, 1973), 5 (Rolf B. Heilman).

f. *Library Journal*, 97 (1 December 1972), 3914.

g. *Listener*, 90 (20 September 1973), 382.

h. *Modern Philology*, 73 (August, 1975), 100.

i. *New York Times Book Review*, 29 July 1973, 6.

j. *Times Literary Supplement*, 27 July 1973, p. 848.

III-B-29  Catherine R. Stimpson, *J. R. R. Tolkien*

a. Howard, II-288.

b. Post, II-510.

c. West, II-710.

d. *Choice*, 7 (June, 1970), 546.

e. *Notes and Queries*, NS 19 (1972), 353–54 (Katherine Duncan-Jones).

f. *Prairie Schooner*, 44 (Spring, 1970), 88.

III-B-30  J. E. A. Tyler, *The Tolkien Companion*

a. "Journeying through Middle-earth," II-314.

b. *American Reference Books Annual*, 8 (1977), 607.

c. *Choice*, 13 (February, 1977), 1577.

d. *Christian Century*, 93 (15 December 1976), 1131.

e. *Kliatt Paperback Book Guide*, 11, Supp. 3 (1977), 4.

f. *Library Journal*, 101 (15 September 1976), 1845.

g. *Observer* (London), 4 July 1976, 23.

h. *Observer* (London), 5 June 1977, 32.

i. *School Library Journal*, 23 (April, 1977), 84 (C. Schene).

j. *SFRA [Science Fiction Research Association] Newsletter*, No. 54 (January-February, 1977), p. 7 (Hal Hall).

k. *Vector*, 82 (August, 1977), 16 (B. Griffin).

l. *Wilson Library Bulletin*, 51 (February, 1977), 537.

III-B-31  Gunnar Urang, *Shadows of Heaven*

a. Barron, II-28.

b. Detweiler, II-156.

c. *America*, 25 September 1971, pp. 215–16 (Edwin D. Cuffe).

d. *Books and Bookmen*, 17 (June, 1972), 72.

e.  *Commonweal*, 95 (29 October 1971), 116–17 (Sallie TeSelle).

f.  *Western Humanities Review*, 26 (Summer, 1972), 286.

III-B-32          Richard C. West, *Tolkien Criticism*

a.  Cheney, II-94.

b.-c.  Christopher, II-107, 108.

d.  Galbreath, II-217.

e.  Homberger, II-284.

f.  Immroth, II-300.

g.  Post, II-531.

h.  Ward, II-695.

i.  Whitmore, II-720.

# IV: Indexes

## A. Tolkien's Writings, Arranged by Title

**B. Anthologies, Books, Monographs on Tolkien, Arranged by Author**

## C. Critical Works on Tolkien, Arranged by Title

## D.  Doctoral Dissertations and Master's Theses

## E.   Tolkien-Related Groups and Publications

Devotees of Tolkien's oeuvre have formed numerous organizations, and they publish numerous amateur magazines (or "fanzines"). This list includes some of the best and longest-established groups and publications, but it is not exhaustive by any means. For further information, write to the addresses given: these should be current as of 1980, but remember that they are subject to change at any time.

American Hobbit Association, c/o Renee Alper, 2436 Meadow Drive North, Wilmette, Ill., 60091. This group publishes the fanzine, *Annúminas*.

American Tolkien Society, P.O. Box 277, Union Lake, Mich. 48055. This group publishes *Minas Tirith Evening-Star*, and until recently published *Appendix*.

*Amon Hen*. Bulletin of the Tolkien Society (British).

*Anduril: Magazine of Fantasy*, c/o John Martin, 3 Aylesbury Crescent, Hudley Green, Nr. Wigan, Lancs WN2 4TY, England.

*Annúminas*. Published by the American Hobbit Association (see that entry for address). This primarily features news and reviews.

*The Eildon Tree*. Published irregularly by the Fantasy Association (see that entry for address), featuring essays and reviews.

*Fantasiae*. Published monthly by the Fantasy Association (see that entry for address). This features news, book and media reviews, and short articles.

Fantasy Association, P.O. Box 24560, Los Angeles, Calif. 90024. This group publishes *Fantasiae* and *The Eildon Tree*. The Association is concerned with the whole field of fantasy, including but not limited to Tolkien's works.

*Mallorn*. Published by the Tolkien Society (see that entry for address), featuring essays and reviews.

*Minas Tirith Evening-Star*. Published by the American Tolkien Society (see that entry for address). This features news, reviews, critical essays, poetry, and fiction.

*Mythlore: A Journal of Fantasy Studies Emphasizing J. R. R. Tolkien, C. S. Lewis and Charles Williams*. Subtitle varies. Published quarterly by the Mythopoeic Society (see that entry for address). This features essays, reviews, and a continuing "Inklings Bibliography" (see Christopher, II-103).

Mythopoeic Linguistic Fellowship. This is associated with the Mythopoeic Society (see that entry for address). The Fellowship publishes *Parma Eldalemberon*.

Mythopoeic Society, P.O. Box 4671, Whittier, Calif. 90607. The Society has numerous chapters, and publishes *Mythlore*, *Mythprint* and other occasional items. This group sponsors an annual conference on fantasy called Mythcon; the proceedings of the first three such conferences were issued separately, but papers from the later Mythcons have been published in *Mythlore*. The Tolkien Society of America merged with the Mythopoeic Society in 1972.

*Mythprint*. Bulletin of the Mythopoeic Society (see that entry for address). This features news, reviews, and occasional short articles.

*Orcrist: A Journal of Fantasy in the Arts*, c/o Richard C. West, 1628 Adams Street, Madison, Wis. 53711. This scholarly journal is published irregularly. It is associated with the Tolkien Society at the University of Wisconsin-Madison.

*Parma Eldalemberon*. Published irregularly by the Mythopoeic Linguistic Fellowship, in association with the Mythopoeic Society (see that entry for address). This journal deals with imaginary languages, especially those invented by Tolkien.

*Tolkien Journal*. This was formerly published by the Tolkien Society of America, but was incorporated into *Mythlore* when the TSA merged with the Mythopoeic Society. Three issues were published jointly with *Orcrist*, and one with *Mythlore*, prior to the merger.

Tolkien Society, c/o Lester Simons, Membership Secretary, 11 Regal Way, Harrow, Middlesex HA3 ORZ, England. The Society publishes *Amon Hen*, a bulletin of news and reviews, and *Mallorn*, a scholarly journal.

Tolkien Society of America. This formerly published *The Green Dragon*, a newsletter, and *Tolkien Journal*, which grew from a small amateur magazine into a scholarly journal. The TSA merged with the Mythopoeic Society in 1972. (The Tolkien Society of America should not be confused with the American Tolkien Society.)